D1566371

Resisting Texts

Editorial Theory and Literary Criticism

George Bornstein, Series Editor

Series Editorial Board

Jo Ann Boydston, Southern Illinois University
Hans Walter Gabler, University of Munich
A. Walton Litz, Princeton University
Jerome J. McGann, University of Virginia
Peter Shillingsburg, Mississippi State University

Palimpsest: Editorial Theory in the Humanities, edited by George Bornstein
and Ralph G. Williams

Contemporary German Editorial Theory, edited by Hans Walter Gabler,
George Bornstein, and Gillian Borland Pierce

The Hall of Mirrors: Drafts & Fragments *and the End of Ezra Pound's* Cantos,
by Peter Stoicheff

Textualterity: Art, Theory, and Textual Criticism, by Joseph Grigely

Emily Dickinson's Open Folios: Scenes of Reading, Surfaces of Writing,
by Marta L. Werner

Editing D. H. Lawrence: New Versions of a Modern Author, edited by
Charles L. Ross and Dennis Jackson

Scholarly Editing in the Computer Age: Theory and Practice, Third Edition,
by Peter L. Shillingsburg

The Literary Text in the Digital Age, edited by Richard J. Finneran

The Margins of the Text, edited by D. C. Greetham

A Poem Containing History: Textual Studies in The Cantos, edited by
Lawrence S. Rainey

Much Labouring: The Texts and Authors of Yeats's First Modernist Books,
by David Holdeman

Resisting Texts: Authority and Submission in Constructions of Meaning,
by Peter L. Shillingsburg

Resisting Texts

*Authority and Submission
in Constructions of Meaning*

PETER L. SHILLINGSBURG

Ann Arbor

THE UNIVERSITY OF MICHIGAN PRESS

A CIP catalog record for this book is available from the British Library.

Library of Congress Cataloging-in-Publication Data

Resisting texts : authority and submission in constructions of meaning
    / Peter L. Shillingsburg.
        p.   cm. — (Editorial theory and literary criticism)
    Includes bibliographical references and index.
    ISBN 0-472-10864-6 (cloth : alk. paper)
    1. Discourse analysis. 2. Written communication. 3. Semantics.
    4. Editing. I. Shillingsburg, Peter L. II. Series.
    P302.R484 1998
    401'.41—dc21   97-28770
                                                                CIP

Every effort has been made to trace the ownership of copyrighted materials
and to obtain permission for their use.

Acknowledgments

Every effort has been made to trace the ownership of copyrighted materials and to obtain permission for their use. I thank the editors of *LiNQ* (Literature in North Queensland), for permission to reuse chapter 2; of *Studies in Bibliography* for permission to reuse portions of chapters 3 and 5; of the *Bulletin of the Bibliographical Society of Australia and New Zealand,* for permission to reuse portions of chapters 7 and 8 (chap. 7 also appeared in *Editio* in Germany); and of *Studies in the Literary Imagination* and *Studies in the Novel,* for permission to reuse parts of chapter 9. All of these previously published portions have undergone revision; chapters 5 and 8 have been substantially expanded. Chapters 1, 4, and 6 have not previously appeared. I also thank Gary Myers and *The New Yorker* for permission to reproduce the image of the poem from the 28 October 1985 issue. And I thank the editors of *The Bulletin* (Sydney, Australia) for permission to reproduce the image of its publication of two poems by Gwen Harwood.

I also thank George Bornstein, Price Caldwell, Paul Eggert, Robin Schulze, Jack Stillinger, and James L. W. West for reading and commenting on parts or all of the manuscript. Its weaknesses, resulting no doubt from my failure to take their advice, are entirely my own.

Contents

Introduction

Is There Anything to "Get Straight"?

It had the power to drive me out of my conception of existence, out of that shelter each of us makes for himself to creep under in moments of danger, as a tortoise withdraws within its shell. For a moment I had a view of a world that seemed to wear a vast and dismal aspect of disorder, while, in truth, thanks to our unwearied efforts, it is as sunny an arrangement of small conveniences as the mind of man can conceive. But still—it was only a moment: I went back into my shell directly. One must—don't you know?—though I seemed to have lost all my words in the chaos of dark thoughts I had contemplated for a second or two beyond the pale. These came back, too, very soon, for words also belong to the sheltering conception of light and order which is our refuge.

—Marlow in Joseph Conrad, *Lord Jim*

This book began—though at the time I had no idea of it—in a Society for Critical Exchange (SCE) conference at Miami University of Ohio in March 1987, which brought together groups of literary critics and theorists and of textual critics and editors to discuss mutual interests. In the final session one textual critic, somewhat frustrated, stood and said, "But we must get the facts straight first." Needless to say, in that crowd those were fighting words, and the conference ended in a royal battle. Battles are stimulating. I went home and wrote what I now see as an introduction to the central concerns of this book.

I

The conference on literary theory and textual criticism provoked a "worry" with the reasoning by which, in some circumstances, historical authors and their intentions are deemed irrelevant to criticism while, in other circumstances, the author's intentions and the originating context of a writing are deemed significant. Two basic approaches to the idea appear to form a barrier separating the critical theorists from the textual theorists. First, for certain kinds of inquiry historical concerns seem irrelevant—it does not matter what was. Second, at a fundamental level of inquiry history is never more than an interpretive construct—which makes appeals to history in a sense illegitimate, not just irrelevant. These two ideas are independent from each other, though no attempt was made in two days of discussion at the conference to distinguish between them. Persons wishing to claim the importance of the facts of historical contexts seldom acknowledge explicitly that "history" is a construct or explain why continued interest in history could be anything more than a disguised manipulation of "interest" in the present.

So, to begin with an obvious and silly instance, suppose that the back leg of a couch breaks and one finds three sturdy novels to put under the corner of the couch to hold it up. It does not matter theoretically or practically who the author was or what state of the text is represented because the purpose is fully met without reference to those issues. The couch will not fall because of a flawed text or because of one's ignorance of historical context. Okay—silly, extreme example.

Suppose a lexicographer studying linguistic patterns in the language or investigating basic functions of grammar finds three sturdy novels of about eight hundred pages each to supply a generous amount of sample text to work with. The authors' messages, notions of the integrity of art, or desires to effect changes are matters to which the lexicographer might be indifferent. Any three or three hundred novels would do. An author's individual use of language is less important than the range of uses found in the whole sampling of language in the novels. Historical context and accuracy of text, however, suddenly does matter more than in the couch case. A concept of authority also matters. If in making a dictionary one bases spelling or definition on a typographical error or an eccentric spelling or use, one perpetuates something individual or accidental as if it were cultural. Dictionary makers protect themselves by insisting that the sample be repeated in unrelated texts. They could also protect themselves by examining the textual history to see if their samples contained any information suggesting whether the reading was consciously intended or accidentally produced. That, however, would not exhaust the possible lexical implications, for we know that new words can be invented and therefore fall within the range of possible forms or perhaps even extend that range. Eccentric spellings and uses are not necessarily expendable and should not necessarily be prevented, though, for the purposes of producing a dictionary that describes the vocabulary currently or historically in use, such accidents or maverick uses might be thought inappropriate.

Similarly, in trying to see if the rhetorical dimensions of a text reinforce or subvert the semantic dimensions, it may not matter what the author was trying to convey; one may instead be interested in what the text sounds like or what impression it creates, or one might be interested in how the text apparently succeeds or fails to achieve one or another potential effect. But insofar as that approach explores the ability of human language to carry meaning from the originator to a targeted audience, or to the extent that it explores the ability of texts to be made meaningful by readers (targeted or not), it has historical, contextual, or structural dimensions. In that case it also matters if the text one uses has been accidentally, rather than consciously or deliberately, altered so as to create another kind of text. If it was altered on purpose, one can form understandings of the text that are unavailable if one knows the text variation is inadvertent. To understand those differences as functions of the way language works, one would have to know the context (particular circumstances, biography, and historical/cultural background) in order to understand what forces were being manipulated or ignored in that utterance. Otherwise, one could only say, within the present context, what the language of the text sounds like and what forces seem to be working in the sample within the limits of present mental and linguistic contexts. If that is what one chooses to do, then, of course, it does not matter that there was an author, an alterer, or an intended meaning.

Yet in both cases—holding up the couch or seeing how language seems to work in samples cut loose from their origins—the fact that one's interest in using the novels is unaffected by their origins, authors, accuracy, or contingent contexts does not mean that the texts had no origins, no authors, no meanings. It only means that those things do not matter for the current purpose.

Suiting the evidence and method of using it to the requirements of a given purpose is one way of relating textual criticism and literary criticism and the varying attitudes they evince toward works of art. It is an act of hubris to say that because something does not matter to me it does not matter period or that it does not exist—likewise, to say that because for my purpose a thing does matter it must also matter to you. Textual criticism does not tell anyone what to do with texts. No one says a couch must be held up with scholarly editions. What textual criticism does say is that, if an inquiry into the text is historical, then the historical context, origin, accuracy, and textual context of the text used is significant and that ignorance of these matters undermines such inquiries. Textual criticism frequently demonstrates that becoming well informed about the origin and context of a text is no easy feat, not the work of a breezy morning.

There is another side to the problem of whether or not originating contexts or authors matter. In addition to the fact that for some purposes the identity, historical setting, and intention of the author are issues of no moment or significance, literary critics and theorists can say it is also true that origins, history, and texts are all extant in the present only as interpretive constructs put together by the accumulation of surviving artifacts (letters, editions, contemporary witnesses), arranged and valued interpretively by the modern scholar driven by modern concerns. Historical constructs of all kinds—our notion of what happened, in what context it happened, the meaning of what was said or written in those contexts—are problematical. Historical constructs, including a great many of what are loosely called facts, may not correspond to history itself, whatever that was when it was the present. Often we act as if there were a definite correspondence between history (a story) and the past (events), but there are only partial ways to verify the accuracy or completeness of such constructs.

This general theoretical insight serves as a warning to all pursuers of historical matters. It is a warning about pitfalls and a caution against acting as if any given construct, whether it be a historical account or an edited text, is or can be determinate or definitive. That does not mean that there is no meaning. Nor does it illegitimatize pursuit of historical matters. In fact, it is impossible to act or speak in the present without reference to the past, for every act or speech or interpretation of the acts of others is influenced by our sense of the past. The fact that our sense of the past and our past may not correspond does not change our dependence on a sense of the past. That sense gives rise to patterns or standards of value and meaning that give stability to our lives as well as providing focuses against which to revolt.

To illustrate the frustration and importance of this gap one can meditate briefly on my act in writing this paragraph and yours (dear reader!)

in reading it. I have written this page because I have a meaning to convey to myself and others. I think it is legitimate—laudable, in fact—for someone to want to know what my message is/was. I think it would be easier for readers to know what I am getting at, why I care about it, and why I have used language in the way that I have if they knew that today as I write is Monday, that this past weekend I spent two days in the company of scholars calling themselves, among other things, textual critics and literary theorists, that we discussed a variety of issues relating to meaning, intention, objectivity, and the physical materiality of fiction and poetry, and that what I am trying to do now is say some additional things that would help us see the relationship between our various uses of texts and our various notions of what can be done with texts, what should be done with texts, and what we think others are doing with texts.[1] The fact that a stranger reading this page is unable to know for sure that I attended that meeting might make her or him wish to analyze this page as a free-floating sample of language; that should not prevent any of the persons who attended the meeting from trying to see in this page something that Peter Shillingsburg is intending to mean as an addition to a historical context the reader is familiar with. To my fellow conferees I would say, on behalf of the one wanting to "get the facts straight first," that I would like you to get this fact straight: I thought these things and wrote these things in Starkville, Mississippi, after the Miami of Ohio conference of 27–29 March 1987. I think that fact stands firmly in the way of anyone reading this page as if it belonged to the discussion that actually took place in the Sunday morning session. Of course, anyone who wants may read it without reference to the conference, to the relation between it and the time of this writing, or to what I mean or want readers to understand. Furthermore, no reader of this page can know for sure that the colon after the word *straight* seven lines earlier should not have been a period, in which case you might wonder if I intended the words *this fact* to refer to the preceding sentence rather than the following one.

Does a reader's inability to know whether that colon was intentional or mistaken mean that my meaning, because indeterminate, is irrelevant to the reader? Does that inability to know what I intended the colon to mean make my meaning an illegitimate concern of the reader? Is what I intended

---

1. It was a matter of curiosity to me to feel the falsity of this sentence, written in 1987, when I came in 1996 to revise this essay for inclusion as the introduction to this book. In anticipation of the reader in who-knows-what year, I feel the added alienation from this attempt, in print, to ape the immediacy of spoken language. The disjunction of speech and script is a central concern of this book.

for this page to convey to its readers less important than what each reader decides to use this discussion for? One conference participant offered as an example the interpretations of the international treaty that might or might not exclude Strategic Defense Initiative (SDI, or Star Wars) research. The Reagan administration's attempt to undermine the interpretation holding that SDI research was banned may, as the participant said, deconstruct the text in such a way as to deprive it of the meaning its opponents say is clearly determinate. But, as another person quickly observed, the president's men did not stop with pointing out that the text was meaningless; all they seemed to want to do was point out that the interpretation banning SDI was not determinate. It would not serve to render the treaty meaningless; the strategy was to loosen the limits of meaning enough to include the administration's construction of meaning. A two-step process seemed to be revealed: first of deconstruction, subverting the "intended meaning" by pointing out internal contradictions; and then a limiting of meaning to what the framers of the treaty might have "intended in view of what they knew at that time." The question of "interest" and the needs of the present in this example weigh much more heavily with the current wranglers over meaning than any real concern over what the framers of the treaty actually meant or intended to mean. The heavy present question seemed to be: what can a treaty-signing nation do now without losing too much honor, face, or credibility? It would appear, then, that the ahistorical critics are right at least some of the time for at least some purposes: authorial meaning is not the central concern. But one cannot help feeling that perspective is both cynical and revolutionary.

I am tempted to provide another metaphor: deconstructive criticism sees traditional critics up through structuralists and perhaps including some Marxists and feminists as operating in a swampland of assumptions about historical meaning and contexts. Deconstructionists come in like the army corps of engineers and drain the swamp, leaving a desert in which there is no meaning, just arid wind and sand shifting aimlessly. It is not a very good image, though. First, deconstruction subverts power by subverting "meaning" and is therefore a guerrilla force, not the establishment army. Second, deconstruction does not drain texts of meaning; it makes room for substitute (though perhaps only temporary) meanings. Even if deconstructive readings insisted that a particular text were nonsense, that would be an alternative meaning: it means nothing; nothing is what it means. The tremendous power to upset comes from the corollary to that: what you said or meant does not matter; you do not matter.

There is a sense in which it is true that language defines us, that interest drives and guides us, that meaning depends on the reading, that the present is more important than the past. But these modern truths are not the whole picture. There is a sense in which it is also true that we live in the rag and bone shop of the heart, that our lives depend on a sense of honor in which a person is as good as his or her word—a dependence that requires that what we said yesterday holds true today—that our interests are social as well as individual. Some of us really believe that what is good for you enhances me, even if very indirectly, and that I can be interested in you for your own sake, for the sake of us all. The first set of truths causes us to be skeptical and humble about certitude; the second set causes us to care about history and one another. To those wishing to take an aerial view it is bad advice to keep one foot on the ground. It is frustrating to those with air sickness to say we can never land.

This is what I learned or had confirmed at the SCE conference:

1. That an interest in the present, in how language works now, in how language presently conceals and reveals moral, political, and social "interests," is important and may not depend on history.

2. That any interest in history is fraught with pitfalls that may make pursuing it seem futile to some people. That all historical research is an attempt to bring to bear critical understanding on the surviving artifacts, many of which, being verbal, are subject from the first moment of their creation to indeterminacy of meaning.

3. That people are nevertheless legitimately interested in knowing what other persons of the present or the past are or were trying to say and mean.

4. That to identify the interpretive and therefore subjective element in historical studies, thus calling into question the significance of every "fact," and to identify the ambiguousness or ambivalence of some facts themselves, does not automatically translate into the despair of saying that facts do not matter or that there are no facts "to get straight." If historical studies are to have any legitimacy at all, the accuracy of the evidence is important. If dictionaries are going to reflect the range of usage of a certain time—even of our own time—then the sources of samples must originate in that time; if statements about the semantic and rhetorical tension in a sample of language are used to illustrate how the tension works, it must do so within a particular linguistic and social context, or by default

it will be a statement only about the scholar's own particular time and place.

5. That artifacts should not be distorted or carelessly identified.
6. That constructs of the past (histories and texts) are interpretations.
7. That ahistorical, objective, disinterested appropriations of artifacts for present uses are historical, subjective, and interested; tomorrow they will be history.

Curiosity about the present and the past, about historically intended meanings and present operative meanings, about specific texts of literature and what we use texts for—all these interests derive from the fact that we are people invested in ourselves and our relations to others, selfishly and generously, with desires to know what others are doing or saying, particularly if that may be helpful, hurtful, or interesting to us. We go on being interested in the past, in what was meant, in what was revealed inadvertently, in how it was in the past, how it is in the present, how it should be, how it could be, and how it can be changed.

Everyone at the conference had legitimate interests and wanted others to share them; some of us wanted also to learn additional cautions, opportunities, and methods from others at the conference. None of us wanted to be told that what we were interested in was nonsense or illegitimate, though we did want to be shown if the way we were going about it or the assumptions we were operating under were suspect.

This book tries to organize various understandings about how texts are generated, produced, and received, with special attention always focused on the implications of such understandings to editorial acts. At best it is an attempt to examine how we avoid the "vast and dismal aspect of disorder" by creating sunny arrangements of small conveniences.

II

> *Language is vehicular; does no good for a homestead.*
> —Ralph Waldo Emerson

The title for this book came to me in 1993 during a sabbatical when about half of the essays contained here were first drafted. Resisting texts, I first thought, was what readers do who appropriate texts, whether willfully or unconsciously, for present purposes. We resist the will of the text and the wills of the author and of the text producers. We resist texts in a sense analogous to the resistance to theory that J. Hillis Miller described in his 1991

Modern Language Association (MLA) presidential address, by insisting on our own uses for texts, regardless of the intentions of authors or publishers.

My next thought was that texts resist readers by yielding their communicative cargo with less richness than they were freighted by their authors. Thousands of interviews with authors attest the notion that readers want authors to help explain the nuances of texts and to reveal the hidden depths of intended meanings. Students in countless classrooms look in awe at the enlightened dexterity their teachers demonstrate in textual exegesis.

Furthermore, texts resist readers by allowing red herring interpretations by readers leading themselves astray, as is attested by many authors who, with shaking heads and wonder in their faces, marvel at the interpretive acrobatics of critics bent on excavating the thinnest veins of trace meanings. "That is not it; that is not it at all," they say.

But these are facile resistances, already familiar to every student of textual and literary criticism who has hashed over the finer points of affective and pathetic fallacies and debated the politics of objective readings and revelled in the joy of text offered by reader response happenings.

It is with no desire or hope to promote a correct or superior form of textuality, with no desire to correct so-called interpretive or editorial textual abuse, nor any attempt to prevent anyone from doing anything imaginable with texts or books, that I have undertaken this book. Rather, I attempt to understand and describe the principles governing the workings of a range of textual engagements. Consequently, much of this book takes the form of "What if we suppose . . ." statements. "If we take such and such to be the case" or "If we assume such and such to be the goal of our exercise" or "If we grant such and such a value to the past or to certain players in a textual history," then "What will be the consequences, what will follow from these assumptions?"

I have discovered that even my good friends and acquaintances sometimes will not play that game with me. When I have sketched out a "What if" condition and begin articulating the definitions of terms that go with that condition and begin drawing the conclusions that follow from it, I am accused of promoting that view as my view and am called narrow or unfortunate in my wording. Of course, it is possible that I am narrow in my views and that my wordings are occasionally or even frequently unfortunate, but it seems necessary, judging from my experience, to caution readers to explore the range of views of textuality and hold in abeyance, as I have tried to do, any rush to judgment about particular views as we take them up one after the other.

Frankly, I do not hold that there is a superior view of textuality. I do not believe the world would be a better place if all textual critics used the same terminology or pursued the same goals or agreed on one methodology for conducting their investigations, promulgating their insights, or editing texts. It would be nice, I believe, if textual critics had a sufficiently broad understanding of the range of views about textuality so that their own preferences could be explained in the context of other views. Unfortunately, many editors and other textual critics present their findings and promote their conclusions with what Paul Eggert has called a tone of "strenuous inevitability." Me likes the phrase, though I half-suspect it was my own tone of voice that prompted the criticism.

This book, therefore, is an attempt to understand why and how we resist texts and why and how they resist us. The result can, I think, be called a theory of script acts. When I first tried to formulate the ways in which speech act theory helped to place resistance to texts in a new light for me, I called written works "write acts"—a term I disliked from the moment of inventing it until it was pointed out to me that it formed a pun for "right acts," after which I actively detested the term.

Speech act theory and, now, script act theory tend to focus on the vehicular uses of language: to communicate, to warn, to enact, to praise and blame, in short, to *convey* meaning. But both speech and script theory must also include nonvehicular uses: to confuse, to conceal, to provoke through obscurity or through misleading transparency, or to amuse or deceive. In the first case an author might feel success if listeners or readers appeared to "get the message" or to understand the speech or script act by getting its "voluntary meanings." In the second category an author might feel successful if listeners or readers failed to understand that they were being misled, or at least that only certain persons were able to understand while others remained in the dark. But even this opposition between communicative and noncommunicative uses of language is restricted to actions for which the success is measured by the fulfillment of the author's intentions. The range of language use accounted for by script act theory must be sufficient to encompass script acts for which any response is equally appropriate, for which there was no attempt to imbue the language with intention to be understood or misunderstood. It is somewhat difficult to conceive of such texts, but analogy with Rorschach tests or certain impressionist or absurdist paintings might help suggest the kind of texts that might be included in this category.

Certainly, a candidate for such a text might be Charles Bernstein's "Lift Off," which I first encountered in Jerome McGann's book *Black Riders*. The title is the only coherent linguistic element in the "poem," which we take to be a poem primarily because it was published in a collection of poems, *Poetic Justice,* and because its overall shape and length is similar to those of conventional poems. The text of "Lift Off" appears to be a random arrangement of letters and symbols and spaces that could easily have been produced at a typewriter or a computer keyboard by a child, a monkey, or a doodling and disengaged typist. It is impossible for me to imagine a "text" of this poem that contained a typo, for it would appear that any apparently nonsensical combination of letters and typographic symbols might do as well as those actually used. McGann speculated that the text appeared to have been generated by a malfunctioning retrieval program attempting to restore a lost computer file and that its recognizable semes but otherworldly unfamiliarity invoke a space age understanding of the title. In *Black Riders* he quotes an anonymous publisher's reader's report suggesting that the text might be the transcription of the correction tape from a typewriter that "lifted off" the errors (109–10). This view is compatible with the rather neat suggestion that "Lift Off" is the un-poem consisting of those parts of texts that had been errors and had been lifted off the paper and hence out of other poems that were meant to convey meaning in more conventional ways. "Lift Off" might thus be thought of as a take-off on "meaning" poems or a send-up of poetic high seriousness. Or it might with equal justice be understood in any other way imaginable.

These interpretations, however, entail the notion that Bernstein "intended" by the title and by the poem to convey a sense of otherworldliness or of the un-poem. As such, each interpretation should be subject to the normal hermeneutical tests of validity, the most obvious of which are: did Bernstein indeed have such a typewriter or computer, was the poem in fact produced in that fashion, and was the ingenuity of the idea of composing a poem entirely from errors an authorial one or strictly a critical one? Of course, some folks would not care, but some readers would be willing to abandon McGann's first notion about the computer retrieval program because the poem's publication date, 1979, predated the general use of home computers, and it seemed more likely that Bernstein had an IBM Selectric typewriter with correction tape in the late 1970s than that he had an early Kaypro or Tandy computer. McGann seems uninterested in verifying the historicity of these interpretations, remaining content with the notion that poetry is "not to be 'read like prose'" and claiming a hermeneutic status for the unhistoricized readings and a mimetic status for the historicized one. Since neither McGann, the anonymous publisher's reader, nor I have bothered to verify the historicity of any of these readings, I fail to see a substantive difference in the modes of speculation that generated them. Without verifying the ascertainable historical facts, none of them can claim to depend on "the text's 'agency of meaning,'" if by that phrase one means the originating agent—the author.[2]

It is probably the case that most of this book is devoted to the ways in which we resist texts and texts resist us as communicative acts. It is important to acknowledge, however, not only that some texts may never have had specific communicative force in their generation but also that readers might with perfect right refuse to care what communicative intention an author might have actually had or professed to have had for a text. One might believe, for example, that Mark Twain intended *Huck Finn* to be an antislavery and antiracist book, but others might not care whether the book was so intended, for they find it to be in fact otherwise. There are examinable reasons for each reaction. It is a desire to understand how these reactions come about that impelled this work. My pursuit led me into a number of dark and tedious corners, for which I apologize and beg the forbearance of readers. Some parts of this book were more fun to write than others, and, no doubt, some will be more enlightening or entertaining than others.

---

2. I should add that I have not tried to verify with McGann whether my reading of his reading has any historical validity either.

Chapter 1

The Hand from the Grave

This living hand, now warm and capable
Of earnest grasping, would, if it were cold
And in the icy silence of the tomb,
So haunt thy days and chill thy dreaming nights
That thou would wish thine own heart dry of blood
So in my veins red life might stream again,
And thou be conscience-calm'd—see here it is—
I hold it towards you.

> —John Keats, Untitled fragment

He, with his copy-rights and copy-wrongs, in his squalid garret, in
his rusty coat; ruling (for that is what he does), from his grave, after
death, whole nations and generations who would, or would not, give
him bread while living,—is a rather curious spectacle!

> —Thomas Carlyle, "The Hero as Man of Letters"

By mourning tongues
The death of the poet was kept from his poems.

> —W. H. Auden, "In Memory of W. B. Yeats"

The "death" of the author as the conceptual authority over the meaning of texts, was, when rightly understood, already a passé idea when Roland Barthes pronounced the last rites in 1968. At least some critics had already long rejected the idea that the central focus of their attention was what the author had meant by a text. Students had already been told to determine what the text said, not what the author meant. In addition, authors had already long acknowledged that anything they wrote was susceptible to misunderstanding by persons too obtuse or too culturally remote to understand authorial meaning. And it seems just common sense to believe that most authors have long been aware that their texts are regularly appropriated by others for uses unrelated to their own original intentions.

But my point is not that Barthes's provocative declaration stated the obvious. I don't think it did, for his idea is complex. He began by pointing to Mallarmé as a writer who had discovered a way to write in which language, and not the author, was the speaker. But quickly Barthes moved from discussion of a new intentionally authorless style of writing to talking of all texts as scripted forever in the present. The author, with passions and a personal history, is replaced by the *scriptor*, a timeless, placeless, authorityless aggregator of quotations from the web of language. An irony manifests itself if we say, then, that in its own right Barthes's essay has been misunderstood and appropriated. Very few people now read it in the light of its original context: a time in which criticism was dominated by authorial hagiolatry, when criticism was devoted to engagement with texts for their "determinate meanings." And few persons who quote the title of Barthes's essay, "The 'Death' of the Author," remember to include the quotation marks around *Death,* which call attention to the special meaning of the word and contramand its conventional meaning.[1]

The next year, 1969, Michel Foucault, in "What Is an Author," acknowledged first that the disappearance, or death, of the author was an old idea but insisted that the "author function" lurked unrecognized in the concepts of "The Work" and "The Writer." Like Barthes, Foucault began with a reference to a modern writer, quoting Beckett's "What does it matter who is speaking?" as the formulation of a modern indifference, which he claimed was one of the "fundamental ethical principles of contemporary writing." The operative word was *contemporary;* for, he again wrote, "we can say that today's writing has freed itself from the dimension of expression." But, like Barthes, Foucault shifted from the contemplation of a new authorless style of writing, reflecting an ambience of indifference and world-weariness, to

---

1. In "Social Discourse or Authorial Agency" Paul Eggert surveys provocatively the concepts of authorship current in library science (particularly for the purposes of cataloging works, almost always by author), in painting (in which the idea of forgery depends so heavily on a concept of authorship), and literary authorship (in which authorly production and readerly performance are forever theoretically and practically separated and linked at the same time). Eggert's observations on the apparent incompatibility to scholarly editing of Barthes's, Foucault's, and Derrida's formulations of text indicate a way to understand the coexistence and complementary nature of editorial and critical agendas.

statements about authorship in general, as if to say that the new way of writing was indicative of the only feasible way of reading.

By distinguishing between the author function, on the one hand, and the signer (of a letter), the guarantor (of a contract), and the anonymous writer (of graffiti on the wall), on the other, Foucault signals the fact that he is concerned with the way the word *author* confers special status on writings in our culture and predisposes us to certain determinate kinds of reading—generally respectful, if not actually reverential.

In the years since 1968–69 that distinction has had a growing influence on our notions of canons and on our increasing patience for misreadings, particularly strong ones. We have become more ready to deal with texts as writings, rather than as literary icons, and to entertain, as objects of study, the cultural impacts of texts without regard to "authorial intention." But I believe we are also beginning to see that Barthes's and Foucault's insights were embedded in the ethos of their time, arising from the expressed desire for expression-less (i.e., content-less) writing of a period, expressive, so to speak, of an attitude at once political and aesthetic, rather than being the universal insights into the nature of texts and writing that so many took them to be.

But for all its complexities and "mis"-applications the idea of the death of the author has a bearing on the work of editors. My point begins with the sense of helplessness to control the life of the text that has always attended authorship; author's have in one sense or another "died" from the beginning of time at the moment they released their texts into the world. And this realization has led them to perform a variety of acts and to stipulate a variety of provisions designed to influence readers to treat their texts as they intended them to be treated. Just read any preface to any book, any prologue to any collection of poems, any interview with any author about her or his works—and you will see authors trying, after the fact, to control how people react to or understand their works. There are exceptions, of course, but the hand from the grave reaches out in prefaces, interviews, and especially in revised editions and in instructions to literary executors in authors' wills, as authors work to overcome the inevitable loss of control over meaning entailed by publication.

I believe, then, that their own death as conceptual authorities over meaning has, with some exceptions, of course, always been anticipated and compensated for by authors who strive to write so as to be understood and who accompany their texts with pilot texts to shore up their eroding control over meaning. And the dead author's hand stretches toward the reaching hands of many critics and ordinary readers, willing and anxious to restore the conceptual authority over meaning to the author. Furthermore, the death of the author does not prevent readers or editors from pursing authorial intention for the exact *wording* of texts any more than it prevents them from seeking the author's *meaning* for texts. Chief among the mediums at the mausoleum doors are scholarly editors "establishing" what the author intended or what the author meant to write or what the author wrote. Social contract editors and documentary editors—rejecting the author's grave but battering at the doors of other tombs—attempt to establish the text according to one or another departed, dead, or otherwise lost standard.

It is fruitless to rail against authors for harboring a forlorn hope to control their texts or the meaning of their texts or to ridicule the efforts of readers and editors to meet the authors, sympathetically, across the gulf. Indeed, as an editor of the works of W. M. Thackeray, I have also tried to create texts that more accurately approximated what the author wrote or what the author appears (to me) to have wanted his texts to say. In interpreting texts, I have devoted myself to reconstructing, as much as possible, the contexts of origination that I believe help clue us into meanings probably authorial.

But most editors and critics acknowledge, first, that our connection with authors and with the past is, if not completely severed, at least irreparably damaged. We acknowledge, further, that our uses for texts frequently make us see them in ways probably not intended by their authors. Every time we analyze a text for what it hides or for what it reveals unwillingly (or unwittingly), we deconstruct the text. Every time we defend or lament an author for apparently holding assumptions about women or race or the environment or politics or poverty or whatever, we take the text in a way probably not intended—we exercise our reading rights without regard to authorial control or in direct opposition to it. Such "hostile" acts are as much a part of what we do as are the more sympathetic ones we pursue when we seek the author's intended meanings.

Editors, however, claim power over the wording and pointing of texts and exercise an authority that has far-reaching effects. Unlike critics who produce new ancillary texts relating to the primary works, editors control the verbal presence of the text itself. Whether the editor exercises this authority on behalf of the author or of the "social condition" or whether the editor consults only his or her own sensibilities and textual whimsies— whether we approve or disapprove of the editor's emendations—the effect of editorial work is authoritative; it is an act of power and appropriation. That is just a fact, not a criticism. Editors are not, therefore, evil people.

But a full realization of the problems arising from editorial power has been growing in our consciousness for some time, for we have had an increasing sense of the fact that different people have different demands to make on texts. Thus, the editor who establishes the author's final intentions by eliminating the misguided editorial interventions and boneheaded errors of the original publishers provides no help for the social historian who may not *just prefer* the text that was read by original readers but whose work *requires* the historical text that formed the basis for original reactions to the work.[2] The editor who establishes a documentary text, reflecting the means of production that "made the work what it became at first publication," provides no help to the student who wants to study the compositional habits or the creative imagination of a particular author.[3] The editor who creates a text fulfilling the "potential inherent in the flawed surviving texts," regardless of how conservative or radical the approach, provides no help to readers who rely on the historical accuracy of the text, regardless of how that is defined.[4] Each of the these approaches has its legitimizing rationale, of course; the point is merely that texts produced to satisfy one view of textuality inevitably disappoint all others.

Any editor who, in establishing the text, relegates any alternative version of the text to a minor position in the reader's assessment of the work has exercised authority over the text in such a way as to determine for the reader what the text of the work is. If the alternative is at the foot of the page, it still appears to have dropped out of the text, as, for example, Jack Stillinger complains about the Cornell Wordsworth edition's presentation of "I Wandered Lonely as a Cloud" (Stillinger, "Textual," 19–20).[5] And if it is in an appendix at the end of the book, it appears tangential at best,

---

2. Striking examples of radical effects on the meaning of works when "properly edited by a modern scholarly editor" can be seen in Henry Binder's edition of Stephen Crane's *The Red Badge of Courage* and James L. W. West's edition of Theodore Dreiser's *Sister Carrie*. Both editions occasioned controversy because traditional interpretations were subverted by the newly edited texts.

3. A famous example is Ian Jack and Margaret Smith's edition of Charlotte Brontë's *Jane Eyre*, which reproduces the first edition punctuation and does not report manuscript pointing—a case made famous by Bruce Harkness's review, though, of course, the same problem reappears in nearly every volume of the Clarendon editions of the Brontës, Charles Dickens, and George Eliot. (See Dale Kramer's insightful discussion, "The Compositor as Copy-Text.")

4. See almost any modernized edition or modern adaptation of any work.

5. To be fair Stillinger also notes that the Cornell edition is "a work of immense practical usefulness" (14).

as I complained of Stillinger's listing of variant readings in his scholarly edition of Keats's *Poems* (Shillingsburg, *Scholarly*, 107–9). It is, however, a condition of the print medium that one text be in the foreground and alternatives be in some permanently subordinate position.

And yet there is a sense in which the *editor* is already as dead as the author. Only a small percentage of the world's literary scholars, to say nothing of literate readers, own full-scale scholarly editions or have access to a library that owns all the volumes published with the seal of approval from the MLA's Center for Editions of American Authors (CEAA) and Committee on Scholarly Editions (CSE). I know of no literary period in which as many as five of ten published essays cite scholarly editions of the texts they seek to elucidate. Few if any teachers can assign scholarly editions or texts derived from scholarly editions for even one half of the works they teach. In a sense, then, the authority exercised by editors has created but a small ripple in the ocean of texts. There are exceptions, of course, such as the battle over *Ulysses*—and in that case the wavelets are not all benign.

The fact remains, however, that scholarly editors, pursuing whatever high ideals and rationales for achieving them, inevitably exercise authority over texts—authority from which readers have little recourse. If no one has already announced the death of the editor as the conceptual authority over what the text says, I announce it here. And if the announcement is premature, I call for the editor's death.

The death of the author (as conceptual authority over meaning) has not stopped new authoring, not stopped attempts by authors to control the uses of old works, not stopped the discovery of the implications of Barthes's announcement, nor has it stopped the denials of that death or the protests that the author is alive and kicking—living on, in, and through the texts, world without end, amen. No more does the death of the editor stop editing. Like Roland Barthes in 1968, I'm overstating my case. But I am driven to overstatement because the moderates among us believe that there is nothing wrong with the system. They rest entirely too contentedly in the thought that listing their emendations and their historical collations makes up for the appropriations they have exercised over the text in pursuit of what can only be labeled a narrow view of textual authority. It does not matter which particular view of textual authority they follow; it is too narrow to meet the needs of the scholarly world. The fact that the print medium gives us no choice but to act as we do is no excuse. I am not asking that we exercise our powers judiciously or responsibly. We cannot do that. The most responsible editor among us is appropriating and manipulating texts.

It is not surprising that editors should feel complacent about their procedures when the medium available offers only the clumsiest of alternatives. At the 1992 MLA Convention, Andrew Brown, from Cambridge University Press, called for the cessation of print scholarly editions in favor of electronic editions.[6] I believe that the scholarly archives and editions of the future will be electronic and ubiquitous, but, at the same time, of the making of books there will be no end.

As a matter of fact, however, my quarrel is not with editors but with users of scholarly editions. There will always be those who do not use scholarly editions, but put those readers aside. What about those who do use them? Their naive reliance on editors, their glib ignorance of textuality leading them to exercise blind faith in the scholarly editions they use, their pious admonitions to their students to use X standard established text causes the more sensitive, or should I say sensible, of us as editors to walk on eggshells when we edit texts, lest in the boldness of our principles we produce a text that the reader will mistake seriously. Years ago G. Thomas Tanselle, reacting to a statement I made in *Scholarly Editing in the Computer Age* about legitimate differences in editorial orientations determining legitimate differences in edited texts, remarked to me in conversation: "No matter which text you edit as the reading text in a scholarly edition, it will come to be known as The Text of the work." He was right. So what is an editor with a keen sense that no text can be *the* text to do?

One aspect of the editor's dilemma can be illustrated with a crisis in my editing of installment number 6 of W. M. Thackeray's *The Newcomes*.[7] Like most editors, I am used to the fact that we work in the absence of absolute knowledge of the historical facts or the intentions of authors. I am used to the fact that from time to time my editorial principles are sorely tested by the circumstances of a particular textual crux. Number 6 of *The Newcomes* tested the weak links in my procedures.

The Newcomes was a monthly serial; each installment occupied thirty-two printed pages; each chapter ended a decent way down the last page; each new chapter began a new page; woodcut illustrations embedded in the text helped to make up extra space when present or helped reduce space when absent. Composition ranged from two to three months ahead of publication, and for the first five installments Thackeray was in London to do the final snipping and adding and moving of text necessary to adjust to

---

6. Incidentally, Brown went on to publish the excellent Clarendon edition of George Eliot's *Romola*.
7. A full account is found in Shillingsburg, ed., *The Newcomes* 2:410–16.

thirty-two printed and illustrated pages. But Thackeray wanted to spend the winter in Italy: he was three months ahead in the writing; he had Richard Doyle in London doing the illustrations; and he appointed Percival Leigh, a fellow regular contributor to *Punch* magazine, as his on-the-spot crisis manager and "editor." So, Thackeray left in December 1853 for Italy, having just made the final adjustments to number 5.

Before stating the problem with number 6, however, I should characterize the kinds of changes Thackeray made in the earlier numbers. They are the same kinds of change one finds as final adjustments in *Vanity Fair* (1847–48) and *Henry Esmond* (1852): additions of whole sentences or paragraphs, deletions of whole sentences or paragraphs, or movement of an episode or description to the subsequent number. More specifically, in number 4 of *The Newcomes,* which was too long, Thackeray divided one chapter in half, postponing the second half to the next number; then he added four pages of manuscript to the first half; and, finally, in proofs that no longer survive he added another twenty-eight lines of text. To help matters a little in this tight number the compositor started one of the chapters a half-inch higher up the page than was normal. Number 5 also turned out too long, but Thackeray cut it by deleting phrases and sentences here and there, cutting large chunks equivalent to two and a half pages of text, and providing fewer illustrations than in any other number of the book.

Then he went off to Italy, sending the manuscript for number 6 in two batches. The first batch arrived safely, but the second, amounting to three pages of text, apparently did not. Whether proofs of number 6 were held up waiting for those three pages or for some other reason, we do not know. In any case proof amounting to "25 pages and a bit" were mailed from London on 11 February to Thackeray in Rome, unusually late for an installment that had to be on the streets on the first of March. The proofs arrived in Rome one day after Thackeray had left for Naples. Thackeray finally got them on 21 February. February in 1854 had only twenty-eight days, and in the best of circumstances mail from Rome to London took five days. So, *if* Thackeray did what he had to do to stretch out the proofs or augment them, and *if* he got them back in the mail by the next day, and *if* the mail moved as fast as it ever did, *then* the London publisher could have received them on 27 February and had one day to correct type, print fourteen thousand copies of two sheets, bind them in their yellow wrappers, and deliver them out of the back door to the waiting booksellers' vans on the evening of 28 February.

All that survives besides the manuscript and the printed book is a letter from Thackeray to Percival Leigh dated 25 February explaining that the proofs were late arriving, wondering what happened to the three pages he sent for the number, and asking what number 6 looked like now. There is an edginess in the tone of the letter suggesting frustration on the author's part at not knowing what actually got published. He was at the time writing number 8, reading proofs of number 7, and wondering what number 6 contained. He laments one particular error in number 6 and concludes: "But what is the use of talking now? I hope you have eked out the number somehow: and trust in the Lord" (Ray, *Letters,* 3:350).

So, we don't know for sure who made the changes in number 6 that successfully appeared on 1 March with thirty-two pages. There are extra pictures in the number, one in particular of three men standing looking like El Greco saints—very tall and elongated, taking up most of the page. One-third of the pages are printed one or two lines short. One chapter begins a half-inch lower down the page than usual. The last pages of the chapters end near the top of the page. One and a half pages cut from number 5 appear in number 6.

All of that is fine, for it is not difficult to accept the fact that Thackeray and everyone else involved in this book intended number 6 to have thirty-two pages. It would be possible, I suppose, to edit the work so as to produce the manuscript version more completely, but the thirty-two-page requirement was a known and accepted boundary, and, for better or for worse, I decided it was a legitimate factor in determining the text for the scholarly edition.

The problem arises when one looks at the other changes in number 6: some phrases cut (including two references to Guy Fawkes and several unflattering descriptions of characters), a number of added phrases (which almost always have the effect of extending a paragraph by one more line), and a myriad of phrases substituting one way of saying a thing for another way of saying the same thing. This last is most unusual. Thackeray did not do that in other situations in which we know he himself was making the changes. There is a high likelihood that Percival Leigh took his task too much to heart and had a field day "improving" Thackeray's prose.

But the point is, we don't know for sure. So, I edited number 6 two ways. Once, accepting the changes that adjust length to fit the thirty-two-page format but rejecting all verbal alterations unless they corrected errors in the manuscript; I called that Thackeray's version of number 6. Then I edited the number to include the changes that I believe—but can not prove—were made by Percival Leigh. I called that Leigh's version of number 6. Every time I added another Leigh change to the text I gritted my teeth because in my opinion the changes are inferior to the original. But my editorial board reminded me that the editor's personal opinion about the literary quality of specific variants should not be the guide for emendations.

I had run into an irresolvable situation in which two texts are, in principle, equally legitimate. But the clear reading text can only represent one of them. And no matter which one was chosen, the other would be seen as a secondary text. One cannot, in a printed scholarly edition, present them with equal force. Even when one declares that they have equal force, it does not have the effect of giving them equal force. As editor of *The Newcomes,* I held in my hand the power to affect readers' experience of the book. The editor decides what readers read.

What can be learned from the concept of the death of the author and the power of the editor that will help us to imagine a responsible and judicious role for the scholarly editor? The literature of editorial policy and procedure is full of analogies designed to characterize the editor. Perhaps the chief of these is the Editor as Restorer and Preserver. This image projects the idea of a once pristine but now damaged artifact susceptible to the ravages of time and inept reproduction. The fact that a preserver of pristine qualities is, by imaginative extrapolation, incapable of restoring anything seems not to bother some editors. To restore, a change must take place; to preserve, a change must not take place.

But our discipline has recourse to other metaphors: the editor is sometimes seen as the midwife of art, caring for the health of the creator and creature, enabling the production of pure texts. The image of midwife is of a humble and indispensable companion of the painful events of generation. Midwives have no creative function, but they ensure that nothing goes wrong. But if the scholarly editor is a midwife, she can only preside at a rebirth; the child will be newly reborn; but, the author absent, one can only suspect that the midwife does have a creative function. The metaphor will not hold.

In a similar ancillary but crucial position is the editor as fiduciary agent to whom the author submits "in much the same way that a patient trusts his physician or a client his attorney" (West, "Editorial," 169). The editor and the client author together face the hostile world of commercial book production. While it is true that authors place trust in commercial editors and producers by signing their contracts, the scholarly editor makes a space for usurping that trust by pointing to its betrayal in case after case of unauthorized and nonauthorial intervention in commercial production processes.

In these metaphoric transmogrifications the editor influences the text benignly on behalf of the author, to whom (the editor, of course, declares) the text and its meanings "belong." But the benignity of the view masks the inescapable fact that the scholarly editor determines the text for every subsequent reader. The fact that the editor expects to be thanked—indeed, that the editor cannot understand why any reader would not be grateful—is no reason to tread softly or to judge lightly the scholarly editor's acts. The fact that editors are proud of their humility and servile self-elimination, accomplished by burying the apparatus and "foregrounding" the author's text, is no reason to forget that edited texts are the work of editors or to fail to recognize the importance of editors as the first interpreters and prime influences on the interpretations of others.

Recently, a critic of textual critics suggested: "We might ... variously view the editor of a ... text as a Bonaventurian compiler, a Barthesian writerly reader, a Bloomian strong reader, a frustrated author bordering on neurosis when faced by decisions, or a revisionary historicist. It should be clear that she cannot be defined simply or dismissively. Now, what if the editor is also a feminist?" (Trigg, "Signature," 172). Experience reveals that it is easier to find fault than to say to the sinner "take up thy bed and walk," but after an attack like this one I must stick my neck out and shall take with as good humor as possible the ax's blow to my preferred metaphors for the editor. The scholarly editor, whether Barthesian, Bloomian, Bowersian, McGannian, or Feminist, is an archaeologist, a historian, and a teacher by turns. An archaeologist finds, describes, catalogs, collects, and stores artifacts; in the editor's case this means archival and transcription work that is only as good as the care, acuteness, and technology employed. Next, as historian, the editor is a storyteller constructing coherences from the scattering of surviving evidence, filling in the blanks with educated guesses and providing from imagination the web of connections that will place each text and each variant in relation to the whole. Finally, as teacher, the editor is one who makes the materials and their supposed relevances and relations available to those less well versed in the matter.

Archaeologists cannot make up new artifacts; they only discover, or rather uncover, them. *Historians* cannot "discover" connections and relationships; their work is not objective. No understanding of the past is without subjective mediation; the historian/editor organizes the material and arranges the data to support a view of the pattern of being and doing that we take for the past—every emendation is such a rearrangement of evidence, every choice of text supports a view of an imagined originary whole. *Teachers* instruct those willing to be led into the historian's view or views of the evidence.

For these reasons I think the ideal scholarly edition should be

1. an archive of historical documents whose iconography is intact but whose words can be searched by computer aid;
2. an archive of edited texts, or at least one edited text, produced to reflect the work of a historian or of several—that is, an edited text newly produced according to clearly articulated editorial principles; and
3. an archive that is introduced historically, critically, and textually. To be a very good teacherly device the archive should have visual and aural presentation and provide space for, or actually demand, scripted interaction from the edition user.

The day is over for the editor as the establisher of a text that shall come to be known as the text of work X by author Y. I wish I could say with equal confidence that the day is over when critics or student readers use scholarly editions as transparent vehicles through which to interact unselfconsciously with the expressions and content of works of art, oblivious to the medium of exchange: the edited text.

Chapter 2

Textual Angst:
Literary Theory and Editorial Practice

I wrote: in the dark cavern of our birth.
The printer had it tavern, which seems better:
But herein lies the subject of our mirth,
Since on the next page death appears as dearth.
So it may be that God's word was distraction,
Which to our strange type appears destruction,
Which is bitter.[1]

—Malcolm Lowry, "Strange Type"

LOSER IN BIBLE CONTEST SOUGHT IN WINNER'S DEATH
DADEVILLE, ALA. —*A man who lost a Bible-quoting contest is suspected of killing the man who beat him, police said. Gabel Taylor, 38, was shot once in the face outside his apartment Thursday. . . . Taylor . . . and the suspect apparently were comparing their Bible knowledge outside an apartment complex, each quoting different versions of the same passage. The suspect retrieved his Bible and realized he was wrong, witnesses said. "He said Taylor did know more and that made him mad," police chief Terry Wright quoted witnesses as saying.*

Associated Press[2]

---

1. Last line thus in *Selected Poems*, ed. by Earle Birney, but as "Which is better" in the scholar's edition, *The Collected Poetry of Malcolm Lowry*, ed. by Kathleen Scherf (Vancouver: University of British Columbia Press, 1995), as reported by Brad Leithauser ("Notions of Freedom," 34).
2. Thanks to Arthur Chandler for bringing this news item to the attention of the PHIL-LIT electronic list.

The textual condition is a condition of angst—the anxiety of the indeterminacy of text. Years of investigation, editorial activity, foundation and government funding, and bibliographical work have left us farther than ever from certainty, for to the indeterminacy of textual meaning we have added orders of uncertainty about textuality itself. Though we find ourselves in the midst of a burgeoning textual theory industry, appalling ignorance continues to feed controversy over the relations between authoring acts, textual documents, and reader responses. Worse, we often assume that what we don't know about these issues does not matter. Literary theory has done little to advance our knowledge of the textual condition, except to ask disturbing questions about it and to increase the level of anxiety. Just when the "New Bibliography" seemed about to establish the definitive edition, along came the serpent, theory, and asked "And is it really so?" Paradise, the innocence of text, has been lost. It remains to be seen whether it was a fortunate fall; it seems clear enough, however, that it was a necessary one.[3]

Textual criticism as it was taught in the 1960s in the United States, particularly at the University of Virginia, Kent State University, the University of Wisconsin, and the University of South Carolina, was the new, developing literary theory of the day. Editors then still used, without conscious irony, the term *definitive edition* and occasionally *definitive text*. They thought of their task as "establishing the text so that it would never have to be done again," unless, of course, new historical evidence in the form of previously unknown letters or authoritative forms of the text came to light. The aim of textual criticism was to prepare a text "as the author had intended it to be." The *New Bibliography* and increasingly large grants from the Health Education and Welfare Office (HEW) and then the National Endowment for the Humanities (NEH) made such goals seem attainable. Editors thought they knew, in any case, that the practices of previous generations of textual critics were frequently based on assumptions about literary production that the New Bibliography was exposing as false.

The reason that established texts were valued (and still, alas, are by many academics who look to editors to provide a simple "best" text) can be suggested by the fact that among the critical statements undergirding textual criticism were W. K. Wimsatt and Monroe Beardsley's essay "The

---

3. An earlier form of this essay was presented as an Elizabeth Wessel Lecture at the University of South Carolina in March 1991. Its point of departure was the question "Of what benefit to practical criticism, and in particular to textual criticism, have been the developments in literary critical theory in the last two decades?" First published in Australia (*LiNQ* 21 [October 1994]: 71–93), it is printed by permission of *LiNQ* and the English Department at the University of South Carolina.

Intentional Fallacy," Cleanth Brooks's study *The Well-Wrought Urn,* and other New Critical works whose central premise was that literary works were "organisms" exhibiting "artistic integrity," "internal coherence," and "wholeness." The critic's job was to reveal the integrity of the work of art. Since "corrupted texts" make that job a difficult one, the task of the textual critic was to insure that the text was free of corruption. In another fundamental critical statement of the time, Bruce Harkness's "Bibliography and the Novelistic Fallacy," the importance of exact textual detail in novels as well as poetry was supported by examples of difficulties critics encountered because of textual errors in, and bibliographical ignorance about, texts by Conrad, Hardy, and F. Scott Fitzgerald. Thus, the undergirding concept of textual criticism was that the work of art was an aggregate of details molded into a wholeness, every part of which was freighted with intended meaning.

The link between New Criticism and textual criticism is worth dwelling on for a moment because on the surface they seemed at war.[4] New Criticism, despite the work of its best practitioners—such as Cleanth Brooks in *The Yoknapatawpha Country,* which, for the work of a leading New Critic, has a remarkable base in historical scholarship—had developed a reputation (not entirely deserved) for its most outstanding feature: attention to "the text itself," frequently with little regard to anything outside the text.[5] Textual criticism was also devoted to "the text itself" but in such a way as to seem opposed to what New Criticism meant by the phrase. To the textual critic the text was the focus of scholarly attention driven by the question of authenticity—what words and what marks of punctuation *should* be there. New Critics all too often assumed the text to be authentic and self-sufficient so that critical attention could all be focused on meaning; the verbal icon was assumed to be an accomplished fact to begin with.

The alliance between textual and literary criticism in the 1960s is illuminated by Fredson Bowers's remark that bibliographers are not the "sons of Martha" or the handmaids of textual criticism. The remark would be

4. The link is not my discovery. Harkness assumes that the New Critics' work is rendered impossible by the use of corrupt texts ("Bibliography and the Novelistic Fallacy"). Michael Groden refers to the connection frequently in "Contemporary Textual and Literary Theory"; David C. Greetham makes similar connections in "Politics and Ideology in Current Anglo-American Textual Scholarship" (1–2); and in "[Textual] Criticism and Deconstruction" (1–2); as does G. Thomas Tanselle in "Textual Criticism and Literary Sociology" (102–3).

5. Actually, of course, New Critics neglecting the "historical" element did bring "from outside the text" all the "intellectual baggage" of their own reading—a point that became central to reader response criticism.

pointless had bibliographical scholarship not been seen already as a secondary branch of study, useful because it helped the textual critic determine what the text should be. Likewise, the feeling among textual critics was that they were not the sons of Martha of literary criticism, merely useful in establishing texts for the benefit of the sons of Mary, the New Critics, who needed textual critics ("drudges who count commas") to provide reliable texts for close reading.

The sexism embedded in this vision of sons of Martha and sons of Mary is worthy of remark, for it recalls the biblical dispute between Lazarus's sisters over which was the proper way to serve and to enjoy the Master. New Criticism and textual criticism were both thoroughly intentionalistic and logocentric, though they may have disagreed over whether the Master they served was the author or the text. If at times some literary critics in those days were careless about which text they used, it was out of ignorance, not out of principle. The closest anyone got to arguing coherently on behalf of the aesthetic superiority of erroneous or accidental texts was James Thorpe in "The Aesthetics of Textual Criticism" in 1965. But even Thorpe argued from the basis of the Text as Master and not from some principle or critical theory that challenged the authority of "The Text Itself."

While in Virginia, Ohio, and South Carolina was fashioning the New Bibliography, in Europe the Imminent Will prepared a sinister mate: a series of leftish critical ideas loosely called structuralism, Marxism, feminism, deconstruction, and reader response. I shall not argue that the collision of bibliography with deconstruction sank the Modern Language Association's Center for Editions of American Authors (CEAA). The first line of defense, however, raised by the scholar/critics in the bastions of the New Bibliography was to snort in disdain and refuse really to understand these new theories.[6] It is understandable that they should have done that. First, the new theories tended to shift attention away from that which they thought should be the center of attention—the author and his or her work—to the language and its work and to sociopolitical concerns. It was bad enough in the eyes of bibliographers and textual critics that the New Critics talked not about the author's meaning but the text's meaning. When other "so-called critics" came along using texts as samples of linguistic usage or as illustrations of how writers can be blind to the chauvinistic hegemonies

---

6. This defense strategy still "informs" much of the resistance to theory, as is amply demonstrated by Dinesh D'Souza's uncomprehending remarks in *Illiberal Education* (51–79, esp. 74).

they benefited from or as clever ways to misread, many declared themselves uninterested in such chicanery. Putting the reader on the author's throne seemed an act of appalling hubris, self-indulgence, and loss of discipline. Literary theorists, it is now almost difficult to remember, were dismissed as charlatans capering on the edges of the profession in which real workers in the vineyard produced historical scholarship and coherent interpretations illuminating the author's achievements and the artistic integrity of the text. Nor would New Critics or New Bibliographers readily acknowledge that criticism was essentially political, for to do so would be to relinquish the objectivity that legitimized textual and historical scholarship. The announcement that the author was dead was the last straw. Old historicists hunkered down and waited for the "fad" to pass. Recent indications are that a great many scholar/critics are coming out of their bunkers to enjoy the death of deconstruction. When asked the question, therefore, "of what benefit have the developments in literary theory of the last two or three decades been to bibliography, textual criticism, and the practice of scholarly editing?" the answer must sift out those responses to theory that rejected its premises from those that have become, as a result, more self-conscious and, I will argue, more comprehensive in dealing with the multiplicity of materials and points of view relative to the nature of literary texts.

The surfacing and success of reactions to theory evident in the American Literature Association and the spate of books by Hirsch, Bloom, D'Souza, Booth, Battersby, and others does not, I contend, indicate that a fad has had its day and is fading. The textual landscape has been irreversibly changed by theory, and failure to acknowledge it would be a sad mistake. Yet literary theory is not one monolithic movement that can be referred to usefully with the third-person singular pronoun. Nor can "its" effects on textual criticism be assessed in some blanket statement. Textual criticism is not a singular movement either. But for some textual critics a number of ideas generated by literary theory have had considerable impact. If nothing else, critical thought of recent years has focused attention on the practitioners and their working assumptions. Linguists have provoked us to look at the medium of literary art in new ways; structuralists have caused us to reconsider our general frames of reference; Marxists, feminists, and "minoritists" have led us to reconsider our choices of works to canonize with scholarly editions because we acknowledge the political implications of those choices; and deconstructionists have questioned our concepts of authority for texts and of the functional existence of works—indeed, deconstruction questions the whole editorial enterprise. Needless to say, different textual critics respond in different ways to the challenges of these ideas, but these ideas have already added to the controversies within textual critical circles, out of which productive discussions have developed concerning editorial methods, goals, and end products and about the uses, and hence the constructions, of scholarly editions.

As a useful preliminary way to view divergent opinions, I will divide what follows into three parts: first giving thumbnail sketches of different approaches to textual critical practice that demonstrate the development of theory within textual criticism; then indicating the implications of some ideas from literary theory to textual theory;[7] and, finally, turning the original question on its head and suggesting some ways in which I think developments in textual theory of the recent past should affect literary theory.

I

The tradition of textual criticism developed in the United States in the 1960s is still a strong influence in the field—was perhaps still the strongest until 1990. Its prime spokesman is G. Thomas Tanselle, who carries the mantel of Fredson T. Bowers, but it includes as major practitioners and apologists many editors connected with or trained by projects supported by the Center for Editions of American Authors and its successor, the MLA's Center for Scholarly Editions (CSE). Their writings have shown at one time or another a shared fundamental idea expressed by G. Thomas Tanselle when he wrote in 1976, "Scholarly editors may disagree about many things, but they are in general agreement that their goal is to discover exactly what an author wrote and to determine what form of his work he wished his public to have" ("Editorial Problem," 167).[8] That claim can no longer be made. Although many textual critics today still locate textual authority in the author and conceive of textual criticism as the attempt to determine a text representing what the author wrote or best conveying what the author intended, other concerns have made their way to the fore, requiring a willingness for editors to develop a variety of editorial objectives. About the only universal criteria left for the Committee on Scholarly Editions to insist upon are that editorial theory for a given edition cohere logically and that practice accurately fulfill stated editorial principles.

---

7. These two areas are developed in more detail in chapters 3 and 5.
8. He repeats this idea in "Recent Editorial Discussion and the Central Questions of Editing" (67), in which he says that the aim of editing is "to emend the selected text so that it conforms to the author's intention."

Perhaps the earliest challenges to the point of view that the author is the center of authority and that the function of textual criticism is to establish the author's final intentions were mounted by Philip Gaskell and James Thorpe, who seemed in general agreement that works of art remained potential works, rather than actual works, until their publication or public performance (Gaskell, *New Introduction,* 339; and Thorpe, *Principles,* 186–88). The primary practical difference between their point of view and that of the so-called Bowers school of thought was that interventions by the original editors, compositors, and publishers were assumed for the most part to be benign acts, rather than necessary evils, and that the polish provided for works of art by the professional ministrations of production personnel were the final touches required before the artist's intentions for the work were fully realized. Of course, Gaskell and Thorpe both realized that glitches in the process did exist, and they argued that the aim of textual criticism was to identify and correct these occasional aberrations by referring to manuscripts and other "pre-copy-text forms" of the work for inspiration in emendation. An interesting elaboration of Gaskell's argument is his application of it to drama, particularly with regard to Tom Stoppard's *Night and Day.* Because Stoppard worked with the acting company during rehearsals and performances in English and American theaters, the text was in a constant state of flux, as that of many plays are, with alterations originating with the author as well as with the actors and directors until it reached a "final" version represented by the fifth printed edition. A similar line of reasoning is followed by Professor T. H. Howard-Hill with regard to Thomas Middleton's play *A Game at Chess* ("The Author"; and "Modern Textual").

It took the writings of D. F. McKenzie and Jerome McGann to elevate Gaskell and Thorpe's preferences for printed works as copy-texts into a bona fide literary-textual theory. McKenzie began by locating the functional authority for texts in the physical objects that textual documents are. By examining treaties and contracts, whose authority resides in the original signed copies and not in any printed facsimiles or transcriptions, McKenzie explores the influence of bibliographical authority and the physical context of texts on interpretive acts (*Bibliography*).[9] Jerome McGann, frequently referring to McKenzie's work, elaborates a social contract theory of texts. Noting that authors enter contracts, occasionally written but always functional, with publishers to produce their work, McGann reasons that the

---

9. See also McKenzie's *Oral Culture, Literacy, and Print in Early New Zealand: The Treaty of Waitangi,* in which he develops more fully the consequences of works as concrete objects in social and physical contexts.

author relinquishes authority over the text.[10] The social contract derives much from Marxist literary theory, showing that authorship is one of several functions in the economic milieu of book production. It can be said that society employs authors to produce its reading matter and that authors are constrained by their social contexts to produce certain kinds of works that do certain kinds of things. The argument includes the notion that the autonomous author, conjured up by our first group of textual critics, is a figment of the romantic imagination.[11] The choice of a printed work, rather than a manuscript, for copy-text becomes a matter of principle, for the work of art embodies the intention of society and is realized by the means of production as represented by the production crew, of which the author is the initiating but not final authority.[12]

The potential for reading the text (the original text) as a socialized product is explored fantastically and humorously by Randy McLeod in "Or Words to That dEffect," in which he explores "a new way to read," by which, in addition to the linguistic text, the reader interprets the physical text, including the evidence of crimpled paper and ink transfers that affect individual copies of a book differently. For example, he calls attention to one copy of John Harington's translation of *Orlando Furioso,* in which at one point the wet ink of an illustration transferred slightly onto a facing page of text in such a way that what I learned in Australia is called a bare bum, legs upward, appears faintly immediately following the colon at the end of a line reading:

And of no breach of honor be suspected:

McLeod notes that "the reading . . . is hereby transvalued forever. The eye, running on its emotionless track at the start of this line, finally leaps from the typographic colon into the pictorial one, and recalls the reader who stumbles over the last type—to *gaze.*"[13] Here we have the critical theories

---

10. See James West's counter-exploration of the "act of submission" in "Editorial Theory."

11. Tilottama Rajan questions the notion that author-centrism derives full blown from Romantic thought in "Is There a Romantic Ideology? Some Thoughts on Schleiermacher's Hermeneutic and Textual Criticism."

12. I explore the logic of this position at length in chapter 5. G. Thomas Tanselle reviews the literature of the sociology of texts in "Textual Criticism and Literary Sociology."

13. Randall McLeod, "Or Words to That dEffect," (as by RandyM cLeod), circulated in photocopy form with additional documentary and photographic attachments. I received my copy in 1985. A version of it was apparently presented in that year at the University of Virginia's celebration of Fredson Bowers' eightieth birthday. In fairness to McLeod he

of McKenzie and McGann carried out with a vengeance, though in defense of McLeod I would add that he knows precisely what he is doing and has both the gall and the humor to carry his method through to exciting and useful conclusions.

Another development in textual criticism since the 1970s is a tendency to think of literary works as process rather than product. This tendency has many names: *versioning, multiple texts, genetic texts,* and *process editing* are a few. Its fundamental premises are that works of literary art typically pass through various stages of development, in which more than one stage can be seen as a completion. Further, the emphasis of this tendency falls on the fluidity and development of works rather than on the work as a final accomplishment. Some textual theorists suggest that physical texts, because they are static, misrepresent the work, which is essentially fluid. But not all editors interested in multiple texts would insist on the work as always in flux. Some merely see that there are a variety of legitimate ways to establish the text of the work, and they recommend versioning or multiple texts as a way of admitting that an "established" text is really often just one of several viable texts.

Among the textual theorists advocating these views are Donald Reiman, Paul Eggert, Hans Walter Gabler, Stephen Parrish, Jack Stillinger, and myself.[14] But every critical editor who ever produced a textual apparatus that made possible the reconstruction of forms of the text other than the edited one has to some extent participated in this view of works of literary art.

The theoretical views of textual criticism that seem to be nearly universally held and that developed as textual theory independent of developments in literary theory are: (1) that differences in texts of works lead to differences in interpretations; (2) that contemplation of variant "authoritative" forms of texts in juxtaposition prompts critical responses that are

---

does not characterize his treatment of the individual copies of works as examples of either McKenzie's or McGann's ideas. For a similar, wonderfully goofy presentation, see McLoed's essay "Information on Information." For commentary on the application of McLeod's ideas to editing see Jeff Doyle's essay "McLeoding the Issue: The Printshop and Heywood's 'Iron Ages.'"

14. Donald Reiman, "'Versioning'"; Paul Eggert, "Textual Product or Textual Process"; Hans Walter Gabler, "The Text as Process"; and "Joyce's Text in Progress"; Jack Stillinger, "Textual Primitivism"; and Peter Shillingsburg, "Ideal Texts." For Stephen Parrish, see the Cornell Wordsworth edition, of which he is general editor. This list could easily be extended with references to critics like Michael Warren and Steven Urkowitz on revisions in Shakespeare, to Daniel Embree and Elizabeth Urquhart on versions of *The Simonie,* and to many others interested in parallel and variorum texts.

different from (and richer than) those prompted by one or another variant text in isolation; and (3) that information about the provenance and accuracy of the text of a document influences the critic's sense of the work. I do not know any textual critics who dispute these propositions. Literary critics seldom explore these matters, either because they deny them or ignore them.

II

Ferdinand de Saussure's ideas about the arbitrary relation between sign and referent opened the way to a structuralist view of communication, in which arbitrary conventions, not objective reality, governed meaning. The implications of structural linguistics include the idea that meaning is relative to arbitrary conventions governing the speech act. That is, coherence within a set of conventions, not correspondence to external reality, produces the sense of determinate meaning. The *langue* is the set of principles or conventions by which *paroles* are generated and judged satisfactory by persons competent with the *langue*. (I shall set aside, for the time being, the implications of the observation that the *langue* can only be inferred from *paroles* and will focus on the implications of the arbitrariness of the conventions of language.) By extension these conventions governing speech acts also function in what could be called "script acts," but because script acts initiate readerly interactions in multiple places and times through the medium of multiple and occasionally physically and textually variant documentary copies, the conventions governing the inscription of any given script act are frequently partially unknown at the time of reading.[15] Put in the terms of the "molecular sememic" system developed by Price Caldwell, meaning in a speech act functions within the parameters of sememic molecules, which, briefly defined, are the conventionalized or socialized "sets" of potential things that can be said and understood in a given circumstance. The sememic molecule is not restricted to syntactic concerns; it encompasses every relevant controlling convention and circumstance that makes speech a social behavior. Violations of the conventions of molecular sememes result in confusion or misunderstandings. For example, if a fan shouts "touchdown" when a home run is hit at a baseball game, what is communicated is

---

15. It is this fragmentation of the speech act into the act of inscription, the material of the script, and the act of "decanting" the script—this fragmentation of the speech act into script acts, in which the written work comes unstuck from the context and moment of inscription—that prompted, as I understand it, Roland Barthes's main idea in "The 'Death' of the Author." I cannot find that Barthes explores the implications of variant copies of the work.

the ignorance of the speaker, not a comment on the event. But because the convention of "American games" seems still to operate, the remark could be taken as ironic. If, however, the fan shouts "spinach," which grammatically or syntactically belongs to the same order of expression as "homerun" and "touchdown" but which violates every known sememic convention, her or his sanity may be questioned as well.

Speech acts, as I understand Caldwell's model, achieve satisfaction within functioning sememic molecules constructed from patterns of speech developed through previous uses, through the contextual circumstances in which the speech act takes place, and through other social conventions governing the human interactions of which the speech act is a part.[16] Many of the clues to the functioning sememic molecules governing spoken discourse, such as physical and temporal locale and pitch, tone, facial expression, and gesture, are missing from written communications (script acts). By Caldwell's schematics a deconstructionist reading interrogates the conventions of the generating molecular sememe in order to understand or expose what went without saying in the parole being examined. What often happens, however, is that the critic merely imposes an alternate sememic molecule that produces a so-called misreading or counterreading. These two activities may look alike but are as far apart as love from lies. In structuralist terms the later (faux deconstruction) amounts to substituting one arbitrary framework, within which conventional values and cultural expectations usually produce satisfaction in communication, with an alternate framework in which, perhaps, other satisfying explanations can be produced. Such acts of so-called deconstruction may be fun and imaginative, but they say nothing about the author or the work or about the social or political conditions of its production, for this treatment of the text hives it off from ordinary language and treats the text as a sample of language, not as a work generated in a historical social context. That is not to say that critics should avoid that activity, but it should not be confused with deconstruction, which interrogates the structuring conventions functioning in the historical social context of a work's generation.

For the textual critic, such a description of communication acts puts a certain light upon attempts to emend texts. So-called demonstrable errors in the text when no textual variants exist are identified by the editor's failure to identify an acceptable interpretation for the sentence as it exists;

---

16. It should be emphasized that speech acts achieve "satisfaction" rather than "communication," for, while each member of the speech act may be satisfied, there is no absolute guarantee of mutual understanding (see chap. 9).

that is, the editor fails to locate a controlling sememic molecule that will produce satisfaction. For example, in W. M. Thackeray's *Vanity Fair*, when the auctioneer knocking down the Sedleys' property realizes that Captain Dobbin's interest in Becky's painting of Jos Sedley riding an elephant is not a bid, the first edition text reports that he "repeated his discomposure." No one in the one hundred and fifty years since that "error" was first printed has gone on record with an acceptable explanation of the line. There is no authoritative variant reading. It has violated all sememic molecules that anyone has offered as the governor of meaning. Early editions eliminated the problem by eliminating the part of the sentence containing it. Another more dexterous emendation suggested that the auctioneer "respected his discomposure" (Saintsbury). And another suggestion is that the auctioneer "repeated his discourse" (Goldfarb). A similar instance is in William Blake's *The Book of Thel* in a reference to the "daughters of Mne Seraphim," which a recent editor left unemended in spite of the fact that he had no idea what *Mne* might mean. Some other editions emend to "daughters of the Seraphim." This editor left it because Blake himself had etched it into the engraving; it was therefore authorial and deliberate—not to be tampered with (Erdman 3, 790).[17]

Such emendations can be seen as attempts "to create meaning"[18] within familiar (i.e., conventional) molecular sememes. Of course, textual critics have understood, in less fancy terminology, that that is what they were doing; they call such attempts "speculative emendation." Literary critical thought, however, as it has applied structural linguistics to its own practices, emphasizes the uncertainty of structured coherences by which such emendations are justified.

A brief example will illustrate why that is so. I have written elsewhere about the editorial problems in Thackeray's *The History of Henry Esmond*, a book narrated in the first person by an eighteenth-century gentleman ("Authorial Autonomy"). Esmond's account is riddled with inconsistencies and errors of various sorts, including what appear to be typographical errors. One editor, John Sutherland, finding all these errors to be unfortunate, emended as many as he could, and for many others he wrote explanatory notes designed to minimize their effect. Another critic, however, has

---

17. Note that Harold Bloom's commentary in the same edition (895) ignores Erdman's decision.

18. This locution, suggesting the insights of reader response theory, emphasizes the fact that Caldwell's communication theory invokes a "generating" molecular sememe separate from a "receiving" molecular sememe, which is "creative" in the sense that it takes text as input and constructs a molecular structure within which to determine meaning. The generation and reception molecules may or may not resemble each other. There is scarcely a way ever to tell.

argued quite convincingly that the substantive errors and inconsistencies undermine Esmond's credibility as a narrator, particularly discrediting the assurance with which Esmond asserts his own personal integrity and personal assessments of truth and his allegiance to it (Scarry). Less plausibly, she even finds in the typographical errors support for the idea that Thackeray, the author, was distancing himself from Esmond, the narrator. Thus, the editor emending "demonstrable errors" might be eliminating clues to the "authorial" narrative strategy. The trouble here is that there is no way to know who is right.[19] There are only alternative sememic molecules within which to create satisfactory meaning and thus justify one procedure or another.

Not only have poststructural literary theories undermined confidence in any general sense of objectivity and historical accuracy in scholarship and interpretation, they have also undermined confidence in specific elements of textual theory and practice of twenty and thirty years ago. The literature of textual criticism has been frequently devoted to arguments about the authority for the text. At issue are the authority for the words and punctuation that are inscribed in documentary copies of the work *as well as* the authority for the meaning of the text. Textual critics have located authority for the inscribed text in a variety of agents and have argued brilliantly over who or what constitutes textual authority. They have not, however, seriously questioned whether there actually is an authority for text and meaning. Literary theorists, on the other hand, while frequently taking the text for granted, have seriously challenged the notion that there is an authority for meaning.

Literary theorists have argued that the work of art is that which the reader "decants" from the book (to use Roland Barthes's expression ["From Work," 62]). Consequently, the authority for the meaning of the text is the reader. Try as one might to reconstruct past circumstances to inform a reading of the text, the reader is doing no more than projecting personal biases and an arbitrary selection, or bricolage, of apparently relevant external data onto the text and finding there what was sought.[20] Caught in the

---

19. This illustration is developed in detail in my essay "Authorial Autonomy vs. Social Contract." In "Thackeray's Errors" (16–27) Sutherland rejects the idea that the errors are put there deliberately by Thackeray to undermine Esmond, but the point is that acceptance or rejection of the theory is a matter of opinion, not fact.

20. It is sobering to modern theorists to find parallel statements in the writings of the supposedly passé historical critics of forty years ago. See, for example, Marvin Mudrick's 1954 remark that, "nose to nose, the critic confronts writer and, astonished, discovers himself" (qtd. by Harkness, "Bibliography," 59).

trap of present existence—prevented, that is, from accessing the past or its authorizing agencies—the reader in all honesty appropriates the text (i.e., the decanted work, not the printed text) and examines it for its potential political, social, or aesthetic implications in relation to contexts perceived and half-created. The result of this playful approach to the text is a loss of interest in historical *re*constructions, for their basis is suspect. Each reading and rereading is a unique experience of the work. Hence, with the author set aside as sole authority for meaning or message, the critic discovers that texts are valuable not according to their authenticity but, rather, according to their susceptibility to rich readings or to the exposure of gaps, particularly ideological gaps—those revealing areas that "go without saying," the identification of which makes the critic by turns so deliciously superior and deliciously humble, for he sees through the mystifications of the text and yet also knows that his own expressions contain the seeds of their own deconstruction.[21]

What can this shift of emphasis—away from interpreting texts as intended messages from the authoring, authorizing past toward an exploration of the rich possibilities of textual appropriation—mean to textual criticism, which has for so long justified itself by producing "authoritative" texts? It seems that, along with the intending authority for meaning, poststructuralists tend also to abandon the authority of the material text. Is this loss of interest on their part a matter of principle, or is it merely an oversight, stemming from a naive assumption about the stability of material texts? It is difficult to find a modern literary theorist who has explored the consequences of this abandonment of the material text in favor of what I call the "reception performance text"—the conceptualized text recreated by the reader in the act of reading. (See chapter 3.) Interest in the indeterminacy of *meaning* has shifted attention away from the indeterminacy of *documentary texts*. It is curious that deconstructionists have failed to take up this question as one inextricably linked to the question of indeterminate meaning.

The degree to which that last observation may be true is, I think, difficult to establish, but it can be illustrated by Sandra M. Gilbert and Susan Gubar's essay "Masterpiece Theatre: An Academic Melodrama," in which two unknown thugs tie an unnamed text to the railroad track, creating a nationwide panic among big-name critics, who congregate in helpless agitation at the scene until an untenured assistant professor, Ms. Jane Marple,

---

21. I admit again that these views oversimplify the arguments and conclusions of many poststructuralists, but the general tendency to focus on "decoding" rather than on "encoding" cannot be denied.

suggests that someone *read* the text. Every currently fashionable critical stance is represented in the crowd, but there is no bibliographer, no textual critic, no scholarly editor, and no historian of the book. Clearly, these "marginalized professions" don't figure on the scene. That Gilbert and Gubar may be satirizing the self-importance rather than the ignorance of the assembled luminaries, who are helpless when confronted with "the text itself," only emphasizes the fact that most critics and most literary theorists take the material text for granted. Further, it is evident that the text in that case has been completely appropriated and tied to the track *out of context*. In Caldwell's terms the text has ceased to be a part of ordinary language and become a free-floating sample text (or perhaps more accurately an isolated and imprisoned text). Whether the thugs who tied it there are alter egos to the crowd of critics, some of whom regularly hive off texts from contexts, remains an open question.

G. Thomas Tanselle has emphasized the idea that the text of the document and the text of the work are two different concepts and the fact that they seldom coincide fully is the problem with which textual criticism occupies itself ("Textual Criticism and Deconstruction").[22] If that is so, and I believe it is, it is crucial to define *work,* for, if the work is not the same as the text, it can be identified in several ways. There are, therefore, also several ways for an editor to determine how the text of the document should be emended in order to bring it into line with the text of the work. And it follows that there are several ways the literary critic can be at the mercy of the physical text in hand. Tanselle says that the task of the textual critic is the "construction of texts of works as intended at some point in the past" ("Textual Criticism and Deconstruction," 26). This formulation acknowledges that the intending agency may have intended different texts for the work at different times or that the intending agency need not be identified as, or restricted solely to, the author. But Tanselle seems to insist that a fundamental characteristic of works is that they are intended.[23]

Jerome McGann seems to deny Tanselle's basic assumption when he finds the work inextricably *in* the material text. McGann does not equate the work with the text of any particular document, but he seems to think

---

22. The distinction is fundamental and useful but not sufficiently analytic. I detail a more complex series of distinctions between conceptual and production texts and between linguistic and material texts and explore the implications of the concept of versions of works to these distinctions in chapter 3.

23. James Thorpe insists on a similar idea when distinguishing between aesthetic objects susceptible to emendation and those not susceptible to it by distinguishing between found or accidental art and intended art (*Principles,* 30–32).

that the work must be in the document, with the document, and of the document for any particular reading event to take place. He is reported to have said to David Greetham:

> You quote this [distinction between concrete "text" and ideal "work"] as if it were a fact about Textual Scholarship that everyone working in the field, whatever their other differences, would assent to. In fact, it articulates one of the key points of the controversy: far from representing an "alien" condition for messages, it seems to me that "the physical" (whether oral or written) is their *only* condition. And of course much of consequence follows from those fundamentally different ways people have of imagining and thinking about texts."[24]

Yet McGann, like Tanselle, vests an intending agency with authority for both the text of the document and the meanings of the work; that authority, McGann seems to insist, is shared by the author and the means of production in a determining social context (*Critique*, 28–94; and "Theory," 20–21).

III

Tanselle's and McGann's propositions do not exhaust the possible responses to the idea that the text of the work and the text of the document may differ. Tanselle's notion is that the work is a conceptual entity resulting from a creative performance (authorial intention). McGann's notion is that the work is a material entity resulting from a production performance (a market commodity). If, however, the text of the work differs from the text of the document because the reading act is always a creative (perhaps distorting) act, we have yet another notion: that the work is a conceptual entity resulting from a reception performance (consumer intention).[25] This notion of the work is one frequently associated with deconstruction and reader response criticism, and it tends to foster a false confidence that the authenticity of the text of the document is of small importance, since the text does not convey meanings from the author that might be betrayed by inaccurate texts. Instead, the text of the document is merely the locus of current appropriations and readerly play.

---

24. Quoted by D. C. Greetham from private correspondence ("[Textual] Criticism and Deconstruction," 9).
25. These ideas are further developed in chapter 3.

Among the results of literary theory relative to textual criticism, then, is the realization that the object of textual criticism is not as clearly definable as we may have thought. It might also be said that the arguments in favor of "established texts" are not as clear as we once thought. Textual criticism has not yet mounted a clear inquiry into the question, if the authority for the meaning of the work resides in the reader, where does the authority for the text of the work reside? Will any text do?[26]

David Greetham, noting that Stanley Fish dismisses both text and author from the classroom, has provocatively rephrased the question: "Well, will it *do*? And if so, *what* will it do?" (Greetham, "Suspicion," 18). But he does not tackle the question head on. Instead, he describes a variety of textual situations regarding uncertain authorship, textual variance, and uncertain agencies of textual intervention. Students, he says, find these matters surprising, and editors take them as matters of serious concern. These observations lead him to the conclusion that a "suspicion of texts" is "one of the fundamental requirements of the critical mind" (25). One is left to conclude on one's own that Stanley Fish must, therefore, lack this fundamental requirement of a critical mind. All of which may be true, but it leaves the challenge of literary theory unmet, for texts *do* the things Greetham outlines only if the author or intending agency somehow matters, and *that* is the question at issue. I think this is an important question to investigate, for, if any text will indeed do, then perhaps we should admit that the object of textual criticism is useless and abandon the enterprise.

One way to approach this question is to ask whether the principles of deconstruction have deferred the intending agency's authority for *text* as well as for *meaning*. It is often assumed that it does, but the question bears investigation. When a theorist says the author is dead, that usually means that the driving objects of criticism are no longer to determine the author's intended meanings or to judge whether the author's wishes are succeeding. But does it follow that the text of the work—what the author inscribed as the text—is also unimportant to the critic's task? I think in some cases

26. There are two rather different ways to understand the implications of this question: (1) There are no essentially literary texts as opposed to non-literary texts: *War and Peace* and a bus ticket are both texts representing the textual condition. This implies that the text is subject to deconstruction regardless of "artistic merit" or the sophistication of the author, and it may also imply that texts traditionally treated as literary texts yield more to this approach if the hagiolatry associated with "the literary" is forgone; and (2) any copy of a specific work will do equally well what any other copy will do. It is not clear whether this second implication derives from a belief that all copies represent the same text or from a belief that differences in the text are immaterial to the reader's response. In any case it is the second implication that I pursue here.

at least it matters a great deal. I think some deconstructionists and some reader response critics depend on the authenticity of the text, though they insist on the indeterminacy of meaning.

First, though deconstructionists and reader response critics seem to agree that the functional authority for meaning lies in the creative relation between text and reader, not in the creative relation between author and document, they do not necessarily agree about the implications of that statement. Some deconstructionists would say, as Umberto Eco did in *The Open Work* (1962) and as the Yale deconstructionists for a time seemed to say, that the reader was entitled to see whatever she or he liked in the work. This position, now abandoned by Eco ("After Secret Knowledge") and by J. Hillis Miller (*Ethics*), was perhaps a necessary overstatement to catch the attention of and dislodge the complacent biases of persons devoted to authorial meanings or verbal icons. That position, if followed to its logical conclusion, would indeed hold that any text will do.[27]

Responding to statements by Jacques Derrida and J. Hillis Miller about the practice of deconstruction, David Greetham concludes that "deconstruction is an *attitude* towards the apparent structures embedded in works (and texts), and an attempt to interrogate those structures, initially by inverting the hierarchies which the structures represent" ("[Textual] Criticism," 2).[28] If the method of deconstruction is to invert the hierarchies of binary oppositions implied by the text of the work, it follows that there was an implied hierarchy that could be inverted or misread. If the new misreading can in turn be misread by reversing the implied hierarchies of its binary oppositions, then each reading (as well as each text) has an implied hierarchy susceptible to misreading. If in spite of the protests of the intending agency crying, "That is not what I meant at all; that is not it, at all," the critic persists in misreading, the *thing* that is being misread is

---

27. It is not necessary to point out to all critics that a reader of a quarto *King Lear* would be reacting to a different set of stimuli from a reader of the folio version and might therefore read differently, but the frequency with which critics are content to base their investigations on the handiest paperback available or to act as if variant versions of the text are not of concern to them suggests that many do not see the relevance of the indeterminacy of text to their work. In fairness one should remember other possible implications of this remark (see preceding note).

28. Greetham goes on to say, "It thus brings to literary criticism a 'suspicion' of texts similar to that long endorsed by most practicing *textual* critics." I would disagree, since textual critics suspect the textual authority of documentary texts and this formulation of deconstruction encourages only a suspicion of the apparent meanings of documentary texts, a different matter altogether. Greetham is aware of that difference, as his next paragraph indicates, though he does not characterize the difference as I have.

the *text* of the intending agency. If the text is not intended, there can be no misreading. Perhaps this is to take advantage of an unfortunate word used by Bloom and others to describe something else they are doing in which the text is in fact essentially authorless, but I think not.

If one looks at the methods of critical analysis employed by deconstructionists, particularly when they are exploring gaps in the text or the things that go without saying in the text, which reveal the unspoken ideologies and internal contradictions of the text, we see that these methods involve close readings of the text. What the text of the document actually says is of primary importance, not because it is freighted with intended meaning but because it is freighted with unintended meaning.[29] This is especially true of deconstructive readings by Marxists, feminists, and minoritists bent on exposing a writer's ideologies by discovering aporias in the text. The way we know that the unintended meanings were inadvertent or designed to be concealed or failed to produce the intended meaning is that we posit an agent of intention who has been betrayed by the aporias (central knots of indeterminacy) of language. Now, in order to be sure that the deferred and different meanings produced by deconstructing the text are actually subverting the intended meaning or betraying the originator of the discourse, the text of the work must accurately represent an intending agency that can be betrayed or subverted. The intended meaning of that text is, perhaps, no longer a matter of critical interest; it certainly is no longer in authorial control. But if the text is going to be read against the grain, the text must accurately reflect the grain.

Of course, some deconstructionists will not be deconstructing any-*body*'s text; they will not be expressing any textual agent's specific self-subversion. The text can be a free-floating piece of verbal flotsam untethered from origin, and the aporias of language uncovered by the reader can be no more than contradictions or variations unconnected with the ideology of any supposed authoring person, time, or place. If it suits the critic to study texts as examples of language rather than as specific *paroles* produced

---

29. It would take a separate inquiry to explore other possibilities, such as the importance of intended texts in which determinate meaning is willfully deferred through the introduction of apparently deliberate inversions of the type I think John Fowles introduces in *The French Lieutenant's Woman* by first stepping into the narrative to warn the reader that the illusion of narrative reality *is* an illusion but then leaving the reader with the impression that the break-in by the narrator is a conjurer's trick as well. The "message" may be that the medium is indeterminate, but enough uncertainty has been introduced to make that assumption suspect as well. One would be rash to suggest that such "meanings" were unintended.

within the confines of a sememic molecule, then indeed any text will do.[30] But no such critic can in good conscience say that the resulting critical commentary relates to a work of art of a particular title by a particular author, for, if the critic truly sets aside the author not only as intender of meaning but as intender of text, then the conventions guiding the production and reception of texts (*paroles*) are likewise set aside or fragmented. And if such a critic were to take up a variant text of the work for a second reading, then new aporias may result and old ones disappear. Deconstruction is tied, willy-nilly, to the documentary text being examined and is subject to the consequences entailed by that text being the one it is rather than some variant text.

We can then ask how deconstruction accounts for variant texts. How would a deconstructionist react to the news that the text under examination did not, in all its copies, say what the critic's copy said. He might say this is another aporia, but that is not an explanation; it is only a reaction. What would that critic call the text being deconstructed, since it was not *the* text of the work normally referred to by a title and author? If any text will do, will the criticism based on one text be applicable to other copies of that work with variant texts? Would the same aporias be visible if the text says that Henry went off with Rachel Esmond "hand in hand," as will be apparent if the text says he went "hat in hand"?[31] Will it make a difference to the potential subversions of the text if it says of Becky Sharp: "Ill-natured persons however say that Rebecca was born before the lawful celebration of her excellent parents' union," as the manuscript says, or if it says, "and curious it is, that as she advanced in life, this young lady's ancestors increased in rank and splendour," as the first edition says?[32] The deconstructionist may be just as willing to work with one text as with the other, but (1) it will make a difference which text is being deconstructed; and (2) if the reading is used to demonstrate what operative inadvertent meanings subvert the apparent embedded meanings of the text, then the accuracy of the text as an intended object is of primary importance. Such a critic, exposing the unintended gaps in a text the author did not write—that is, in a corrupt text or one revised by an editor—will end up like Emily LaTella, the goofy

---

30. Linguists examining texts often are unconcerned with the specific molecular sememe that "authorized" the text's initiation. That is, they examine sentences in isolation or construct "sample sentences." The method is open to the charge that it murders to dissect and that comments on language resulting from the method apply only to artificial "laboratory" language.

31. The example is from Thackeray's *History of Henry Esmond* (bk. 1, chap. 11). Printed editions all say "hand-in-hand"; the manuscript reads "hat in hand."

32. The example is from Thackeray's *Vanity Fair* (chap. 2).

news commentator on the original "Saturday Night Live" television show, having to smile and say, "Well, never mind."

Reader response critics might look at the problem differently. Some, in locating the authority for the meaning of the work in the reader, deny that anything interpretive can be said about the author. But some critics are interested in "reader response" simply because they are aware that the reception performance influences what the work is perceived to be, and they wish to investigate the machinations of the reception processes. Reader response theory is interesting as an added interpretive consideration, not just as an alternative to other interpretive agendas. Every given reader's level of competence probably influences the reception performance of the work more than does the accuracy of the documentary text, but competence does not obviate the effects of variant texts. As in the case of deconstructive readings, not only will the reader's response be different because of text variation, reader response commentary on a work will be thought appropriate or not according to whether the reader of the criticism is reading an identical document or a variant one.

The general drift of this attempt to meet head on the questions "Well, will any text *do?* and if so, *what* will it do?" is that any text may do, but variant texts will not do the same thing. Of course, some variants will make less difference than others. Most obvious typos, for example, are edited automatically by the reader and discounted. But revisions and typos that produce viable variant readings will make a difference regardless of what literary theory informs the reader's sense of what is represented by the text of the work.

Theory, both literary and textual, concerns itself with the way we think about works of art. The way we think about works of art influences what we do as editors and as critics. Even if we do not know what our theories are, our assumptions about the nature of art and the nature of interpretation influence our interpretations. It behooves us, therefore, not to be just editors, just textual theorists, just literary theorists, just literary critics, or just scholars. There are consequences, undesirable I think, in compartmentalizing ourselves or in thinking that basic questions in our field have only one correct or natural answer. Optional answers to the question about whose intentions the work really represents legitimately include the author's; the society's; the production complex, including author, publisher, editor, and printer; the verbal icon's; or the reader's. There may be more. If we ask what rationale exists for thinking of works as intended, we have the models of messages, contracts, sermons, decrees, and other forms of communication in which a speaker or writer wishes to convey ideas and feelings to the understanding of an audience; therefore, literary art, like those communications, might also "say something to us from the writer," though we know enough about treaty disputes and contract litigation to know that meaning is not always conveyed unequivocally. And we know enough about sermons and political speeches to know that authors may "intend" to mislead.

Optional answers might say that the work of art speaks its piece regardless of authorial intention or that the work of art speaks by revealing the assumptions of its author and producer or that the work of art actually reflects what the reader brings to it. If we ask whether it is possible to recover intended texts of works that may be misrepresented by received texts of documents, the answers range from yes to partially to no. We need to know why that range is viable. And if we believe that intended texts cannot be recovered and ask, why go on treating the work as an intended entity? the answers range from, "Well, we can't be perfect, but we can approximate it," to "Well, we should just do with texts as we will."

As editors are we left at an impasse? Should each subset of the scholarly community impose its own operating definitions on works of art and create texts for its own consumption? Scholarly editions of twenty years ago were intended (pardon the word) to fulfill the needs of scholar-critics. Can an edition do that if it represents one set of answers to the questions I have posed and, therefore, represents only one of several viable ideas about what the work of art is and how the work of art can or should be used? Or can scholarly editions be developed more like Swiss army knives, capable of fulfilling needs of a diverse clientele? I think the question may reflect a common belief or hope that the scholarly editor can produce all that is needed for a critical understanding of the work. Scholarly editions are open texts in ways that single texts sans apparatus are not, but in the whole scheme of things a scholarly edition is a tool, not "the work itself." Scholar-critics, like professionals in other walks of life, will want the best tools and will not be content with just one.

Literary theories add welcome tools serving the common purpose of understanding what literary works are and how they function and what they may mean. The anxiety of text is a good and normal anxiety, best expressed as suspicion and best relieved, but never cured, by open investigation by critical minds. It is not enough to have and use a "definitive edition" for sound practice in literary criticism. Regardless of the critical approach employed, it matters whether or not the critic has knowledge of the provenance of texts, of the circumstances of their inscription and reinscriptions, and of the sememic molecules governing those inscriptions. Sure cures for textual angst, such as definitive or standard editions, should be treated with the suspicion afforded to shortcuts and get-rich deals.

Chapter 3

Text as Matter, Concept, and Action

no relation of a dream can convey the dream's sensation, that com-
mingling of absurdity, surprise, and bewilderment and a tremor of
struggling revolt, that notion of being corrupted by the incredible . . .
—Marlowe in Joseph Conrad, *Heart of Darkness*

Textual criticism and scholarly editing have not occupied conspicuous positions on the cutting edge of literary theory because, until the late 1980s,
theory and practice in these disciplines seemed largely unaffected by several
fundamental propositions of modern literary theory and, indeed, scientific
theory and philosophy as well. Consequently, the science or art of detecting and removing textual error, the discipline of establishing what the
author wrote or final authorial intention, the work of purifying and preserv-
ing our cultural heritage—textual criticism, in short—appeared to occupy
an intellectual backwater concerning itself with goals and a methodology
challenged or abandoned by modern communication theory, principles of
relativity, and concepts about the nature of knowledge.[1] If to traditional-
ists modern literary theory seemed to have lost its moorings in reality, to
literary theorists textual critics seem moored to a chimera.

   Three fundamental propositions underlying challenges to old certain-
ties about textual materials and the editorial goals and methods revolution-

---

1. If, as G. Thomas Tanselle contends, this is an unfair characterization of the work of
McKerrow, Greg, and Bowers, it is, nonetheless, a characterization of such wide circulation
that it accounts in part for the lack of success scholarly editions have had in promoting an
effective integration of textual criticism with literary criticism. It is a prime motive for the
present book to show that the concerns of textual and literary criticism, rightly understood,
are inextricably joined.

ized textual critical theory and practice in the 1990s. The first fundamental proposition questioning factual, historical, and scientific knowledge holds that objectivity is a chimera and that statements about facts, history, and truth are relative—not objective or "knowable"—because of the gap in perception between object and subject (an inability to verify correspondence between mental constructs and "real" objects). This is not a new idea, of course. The second proposition is the structuralist notion that language provides the vehicle and imposes the limits for mental constructs of "reality"; therefore, recent investigations of the nature of "facts," "history," and "truth" have been focused on the structuring effect of language. The relevance of these fundamental propositions to any form of speech or writing is quite obvious. In communication, whether or not the listener/reader receives into understanding precisely what the speaker/writer sent from intention is problematical—not ascertainable, not verifiable.[2] The third proposition is, then, that the reader, listener, or perceiver is the most important, or some might say the only important, functional authority for meaning or understanding. That is, it is impossible to conceive of a work of art apart from a perceiver's perception of it. *Moby-Dick,* for example, as it "exists" between the covers of a closed book has no functional existence as a work of art, remaining potential until someone reads it.[3] These three propositions entail one another. The reading, which "creates" the functional existence of the work, is subject to the perception gap and determined by the structuring nature of language, as was the writing that created the "potential" existence of the work.[4]

---

2. It should be acknowledged at the outset that all any reader, editor, or philosopher can know about "authorial intention"—or intentions of any kind, all of which are irrecoverable except tentatively through inference and speculation—is based on personal experience in having intended and written down texts, which produced more or less satisfaction. Anyone's analysis of "intention" is analysis of personal experience of intention. No one has analyzed directly the intentions of any other person. But one should also acknowledge that inference and speculation are two important and necessary, though fallible, tools of scholarship. In short, the fact that intentions are inaccessible *definitively* is not a reason to consider them nonexistent or unimportant.

3. Parallel to the acknowledgment that anyone's perception of another's "intentions" is personal, is the observation that any reader's perception of a work through the act of reading is personal. This is a truism, for it affects every person's perception of every thing. It is an important point that perception is always partial but that there can be degrees of partiality. The point will be made that the work is only partially represented in any given text and that a reader's perception of this partial text is influenced by partiality consisting of biases, skills, and incomplete exposure to the evidence relative to works.

4. Perhaps it "goes without saying" that a commitment to the first of these propositions prevents any attempt to "use" structuralism as a means of approaching objectivity. Poststruc-

The question ultimately is how these propositions, when taken seriously, affect specific ideas about the materials, methods, and goals of scholarly editing and scholarly reading—how they affect the making and using of scholarly editions. But a question that to a textual critic appears natural, such as "What difference does it make to a deconstructive reading what text the critic starts with?" might appear irrelevant to literary theorists, for deconstruction is a means of seeing how meanings are generated from a text, not a means of detecting the intent of a specific text. But what follows does attempt an answer to the question. If textual criticism and scholarly editing are to provide texts and insights that are valuable to literary criticism, they must be conducted in the light of what literary critics find valuable to do. A great deal of the textual criticism of the past twenty years seems to have been conducted in the light of literary critical practices of the 1930s to early 1960s. I begin, then, with an attempt to characterize some of the fundamental ideas of modern literary theory, though that field is such a seething sea of conflict no summary can be adequate. Crucial differences in the basic assumptions literary critics and textual critics hold about texts, however, will emerge.

I. LITERARY THEORY AND THE WORK

In literary criticism the indeterminacy of meaning was long seen as the problem, and, until acceptance of relativity changed the aim of criticism, it was the goal of historical criticism to develop means to interpret texts so that they would be understood as they were intended. When structural linguistics began affecting the practice of literary criticism, faith in recovering intended meanings through strenuous biographical, historical, and philological study began to erode. The *word* no longer could be used as a stable semantic unit or as access to "reality," since the word (signifier and its component phonemes and morphemes) bore an arbitrary, not "natural," relation to the signified, which was itself a concept, not the "object in reality." Attempts to link the phonemic elements of language to physiology or neurology so as to demonstrate that they were not entirely arbitrary have not proven very fruitful. Structural relations between words (syntax) was seen to govern their meaning, and the structuring aspect of language governed what could be meant. The Author as Authority for meaning lost ground to "the text itself."

---

turalists' supposed rejection of structuralism is, I believe, a reaction against such attempts and not a denial of the fundamental concepts of structural linguistics.

Rumblings about intentional and affective fallacies focused attention on the text's meaning as opposed to the author's meaning, for the latter was both inaccessible and perhaps subverted by a failure to achieve that which was intended, though the text might well witness the success of other perhaps unintended meanings (Wimsatt and Beardsley). Literary theorists abandoned the author by defining texts as acquiring "determinate meaning through the interactions of the words without the intervention of an authorial will" (Beardsley 30). The phrase or sentence replaced the word as the irreducible semantic unit, and the intentional fallacy became something to avoid or disguise carefully. Yet faith in syntax as a reliable semantic unit continued, as is evident in Beardsley's definition, and "the text itself" seemed a stable and concrete object amenable to disciplined analysis, though authorial intention seemed remote and problematic. The idea that meaning is created by the relations between the words and by the perceived choices among words that could, grammatically, have been used instead made texts seem even more complex and at the same time apparently more able to communicate successfully. Bakhtin's ideas about a dialogical interaction between/within texts and Claude Lévi-Strauss's concept of "bundles," which included societal and behavioral elements in the "sets" that defined the choices by which differentiations in structural relations were identified and understood, can be seen as means by which communication can work more effectively (by narrowing the appropriate range of possible meanings) or to increase the amount of slippage (by multiplying our awareness of oblique references—that is, we become more aware of the potential counters *not* chosen). In either case the need for an author is diminished.

With poststructuralism, and particularly with focus being placed on the creative act of reading, came a second wave of reaction against the author that exceeded the new critics' distrust of the intentional fallacy. The author was proclaimed dead because meaning was seen as located and created in the readers' interaction with the text, making any meaning the text "has" or "is witness to" functional only in reading acts—the intending acts of authors having receded, so to speak, into the inaccessible past. Thus, scholars' attempts to recreate the moment of authorship were seen as futile; historical criticism had beached itself like a disoriented whale. Furthermore, faith in the semantic stability of syntax became as problematic as faith in the meaning of the word had become with the advent of structuralism.

A strong undercurrent of thought accompanying the wave of poststructuralism and deconstruction indicated that, because the past was unknowable and because speech acts, writing acts, and reading and listening acts have (or create) their meaning *now* in a cultural or social setting fraught with power struggles, hegemonic structures, and political agendas—including very local, perhaps even domestic ones—therefore (1) the meanings we create for a text now matter more than the supposed original or historical meanings; and (2) the way in which meanings are generated and the uses to which meanings are put are a more interesting study than are the texts or the authors or the meanings they may originally have tried to produce. Overtly political forms of literary criticism, particularly Marxist and feminist criticism, received a boost of energy from this line of reasoning. Such criticism focuses on the economic power structures at work in diction and syntax and on the patriarchal and class structures, both linguistic and social, that can be seen embedded in texts. To some literary theorists it seemed logical to conclude that this line of thought set aside the major concerns of textual criticism and scholarly editing as they had been understood and defended traditionally, since the most interesting aspects of texts are not the alleged authorial intentions but, rather, the unintended revelations the text is witness to.[5]

The so-called new historicism of the 1980s, while profiting from the insights of structuralism and relativity theory, resurrected some of the interests of historical criticism. The result was radically different from the old historicism, for, in developing accounts of the past, the new historicist was very conscious of the absence of any means to validate the correspondence between the past (whatever it was) and the historian's account of it. Further, new historicists were often very concerned with the structuring influences of language and the political, social, and mythological "realities" it framed. New historicism, though subject to abuses and unconvincing practice, provided several fruitful means of investigation. One was that the understanding of a text derived from even indeterminate historical investigations is often palpably different from "readings" that relate the text only to the present reader's experience. It suggested that the richness and complexity of a text (and of language) is more fully experienced by contrasting the text as a product of a partially known (i.e., constructed) past with the text as free-floating in the present and as it seems to have been experienced at significant moments in intermediate times.

---

5. Lost in the discussion, often, is the notion that these revelations are about meanings unintended *by someone* and that the text is being treated as witness to a designated historical event. In other words, the current political agenda of the modern critic attempts to derive strength from contrast to a supposed historical "actuality" about which the writers in question were supposedly unaware.

Another rationale for new historicism considered that structuralism's undermining of authorial autonomy and poststructural emphasis on the death, absence, or self-subverting of the author had taken the reaction against belief in objectivity about as far as it seemed likely to go. Furthermore, by concentrating its efforts on the creative act of reading, deconstructive criticism provided a methodology that concerned itself with only half of the picture. A returned interest in the idea of texts "conveying meaning" from an "originator of discourse" and belief in the possibility of "fiduciary trust" between author and reader was defended in several ways. First, it was a demonstration of interest in the workings of culture and tradition—an interest that did not necessarily entail belief in the objectivity of their reconstructions nor a nostalgic reactionary hope to "reestablish" or "restore" anything but, rather, a genuine interest in roots and differences and a fascination with the malleability and tensile strength of histories and ideologies. Curiously, this approach considered both "history" and "the present" as current constructs, which are nevertheless useful as a means of exploring the sense of continuity and change in human feeling and thought. Second, some new historicists attempted to explore the concepts of utterance and discourse as functional links between the verbal text and its social, economic, and material contexts. The aim of the approach was to study behavior rather than to ascertain and pin down definitive meanings or interpretations. In these ways new historicism emphasized the link between the text as a material object and the meanings created from its physical format.[6]

Deconstruction, recognizing the futility of regaining or understanding intention, has focused on the independent life of the text as it is confronted by actual readers (who might, in spite of themselves, be trying to conform to the roles of implied readers). To this deconstruction adds the concept of ideological influences (structured "realities"), mostly subconscious, which make texts self-subverting in ways probably contrary to authorial intention but nevertheless very important to the reader. One should note that

---

6. A particularly interesting theory of a basic semantic unit was presented by Price Caldwell in "Molecular Sememics," in which meaning is seen as determined by the rhetorical "molecule" within which what is said is contrasted by speaker and listener alike to that which is not said within the limits of the molecule. This is a rejection of syntax as the primary meaning unit and acknowledges a context socially conventionalized and thus accessible to socialized speakers and listeners to insure reasonable success in communication. The structure of a molecule is similar to, but not identical with, Lévi-Strauss's bundle. One very attractive feature of molecular sememics is its ability to explore the richness of subtle usages such as irony, analogy, metaphor, and even rhyme and lies.

this way of putting it suggests that deconstruction "reinstates" authorial intention as something that can and must be inferred in order that it might be "decentered"—that is, authorial intention is identified but not treated as an authority for meaning.[7] It should further be noted that decentered meanings are not dislodged by nothing but, rather, by other provisionally centered meanings, each of which must be justified before it can in turn be decentered. Some Marxist and feminist critics have capitalized on these two principles to read texts politically and to value or discard texts according to the ideologies revealed in the "subtexts." As we shall see, however, release from the bondage of an impossible objectivity is not an escape from the physical object, the book. Nor is it an escape from the consequences of using one edition or copy of the book rather than another.

The full impact of relativity, structuralism, and reader-oriented theory has been slow to affect textual criticism, but it has begun to rock the boat. Textual criticism and its "handmaidens," bibliography and paleography, have had a strong positivist tradition, which manifested itself in former times in phrases like "the calculus of variants" and "definitive editions" and more recently as "determinate meanings" and "social contracts."[8] The discipline has made some accommodations to the "truths" of relativism: the concepts of "critical editions" and "eclectic texts" as Fredson Bowers and G. Thomas Tanselle have developed them, for example, diminishing the positivist force of "solid historical research" that supposedly resulted in "established texts that will not have to be edited again." In addition to acknowledging the indeterminacy of the meaning of the text, discussions of multiple texts and problematic texts refer specifically to indeterminacy of the words and punctuation constituting the work of art. It seems, furthermore, apparent that the emphasis on "process texts" and "versioning" that Michael Warren, Donald Reiman, and Paul Eggert, to name only a few, have undertaken, is an accommodation of structuralism—though to my knowledge none of them has characterized it as such. The result has been a slight shift (to some editors it seems a great shift, perhaps even a sell-out)

---

7. One asks what self is being subverted when a text is described as self-subverting. Is it the author's apparent meaning or the text's apparent meaning that is subverted? In either case how can a reader "know" that the *text* is subverting a meaning? What meaning is being subverted? How can the reader know that the subversion was *not* itself intended and, therefore, itself be the meaning of the text? Or is it that the *reader's* meaning is subverted by the text? The whole question of agency of meaning is, in spite of protestations to the contrary, central to deconstruction: one can hardly deconstruct what is not there.

8. These phrases were used by a variety of writers but were given currency, respectively, by W. W. Greg, Fredson Bowers, Hershel Parker, and Jerome McGann.

in the aim of textual criticism from considering the text as an established (or establishable) locus of authoritative stability to a concentration on text as process.

What this means in practice is that the editor or critic declares an interest in multiple texts for each work rather than restricting interest to just one true or final text. It means authorial revision and production influences on texts are seen as having potential "integrity" as representations of the work at various stages in the process of composition, revision, and production. It has meant, moreover, that for some works the editor posits two or even more texts to be read and studied in tandem. It has also, however, meant that the concept of textual purity has been rescued by making it necessary to "edit" correctly each stage of the process or to make the process visible by some means that distinguishes between the various agents of change and evaluates the changes not only according to the perceived effect made by the change but according to the "authority" of the agent of change. In short, "process editing" has not embraced deconstruction as an approach to texts. It retains the idea of the author and of authority, though in the theory and practice of some practitioners process editing has loosened its grip on the text as sacred icon or as the well-wrought urn.

A great deal was published on these subjects, and radical changes had occurred in the way new postmodernist works were written and produced before scholarly publishing itself as a technical practice began responding to the influence these ideas about communication had on the nature of publishing and on the notions that publishers have about what a book is and how it should be printed. Editions continued to be published (and read) as if written works were stable, achievable, objective, tangible substances, though these are the very concepts about reality that have been challenged by the propositions with which I began. Electronic publishing, to be taken up later in this book, has begun to thrive on the reimagined notions of texts developing from this reexamination of the assumptions of textual criticism.

II.   THE HOLE AT THE CENTER OF TEXTUAL
       AND LITERARY THEORY

One weakness of much literary theory and textual criticism is that practice proceeds without the advantage of a clear taxonomy of texts. Textual critics have not had a clear enough vision of the varieties of viable answers to questions about who has the ultimate authority (or even the "functional authority") over what the text becomes, whether it is possible for a work to have a variety of "correct forms," or the extent to which the editor's decisions about the authority of textual variants is a function of reader response rather than evidence. Likewise, literary critics have not had a clear enough vision of the problematic nature of physical texts and their assumptions about textual stability (e.g., that a work is a text and a text is a book and the book at hand is, therefore, the work itself).[9]

The "structure of reality of written works" implied by the three propositions with which I began places the writer, the reader, the text, the world, and language in certain relationships and locates the focus of experience of that reality in the reader. This relationship has been mapped by a number of theorists, some of whom will be discussed presently, but these maps reveal a gaping hole in our thinking, around which swirls a number of vague and sloppily used terms that only appear to cover the situation. The lack of clear, focused thinking on this question is revealed graphically when the physical materials of literary works of art are located in a center around which scholarly interests in Works of Art can be visualized. To the West of this physical center is found the scholarship of interest in creative acts, authorial intentions and production strategies, biography, and history as it impinges on and influences authorial activities. To the East of the physical center is the scholarship of interest in reading and understanding, interpretation and appropriation, political and emotive uses of literature. To the North of the physical center is the scholarship of interest in language and speech acts, signs and semantics. All three of these segments of our map tend to treat the work of art as mental constructs or meaning units; the physical character of the work is usually considered a vehicular incident, usually transparent.[10] To the South is the scholarship of interest in physical materials: bibliography, book collecting, and librarianship. Only in this last area do we detect the appearance of special attention on the Material Text, but,

---

9. I note, for example, that in "From Work to Text" Roland Barthes wanted to talk about the work "at the level of an object" and distinguished between *work* (by which he most of the time meant *book*) and *text* (by which he sometimes meant an area of play, sometimes the players in that area, sometimes the way the area plays with readers, and sometimes an object located at the intersection of propositions—in short a variety of "things" more or less abstract). But, in fact, Barthes did not discuss the physical object in any sophisticated way at all, treating the book (work) as a single unproblematic given. He apparently was not interested in work and did not see its relevance to text except as a something to be decanted. I have no quarrel with Barthes's useful exploration of his term *text*—though I prefer to use several different terms for the various things he denotes by it.

10. This map is adapted most immediately from two models by Paul Hernadi designed to illustrate the questions What is a work? and What is criticism? but the similarity to models of language by Roman Jakobson is apparent. (See fig. 2.)

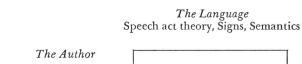

The Language
Speech act theory, Signs, Semantics

The Author

Time,
Place,
Intention

The Physical Documents
for the Work

The Reader

Time,
Place,
Interpretation

The Book
Bibliography, Librarianship, Book collecting

Fig. 1

because traditionally scholars in these fields have made a sharp distinction between the Material and the Text[11] and because they have focused their attention on the Material as object, their work has seemed tangential to the interests of the West, North, and East.

The "Southern" interest has traditionally been looked upon by the others as dull and supportive—we must have libraries and bibliographies— rather than as full-fledged fields of significant interest.[12] Textual criticism has tended to occupy itself with the concerns of the West (intention) and the South (documents), but, if it took seriously the propositions underlying relativity and structuralism, textual criticism would be in the center of the "structure of reality" depicted in figure 1, drawing upon all sides and informing all sides. It would not be self-defensive and apparently narrow-minded or subservient, as it has often appeared, clinging to questionable notions of objectivity and stability.[13]

---

11. Note particularly W. W. Greg's often quoted definition: "What the bibliographer is concerned with is pieces of paper or parchment covered with certain written or printed signs. With these signs he is concerned merely as arbitrary marks; their meaning is no business of his" ("Bibliography—an Apologia," 247).

12. G. Thomas Tanselle surveys a number of approaches to the problem of relating intention to texts in "The Editorial Problem of Final Intention" (309–53, esp. 312–19).

13. The degree to which textual criticism is breaking out of this narrow mold has gained

This particular map of textual concerns leaves out entirely the data world—the objective referents of language, probably because knowledge about that part of the picture has been recognized as objectively inaccessible, beyond the perception gap, and structured by, or constructed through, language. This worldview may not be the true one, but it is the purpose of this chapter to explore its implications to the concept of texts or works as attested by, or extant in, physical documents.

The specific questions to address next fall within a narrow band at the center of the related questions implied by this brief survey. One cannot here deal with the whole range of interesting questions outside that band. I am not, for example, raising any questions about what a particular text means or what the author or other issuer of the text might have meant by it or even what a reader might have understood it to mean. I am supposing that the author and other purveyors of texts did mean something or some things by them and that texts are understood by readers to mean certain things. The fact of these meanings is important, but the meanings themselves are not the concern here. The answers to such questions lie to the West and East of my concerns.

The questions I ask have to do with the mental and physical acts and the material results of acts attending the processes of composition, publication, and reception of written texts. The questions are about what these acts and results can be, not what they should be. Further, I assume that whether the author and reader understand the same thing by a text is not ascertainable. Moreover, I am not asking questions about whether an author's or publisher's "sense" of the work is individual or culturally determined, nor am I asking if the readers' reactions are culturally bound. It does not seem that any specific opinion about these notions bear significantly on the proposed taxonomy. Nor am I asking how the meanings of author and reader

---

very slow recognition, for many edition users still look for a "standard" or "established" text to use uncritically, but there are new movements afoot. What I see as a problem is that proponents of the breakouts tend, unfortunately to view their new insights as new, replacement orthodoxies—Jerome McGann and Hans Zeller, for example, bringing in and then overvaluing book production as the milieu of meaning, Hershel Parker bringing in the psychology of creativity and turning it into a determiner of text. The common problem appears to be that, though textual critics are very well aware of the distinction between the work and the book, they have been obsessed with the notion that the work should be reducible to a book. The focus here, however, is not upon what is wrong with textual criticism or textual critics but on what a taxonomy of texts reveals about the connections between textual criticism and its related fields of interest and on what such a taxonomy can show about the nature of works of art that might change the aim of textual criticism and the way copies of works are used in study regardless of one's position of approach (East, West, North, or South in fig. 1).

are generated and how they either succeed or go astray. The answers to these questions lie North of my concerns and are explored in other chapters. On the other hand, I am not confining my interest to documents and books as items for bibliographical description or cataloging for shelving.

The questions essential to textual criticism involve all of these other fields at their margins, for texts—both as physical and mental constructs—lie at the center of any attempt to record or communicate any knowledge.[14] The two propositions underlying much of literary theory with which this study begins (the perception gap that holds that our knowledge of the real world is restricted to our mentally inferred constructs and the view that language is the structuring tool through which knowledge is constructed) entail two corollaries: first, that the text of a work as found in a document (what I will call the Material Text) is the locus and source of every reader's experience of a written work of art and that, regardless of what concepts of works are inferred from the evidence of the Material Text, there is no channel other than inference by which a reader may reach out to the mental forms of works as they may have been experienced by authors or other agents and originators of texts; the second corollary is that the mental construct of the work derived by a reader from the Material Text in the act of reading (what I will call the Reception Text) is the only "thing" that a reader can refer to when making comments about a work.

These two fundamentals—the physical documents and the reading experience of them—are the irreducible core of literary works. Without the reader the physical documents are inert and inoperative; without the physical documents there is no reading.[15]

For most practical purposes the words *work of literary art, book,* and *text* are thought to be vaguely synonymous, which leads to a great deal of confusion: whenever anyone means something specific by them, qualifications become necessary. So, we talk about classroom texts, standard texts, established texts, inscriptions, or revised editions, and we add other concepts relative to production economics or reader response theory. Even these qualifications do not clearly distinguish the many concepts invoked

---

14. All communication of knowledge, that is, must pass through a physical medium as sounds or as signs to be seen, heard, or touched. Communications of any other sort are called telepathy, about which I have nothing to say.

15. This is obviously not true of literary works held in the memory and that "live again" as they are remembered or recited without the aid of physical documents. It is perhaps a little too literal to define reading and writing in relation to physical documents, but textual criticism and scholarly editing seldom are able to concern themselves with memories and recitations. (See also n. 32.)

by *text* and *work*. Arguments about how to edit works are fueled by confusions about what are or are not textual corruptions and by what aspects of book production are or are not legitimate "enhancements" of the work. And these confusions and controversies become heated to the extent that one or more parties believe there is a correct or optimum definition of *text* that is a guide to the desired good, correct, standard, or scholarly edition.

These confusions have not helped to overcome the already difficult task of bridging the gap between concepts of works of art that are abstract, ideal, or mental and the material manifestations, the records, of these concepts in paper and ink documents and books. One could try to put this in terms familiar to textual critics as an attempt to draw more clearly the relationship between intended texts and achieved texts, but that puts the question too narrowly (and too Westerly on my map). Or one could try to put it in the language of the English philosopher and linguist J. L. Austin as an exploration of the relationships between perlocution, illocution, and locution, but that tends to emphasize the Westerly and Northerly aspect at the expense of the physical center.[16] Most of the work upon the mental and abstract aspects of works of art is marred by vague or coarse notions of what the material texts are. And much of the work upon the physical materials of works of art has been marred by a parochial adherence to notions about objective reality.

Saussure did explore the relation between mental concept and physical sound-image in speech, and a good deal of thought has been applied to that relation in linguistics; so, what is proposed here for literary works is not entirely new. But confusion arises for at least two reasons when applying Saussure's model of speech to written works. First a speech act takes place in the presence of speaker and listener as a single event in time and in a shared space: a unitary physical and historical context. Written works do not. Second, written works, contrary to folk tradition, are not stable, singular, verbal texts. They tend to change in "transmission" (to use one of textual criticism's least elegant terms) either by revision, by editorial intervention, or by accident. The implications of these two differences between

---

16. *How to Do Things with Words*, 99–130. Illocution, the way an utterance is used (as warning, advice, etc.) and perlocution, the effect aimed at by the utterance (as persuading one to respond appropriately) are just two of a number of possible ways to categorize the intentions that might constitute the thoughts and feelings preceding and leading to utterance, locution, or creation of a delivered text. See appendix A for further analysis. The concept of intention is slippery and has been discussed in connection with literary texts by me (*Scholarly Editing in the Computer Age*) and others (see works cited by Bowers, Tanselle, McGann, and McLaverty).

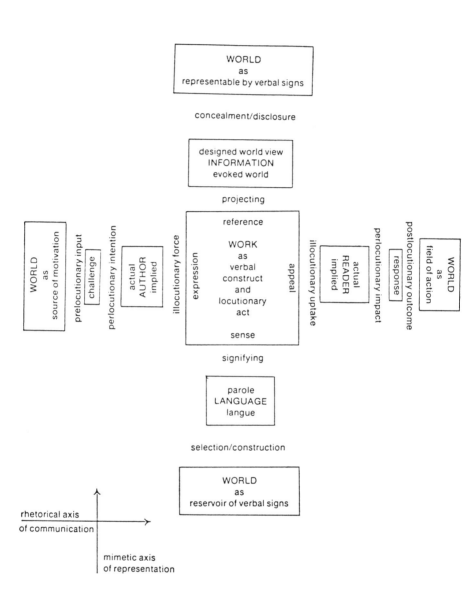

Fig. 2

Reprinted by permission of the Modern Language Association of America from Paul Hernadi, "Literary Theory," *Introduction to Scholarship in Modern Languages and Literatures* (New York: Modern Language Association, 1981).

speech acts and "script acts" will be developed in due course. For the moment, however, I merely emphasize that the alleged similarity between the two has led many practitioners of literary and textual criticism and linguistics to treat the physicality of the written text as unitary and unproblematic.

Theorists are, of course, greatly concerned with the complexities and problematics of "intention" and "interpretation," which precede and succeed the text, but the supposedly stable, unproblematic physical signifier between them, the written text, is simply missing from most diagrams of the problem. Paul Hernadi's adaptation of J. L. Austin's speech act theory is one of the most useful and enlightening of such diagrams (see fig. 2). He elaborates both ends of the author-work-reader equation and indicates relevant concerns about language as a communication system and its function in the "world as representable by verbal signs," but the center of Hernadi's chart identifies the "Work as verbal construct and locutionary act." As such, it is the work of the author and a field of reader response and is described as *verbal*, not as *physical*. The paper and ink Work, as a repository of signs for the verbal construct and locutionary act, untethered from its origins, does not exist on the chart (Hernadi 103–5). This physical absence (or transparency) is typical of speech act and literary critical formulations of the communication process. See, for example, Roman Jakobson's model:

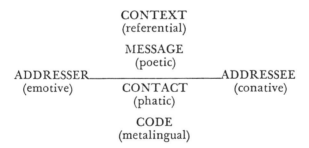

What should, perhaps, be the physical text is apparently a straight line. That line, like Dr. Who's Tardis, may look small and ordinary from outside, but it is spacious and complex inside. From the outside, so to speak, written communication looks like spoken communication, but the differences are so startling as to make conclusions about speech seem simply inapplicable to writing. The problems can be easily demonstrated.

I was spring-cleaning the family deep-freeze and came to three jars of frozen grape juice. The labels said: "This year's juice." When the person who preserved and labeled the juice wrote the label, it was natural and perfectly unambiguous to say "This is this year's juice." Considered as a speech act rooted in time and place, the labeling had a speaker, a hearer, a place of utterance (the kitchen), a time (the year and moment of placing the juice in the freezer), a richness of social and physical context that identified the relevant "bundle" (Lévi-Strauss's term), or "sememic molecule" (Caldwell's term), that prevented any misunderstanding or sense of inappropriateness or inadequacy in the phrase "This year's juice." Only when seen as a written message, a script act, untethered from speaker, from moment and place of utterance, and from designated hearer, do we find it risible, inadequate, or frustrating to imagine this label as capable of signifying something specific at any time it happens to be read.

Another example: I was reading excerpts from some articles that had been photocopied and bound together for student use. One of the sources photocopied was itself a compilation of essays. At one point a cross-reference suggested: "See p. 33 of this book." When it was first written and printed "this book" probably was meant to distinguish the compilation from the original works being excerpted ("those books"). Now, in the photocopy of excerpts from various sources, the reference was inadequate and frustrating. The statement "This office will be closed until tomorrow" is perfectly clear when announced to a waiting crowd but totally ambiguous when posted on a locked door and read in the early morning. The bundle, or molecule, changes with reference to written material in ways not experienced in a speech act. The difference and ambiguity can be consciously exploited—as in the pub sign announcing "free beer all day tomorrow." Thus, an exploration of the relation between mental concepts (signifieds) and physical texts (signifiers) for literary works leads to problems Saussure never discussed (that I know of) and will lead to descriptions of writing and reading acts in ways that clarify some of our disagreements about what they are and how they are. Perhaps it can also defuse some of the vehemence of our disagreements about what and how they ought to be.

III. A TAXONOMY OF TEXTS[17]

In 1984 I made an attempt to delineate the gradations of concepts from the ideal to the concrete, which I thought clarified the editorial materials

---

17. This is not really a taxonomy, for I am not classifying kinds of literary works; rather, it is an anatomy but only of a narrow band of what a literary work is. It is more accurately an ontology of texts but a suggestive and tentative one. Most definitely, it is a proposal for a partial nomenclature of textual criticism.

and goals sufficiently so that disagreements among scholarly editors about editorial policies could be understood clearly and not result from vagueness or confusion.[18] Disagreements could thus be resolved or brought to a truce in which the parties at least knew why they disagreed. I have been gratified by the response to this effort from editors who expressed feelings of relief and release from conflicts between what their common sense inclined them to think was a desirable editorial solution and what standard editorial practice and principles seemed to dictate.

Now it seems profitable to raise the question again because the arguments about what constitutes the work of art rages not merely among textual critics but among literary critics generally. I found inspiration to elaborate the ideas in this chapter in the writings of Jerome McGann, D. F. McKenzie, Joseph Grigely, and James McLaverty.[19] The distinctions between concepts will be shown primarily though definitions designed first to provide a system for describing the range of materials that are commonly referred to vaguely as books or works of literary art and, second, to provide a ground for discussing the various sorts of acts undertaken in response to these materials. Clarity of distinctions through definitions should enable the conflicts to be focused more clearly on substantive differences of opinion and judgment rather than on confusions about what is being said. Although taxonomies are by definition logocentric and tend to pin down concepts or objects in a conventional way, the drive to arrest and codify Works of Art is surely futile. This taxonomy suggests that the work is partially inherent in all "copies" of it. The work is neither this nor that

18. *Scholarly Editing in the Computer Age*. An earlier, less developed presentation is in my essay "Key Issues in Editorial Theory." Additional comments focused particularly on what might be called production texts or the sociology of texts are in chapter 5.

19. Jerome McGann began elaborating his ideas about production versions of works in *A Critique of Modern Textual Criticism* (1984) but makes a clearer statement of them in "Theory of Texts" and *The Textual Condition*. D. F. McKenzie explains his views of works as cultural artifacts with specific spatial and temporal appropriations and functions in the Panizzi lectures, *A Sociology of Texts*. In "The Textual Event" (*Textualterity*, 89–119) Joseph Grigely presents his ideas of texts as occupying literal, historical, and mental spaces and discusses the consequences of literary works being both objects and events or performances. James McLaverty published two informative articles in 1984 ("The Concept of Authorial Intention in Textual Criticism" and "The Mode of Existence of Literary Works of Art") on concepts of authorial intention, and his STS conference paper in New York in 1989, published as "Issues of Identity and Utterance" suggests several concepts that might be used in identifying different forms of a work; these include identity, survival, function, and utterance. I am especially indebted to McLaverty for sparking off the ideas elaborated in this essay, though his definition of *utterance* and mine are quite different. I should add that conversations with my colleagues Paul Eggert and Jeff Doyle (at University College, Australian Defence Force Academy) have been influential in ways too numerous to point out.

but both and none. The work is partially in the copy of the book but is not the copy. Works are known through proliferations of texts, not through their refinement or concentration. Every experience of a work is, therefore, partial. This taxonomy helps reveal what parts remain unknown or unexperienced.

A. Methods of Classification

It is customary to speak of a work of literary art, such as *Moby-Dick* or *Dombey and Son,* as though such titles designated something definite. That they do not is easily demonstrated by asking, "If the *Mona Lisa* is in the Louvre in Paris, where is *Hamlet?*"[20] The term *work* is used to classify certain objects, so that we can say, "This is a copy of *Moby-Dick,* but this over here is a copy of *Dombey and Son.*" The term *work* and the title *Moby-Dick* do not refer to a thing, an object, but, rather, to a class of objects. We can see this by saying, "This is a copy of *Moby-Dick,* and that, too, is a copy of *Moby-Dick.*" We might try to push the limits of this insight by defining the work as that which is implied by and bounded by its physical manifestations.[21] This statement suggests both that a work can have forms other than that of one of its physical manifestations and that its potential forms are limited by the forms of its physical manifestations. It suggests, further, that a work is in important ways both plural and fragmented. These are not simple or comfortable suggestions, and the reaction of some critics and editors is to limit their attention pragmatically to the physical manifestations of works, the book in hand, as if the *book* and the *work* were coeval and congruent. They are not interested in abstract notions of intention or in fragmentary forms of the work, which if they encounter they label "pre-utterance forms" or "pre-copy-text forms" or "shavings on the workshop floor." For them the work *is* the book in hand. It is simple; it is practical; it is achieved by willfully ignoring certain sets of questions about the work.

But for those who stop to think that not all copies of a work are identical (which is particularly true of well-known, often reprinted, works) and that what person X says is the work (because he holds copy X in his hand)

---

20. The question has fascinated me since I first encountered it in James McLaverty's essay "The Mode of Existence of Literary Works of Art," in which he credits it to F. W. Bateson.

21. This is probably not always true for the author who might consider "the work in his head" to be better than and independent from any of its physical inscriptions. It might also be untrue of readers who, having appropriated a work, rewrite it according to their own inspiration either as adaptations, abridgments, or retellings with augmentations. Most people would hesitate to include in their concept of the work either what remains in the author's head or the lucubrations of others, but it is astonishing where some folks draw the line.

is different from what person Y says is the work (because she holds copy Y), there is a problem worth resolving, because what person X says about the work, referring to copy X, might be nonsense to person Y, checking the references in copy Y.[22] A fruitful approach to this problem is to examine the concept that the work is implied by and limited by its physical manifestations, rather than being identical with them. This examination requires that we contemplate, if only for argument, the idea that the work is an ideal or mental construct (or constructs) separate from but represented by physical forms. We can do this without arguing that the work is either the mental construct or that it is the physical form, and we need not argue that one or the other has a greater claim. Instead, we might pursue the implications of defining the work as a mental construct that can be known only through its physical forms and the effects they create or allow.[23] Note carefully that I do not mean, by this distinction, the difference between a sign and its meaning or referent. I mean, instead, the difference between the physical sign sequence as recorded in copies of a work and the sign sequence a user of the copy of the work takes to be the work. The latter sign sequence is a mental construction deriving from the former with the added proviso that the user may consider the physical copy of the work to be marred by error or abridgment or to be partial by reason of revisions not recorded in that copy or even by reason of inappropriate packaging.

When two or more of these physical forms of a work disagree, it is patently obvious that, if the work is a single ideal entity, they cannot both accurately represent it. Two possible explanations for differences between two physical manifestations of the work can be suggested. The first is that one is corrupt and thus misrepresents the work (or both copies could be corrupt in different ways). The second is that the work exists in two (or more) *versions,* each represented more or less well by one of the physical

---

22. There are, of course, many other reasons why X and Y disagree, many of which are explored quite revealingly in works on reader response. I am here concerned with those disagreements arising from differences in the physical manifestations of works. (See also fig. 4.)

23. I do not think that textual criticism is a "science" if by that term one implies something objective, but there is a pleasing similarity between the scientist operating as though photons and quarks exist, though they cannot be seen, and a textual critic operating as though works exist, though only signs for them can be seen. I would distinguish in this way the relations between the concept of a work and sign for a work from the relation between Platonic ideals and realities, which seems more whimsical and better represented by, I believe, Christopher Morley's fiction about a limbo of lost works, a place in which works continue to exist after all physical copies have been destroyed and forgotten.

copies.[24] We can think of the work, then, as existing in more than one version and yet be one work. This does not, however, help to resolve the problem of whether the work or a version of it is accurately represented by the physical copy held by person X or person Y.

Before pursuing that problem, there are some difficulties with the concept of version to try to clarify. First, like the term *work*, *version* does not designate an object; it, too, is a means of classifying objects. In the same way that the work *Dombey and Son* is not *Moby-Dick*, so too a first version is not a second, or a magazine version is not a chapter in a book, or a printed version is not a version for oral presentation. The term *version* in these formulations is a means of classifying copies of a work according to one or more concepts that help account for the variant texts or variant formats that characterize them. Second, it is not just the existence of different texts of the same work that leads us to imagine multiple versions of a work. What we know about composition also suggests versions. And to help distinguish various concepts relating to version, I would suggest the subcategories *potential version, developing version,* and *essayed version.* These categories correspond to ideas we have about composition and revision. Potential version refers to the abstract incipient ideas about the work as it grows in the consciousness of the author. The potential version has no physical manifestation, but we judge from our own experience in composing that such a version exists at least in outline, and we imagine this version capable of being developed, abandoned, or changed. The potential version is unavailable to us except as an idea. Developing version refers to a process that does have physical outcomes. The potential version processed by thought and inscription produces, in the case of many authors, drafts or notes, which when added to more thought, more inscription, and perhaps some revision results in additional drafts. When the developing version has progressed sufficiently and been consolidated into an inscription of the whole, we have a physical representation of what I would call an essayed version.

The point at which the developing version reaches sufficient wholeness to be thought of as representing the first essayed version is, of course, a matter of opinion and, therefore, of dispute. This problem is another

---

24. It is theoretically possible with this concept to imagine that a work represented by only one physical copy in the whole world might be misrepresented by that copy. That is an important problem. We can imagine further that other versions of the work might have existed, but if we stick to our original proviso—that if the work is a mental construct it can only be known through its physical manifestations—we will spend little time with this possibility.

demonstration of the fact that the term *version* refers to a means of classification, not to an actual stable object. The first essayed version can be thought about and revised and used as a basis for producing a second version, etc. It might also be thought of as a provisional version or a finished version, but it is a version of the work in that it represents the work. Though the essayed version has physical embodiment in a text, it is not the physical text. We can imagine the essayed version in the author's imagination as more perfect than the ability to record it in signs, thus requiring compromise in a process also liable to inscription error. Even if there is only one physical copy of the work, one could not say that the Version it embodied was the work, for as soon as a new version appeared the distinction between version and work would become necessary again.

We should pause for a moment here, suspended in the ethereal realm of ideal forms, to observe that the idea that "a work is implied by a series of versions" is based on ideas about composition, revision, and editorial interventions. That is, these ideas depend upon imagining the processes of composition rather than emerging from a contemplation of finished copies of the work and inferring the processes "backward" from them. To think in this way about a work entails also believing that each new version has integrity, or "entity," as an *utterance* of the work. If two copies of a work differ in ways that are explained by "infelicities in transmission," then one does not need a concept of version to explain the differences. But if each is thought to be desirable or "authoritative" in its own way, then the concept of version is useful for classification. One could think of a version, then, as the conception or aim of the work at a point of utterance. But version is a very complex and slippery concept requiring further definition and discussion in detail later. Where there is a well-established convention for using the term *work* to distinguish between *Vanity Fair* and *Jane Eyre,* there is not an established convention for distinguishing versions of *Vanity Fair.*

Of the problems concerning the concept of versions that must be discussed in detail later, there are two that should be mentioned before moving on to definitions of *text* and making clearer the connections between ideal concepts of works and their physical manifestations. The first is the problem of determining when the developing version has reached a degree of coalescence that can be identified as an essayed version. The second is the problem of determining if and when a second version has coalesced that should be considered as separate from the first. To discuss these problems we need several related concepts: *time, content, function,* and *material*. One should also note that concepts of *intention* and *authority* are crucial to the idea of versions; neither of these concepts is simple.[25] Needless to say, I think the idea of versions is a very useful one, in spite of its problems.

B. Texts: Conceptual, Semiotic, and Physical

Although discussion of some of the problems with the term *version* are being deferred, it is helpful here to imagine the writer composing a version of the work in order to pursue the taxonomy through various concepts that are too often hidden in the use of terms such as *work* or *version*. One should note, then, that an essayed version is a conceptual entity, not a physical entity; it is not equivalent with the physical embodiment of it, because its embodiment can be and usually is an imperfect representation of the version. The contortions of that last sentence bear witness to the fact that *version* is being used in two ways: it is a classification system for those texts that represent version X as opposed to those that represent version Y, and it is a conceptual text that copies of version X or version Y represent. This latter notion, the conceptual text, is not a system of classification but more like an ideal form of the work. But it is not a Platonic ideal, for it develops and changes, and probably does not "preexist" as an ideal, and it probably does not last very long either. The imperfections of physical texts are of various origins, including failures of creative imagination, failures of inscriptional skill or care, use of elisions and abbreviations to be filled in later, or unhappy interventions by scribal assistants. The essayed conceptual text, insofar as it can be known by editors and other readers, is always manifested in a physical form, but it is not a physical, material text, for the conceptual text that is essayed remains (as the author's mental concept) invisible and probably not stable, but the embodiment of the conceptual text is visible and fixed in a material medium.[26] The concept of fixing, or

---

25. I have discussed them elsewhere (*Scholarly Editing*, chaps. 1 and 3), but I will return to these problems again.

26. Two objections that I consider unfortunate misreadings of my definition were prompted by an earlier version of this chapter. The first is that an essayed conceptual text existing in an author's mind does not have to be recorded in a document in order to have existed. That is true but of no moment to editors who can only infer the text of an essayed conceptual text from an attempt to record one. The second objection is that an essayed conceptual text, and indeed any conceptual text, of a long or complex work cannot be "held in the mind" as a whole or as an "ideal." I can only say that I thought that is what I meant by the comments about the ephemeral and unstable characteristics of essayed conceptual texts, but I could reinforce that idea by saying that a conceptual text (whether in an author's mind or a reader's) probably "exists" as does any large object or idea as a functioning "focus of attention" a little bit at a time and that significant elements of initial parts of the conceptual text of a work have already ceased to be held in the mind when the middle or later portions are

stablizing, suggests another reason the material text may misrepresent or at least only suggest the work: version (potential, developing, and essayed) is fluid conceptual process, but the material text is physically static, fixed. Yet since the essayed conceptual text cannot be known except through a material text, people tend to equate them for practical purposes. But the material text can misrepresent the essayed conceptual text, and hence that equation is not exact. The ways in which the material text can misrepresent the conceptual text are many and often are indeterminate, but some might be revealed in the drafts or by violations of syntax, grammar, or orthography that cannot be justified as accurate representations of the ideal version.[27]

It is common, at least among textual critics, to think of a text as consisting of words and punctuation in a particular order. This concept of texts has been called the *linguistic text*.[28] It refers to the semiotic dimension of texts—the specific signs for words and word markers that stand for the work (or the version of the work). Linguistic texts have three forms: *conceptual, semiotic,* and *material*. The author's conceptual linguistic text consisted of the signs he "intended to inscribe." A semiotic text consists of the signs found recorded in a physical form of the work. If a version represents the conception or aim of the work at a point of utterance, the linguistic text is the execution or achievement of that version, first as a conceptual text (thought), then as a semiotic text (sign), and then as a material text (paper and ink or some other physical inscription or production), at that point of utterance. The material text is the evidence that a conceptual text was formed and uttered as a representation of a version of the work: in short, if there is no material text there is no linguistic text and hence no version available to a reader.[29] The conceptual text can be materialized in spoken or written form, and it can be recorded in a mechanical or

---

occupying center stage. But their evanescent existence does not imply that conceptual texts do not have historical existence nor that they cannot be inferred from surviving evidence nor that the differences between them and material texts are unimportant.

27. See Fredson Bowers, *Bibliography and Textual Criticism* and *Essays in Bibliography, Text and Editing* for fuller discussions of means to detect and correct textual error.

28. This is Jerome McGann's term and corresponds to his distinction between *linguistic texts* and *production texts*. I prefer *material texts* to *production texts,* for it identifies an entity without regard to the agency responsible for its production. McGann, if I understand him, defines *production text* as the product of nonauthorial book production procedures, but a *material text* is any union of a linguistic text with a physical medium that "fixes" it, whether it is a manuscript or a printed book.

29. It has been objected that a linguistic text can exist without being "dispalyed in a document"—which is true but of little use to an editor or other reader. What is of importance is the distinction between the linguistic text as it was in the conceptual text and as it came to be

electronic way. It follows that the linguistic text can have more than one semiotic form—spoken, written, electronic, and Braille, for instance. The linguistic text is not, therefore, physical; it is a sequence of words and word markers, conceived before spoken or written, and taking its semiotic form, when written, from the sign system used to indicate the language in which it is composed. We must also distinguish between the linguistic text and the documents that preserve them, for as long as the sequence of words and markers is the same the linguistic text is one, regardless of the number of copies or number of forms it is manifested in. All accurate copies, whether facsimiles, transcriptions, or encodings, are the same single linguistic text. An inaccurate copy, however, is a different linguistic text, for it is a different sequence of words and word markers, though it might still represent the same version. The new linguistic text might represent the essayed conceptual text more faithfully or less faithfully.

It should be noted that a linguistic text representing an essayed version (the ideal aim of utterance) runs the risk of error at each transformation in production, both through a failure of articulation (we've heard authors complain that they just couldn't put what they wanted into words) and because the author or a scribe failed to inscribe it accurately or completely. The linguistic text, therefore, corresponds to the essayed version only to the extent that its production was perfect. "Authorial intention" editors have understood their job to be the production of a newly edited linguistic text that accurately represents the final version of the author's intentions. Put in the terms defined here, the traditional "intention" of scholarly editing has been to create a new material text editorially, the linguistic text of which coincides with the author's essayed conceptual text. But because the author's essayed text is available to the editor only through material evidence for it, the editor can do no more than construct a new conceptualization of it (i.e., the editor does not in fact "recover" the author's conceptual text). The resulting edition is then a forward construction rather than a "backward" restoration.

To speak of the linguistic text as a sequence of words and word markers is to emphasize a distinction already made but one that is of primary importance: that the linguistic text, being composed of signs, is a representation of the work and is not an embodiment of everything that is encompassed

---

recorded in the material text. This distinction indicates a space where two things can and often do happen. First, the linguistic text recorded as material text can misrepresnt the linguistic text of the author's conceptual text—in ways that can be inferred as well as in obscure ways. And second, the material text's physical characteristics modify the lingustic text in ways that affect it when a reader performs it into a reception text.

by the term "work." It represents a version; it is not the version itself. It is the result of an encoding process undertaken by the author or the author and her or his assistants. The linguistic text is, therefore, a sign and not an object, though it is always manifested in an object. To speak this way about the linguistic text is also to emphasize the act of decoding that is necessary before another person can be said to have seen or experienced the work of art. It should be equally evident that such a decoding experience cannot take place without a physical manifestation of the text as a starting point.[30]

The word *document* can be used to refer to the physical vehicle of the linguistic text. It might be paper and ink or a recording of some sort, including, for example, a Braille transcript that can be just paper. Records, tape recordings, microforms, and computer disks are also documents, though decoding such documents requires mechanical or electronic equipment. Documents are physical, material objects that can be held in the hand. Each new copy or fresh embodiment of the linguistic text is in a new document. Two documents containing the same linguistic text are still two separate entities but only one linguistic text. This physical form not only provides a "fixing medium" (to borrow a concept from photography), but it inevitably provides an immediate context and texture for the linguistic text. It will be useful, therefore, to have a term for the union of linguistic text and document. I call it the *material text*. It seems clear that a reader reacts not just to the linguistic text when reading but also to the material text, though it be subconsciously, taking in impressions about paper and ink quality; typographic design; size, weight, and length of document; and style and quality of binding; and, perhaps from all these together, some sense of authority or integrity (or lack thereof) for the text. These aspects of the material text carry indications of date of origin and social and economic provenance and status, which can influence the reader's understanding of and reaction to the linguistic text (see fig. 3).[31]

---

30. It is interesting to note that the mistake of equating literary art with the printed representation of it is never made in music: a score is never confused with the sounds it signals, nor is a record or tape ever thought of as the music; every one knows it "must be played." Yet recordings and scores have nearly all the textual problems of literary works. The relationship between "playing it" for music and "reading it" for literature is very close.

31. The importance of the material text has been the special theme of much of Jerome McGann's and D. F. McKenzie's discussions of textual criticism and bibliography. McGann, by calling them "production texts," emphasizes the agents of production rather than the mere materiality of the texts. I believe he does so to help validate his contention that nonauthorial agents of textual change and nonauthorial creators of textual contexts have a legitimate role in making the work of art. The taxonomy presented here remains neutral on this point and is useful as a description of process and phenomenon regardless of what one thinks is "legitimately" the work.

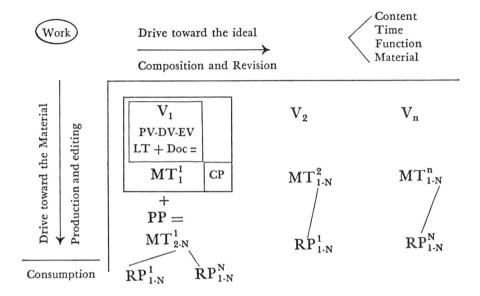

Fig. 3

There are as many Versions (V) as the Receptor can convince himself were created.
There are as many Material Texts (MT) as there are copies of the work.
There are as many Reception Performances (RP) as there are readings of the work.
Each Reception Performance is conducted in relation to one Material Text.
No Material Text is the equivalent of the Work but is one representative of it.

We should pause again for a moment, this time with our feet firmly planted in the material realm. A material text, any material text, is the reader's only access route to the work. A linguistic text cannot exist for anyone (who does not already hold it in memory) without a material medium;[32] the linguistic text and its medium are the material text with all the implications of that union. Material texts are the production of utterance. The first material text (say the manuscript) is the first attempted union of the essayed version and a document. There might be a prob-

---

32. This is true even if one hears a recitation produced by someone else's recollection of the text, though the physical medium in such a case is air molecules vibrating in sound waves rather than printed signs. One might add that any recitation, whether from memory or from a written text, is a new production of the text susceptible to "transmission error" or embellishment.

lem in distinguishing that first material text from draft fragments, and it might be possible to reconstruct archaeologically a version buried in drafts in early manuscripts or in the canceled and altered passages in a manuscript or typescript whose final revisions represent essayed version one. Material texts numbers 2–*n* are transcriptions made by anyone including the author. These material texts might incorporate the results of revisions, editorial interventions, or errors, or they might be accurate transcripts.

It would appear from the concept of material texts that, when an editor has extracted or edited the linguistic text believed best to represent the version being editing, that linguistic text must be embodied in a new document that will be a new material text with implications all its own. The editor cannot reincorporate a new linguistic text into an old document to present a "restored" material text. The force of this idea came to me while reading Jerome McGann's explanation of the work as a product of social contract in which the production process was described as an integral and inevitable aspect of the concept of the work of art (see chapters 5 and 9).

C. Texts Again: Physical, Semiotic, and Conceptual

The terms *version, text,* and *document* have brought us in the life of a literary work of art only through the downswing of the pendulum from the "mind of the author" to the concrete manifestations of the work in material texts (i.e., books). And it should perhaps be emphasized once again that a work may be "implied" by more than one version and by more than one swing of the pendulum. But now we must face the material text in the absence of the author and with a realization that, as we approach the material text, we are not before a verbal construct and that we cannot see prelocution, perlocution, or illocution or even intention or meaning. What we have before us are physical molecules compounded in paper and ink. Everything else must be inferred from them, beginning with the recognition of the sign shapes, which the ink shapes materially represent. The material text is the starting point for further processes, the upswing, necessary before the work can be perceived, for the material text is not equivalent with the work but is, instead, merely a coded representation, or sign, of the work. Furthermore, the material text in hand is only a single instance of many possible manifestations of the work. Not all material texts are necessarily representative of the same version of the work, nor are they all equally accurate representatives of the work. Nevertheless, a material text is where the reader begins the process of perceiving or experiencing the work of art. This process is one of decoding or dematerializing the material text into some mental construct of it. It is in this decoding process that the work can be said to function.[33]

IV. TEXTUAL PERFORMANCES AS script actS

It seems useful here to add the term *performance* to our taxonomy of concepts related to works of literary art.[34] Performance is an act, an event. Performances take place in time and space. They are not material objects, though they might produce results that are material and that can be used as records of the performance. Yet these outcomes of performance are not the performances themselves. It will be useful to distinguish between at least three types: *creative performance, production performance,* and *reception performance.*

Creative performance refers primarily to acts of authority over linguistic texts, determining what shall be encoded as the inscription representing a version.[35] Creative performance includes all the activities indicated by the entities potential version, developing version, and essayed version. Creative performance is primarily inventive but usually involves some sort of mechanical work to inscribe through writing, typing, or dictating. This mechanical aspect should perhaps more properly be called production performance, but when the author is inscribing new material it is clearly primarily a creative activity. One might say, however, that when the author makes a mechanical error in inscription it might be a failure of production rather than of creation. To a casual reader this difference makes no dif-

---

33. Barthes says "the Text is not the decomposition of the work" ("From Work to Text," 56), which sounds like a contradiction of what I just said, but in fact we are saying the same thing. Barthes's *work* (my *material text*) cannot be experienced until it becomes Barthes's *text* (my *reception text*). Since Barthes is interested only in the experience, or play, of text, he would, of course, define the real aspect of the work of art as the experience of it. That experience of it (Barthes's play) begins with decoding or dematerializing the material text (Barthes says "decanting the work").

34. Joseph Grigely in "The Textual Event" uses the word *performance* to apply to those things people do when they engage with a copy or text of the work (100). His emphasis is, however, on the events of text production, reproduction, and reading as moments with historical contexts such that even identical physical texts are not "iterations" of utterance. His conclusion is that the editorial goal of a stable product is misdirected—a proposition I fully agree with.

35. By the term *creative* I do not mean to imply that authors make something out of nothing. They may be manipulating givens or they may be manipulated by forces over which they have no control. The "nature of creativity" is not the issue here; rather, I am distinguishing acts of authority over linguistic texts (determining what words and punctuation and the order for them that will constitute the linguistic text) from other acts such as determining the format and design of productions or acts of interpretation or appropriation of meanings.

ference, but to the editor who holds production authority over the work it makes a significant difference, since a production error will probably be corrected, but a creative failure, because it might be a creative innovation, is usually allowed to stand. An editor might, of course, mistake the one for the other.

Production performance refers primarily to acts of authority over material texts, determining what material form the linguistic text shall have and reinscribing it in those forms for public distribution. Production performance can have a variety of methods and outcomes; they can be nurturing or negligent, skillful or clumsy, well intentioned and wise or well intentioned but ignorant. Production performance often affects the linguistic text and always affects the material text, but it differs from creative performance in that its primary purpose is the transmission and preservation and formal (not substantive) improvement of the linguistic text. It is a process of transcription, not one of revision. Creative performance and production performance are often carried out simultaneously by the same person, but, traditionally, creative performance has been associated with authoring and revising the linguistic text, and production performance has been associated with manufacture and publishing the material text. In practice these two processes are not always easily separable, for authors occasionally perform production acts, and publishers, printers, and editors quite often perform "authoring" acts. The results of these crossings are sometimes "happy" and sometimes not—often the judgment depends on who is judging.

Reception performance refers to acts of decoding linguistic texts and "conceptualizing" the material text; that is what we do when reading and analyzing. Reception performance differs from production performance in that its primary purpose is not the reproduction of the linguistic text in a new material form but, rather, the construction of and interaction with the linguistic text in the form of a conceptual text. Readers do not normally distinguish consciously between the material text and their conceptual text derived from it. They are also often unconscious of the ways in which the material text is more than just the linguistic text of the work, so that their conceptual text is formed under the influence of material contexts that did not attend the process by which the author materialized the essayed conceptual text by inscribing it. To put this in a simple model, the author's essayed conceptual text takes form as a material text that the reader uses to construct the reception conceptual text. If we imagine, then, that the specific copy of the work that reader X is using is material text X, that copy with its textual limitations and errors is what the reader is reading.

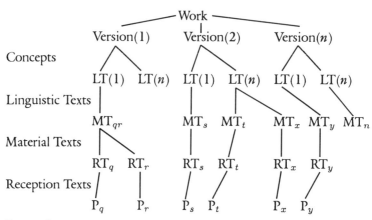

Fig. 4

(*n*) represents any number.

Critics q and r disagree from the same copy of the Work (MT_{qr}).

Critics s and t disagree from different editions of a single Version of the Work.

Critics x and y disagree from different Versions of the Work.

If *q, s,* and *x* each think the Work *is* Reception Text RT_q, RT_s, or RT_x; and if *r, t,* and *y* think it *is* RT_r, RT_t, or RT_y, they will always disagree. (In a way each is right and wrong.)

All that each critic knows of the Work is what finds its way into the Reception Text.

All that each critic can share with another reader is what finds its way into the Protocol.

It is a material text, not the work, though the work can only be known through a material text. It need not, however, be known through this particular copy; the imperfections of the particular linguistic text as well as the implications of the particular material text contribute to the uniqueness of this particular representation of the work. Furthermore, it is not the work as some ideal form supposedly behind the material text that is known through the material text but the reader's reconstruction of the work, the "reader's conceptual linguistic text as mediated by the material text," or, in short, the reception text. It should be noted that the reception text is still what Saussure calls a "signifier," for it is no more than the linguistic text in internalized semiotic form. It is then reacted to in a variety of ways and according to a variety of principles of interpretation that, taken together, can be called the reception performance. The point to emphasize and then to elaborate is that these are reactions to the reception text, not to the material text. See figure 4, in which critics *Q* and *R* read the same copy of the work and may disagree about interpretation because of their different skills in performing the reception text, because their experiences of life and reading differ or because they employ different interpretational principles. Critics S and T, who read two different editions reproducing more or less well the same version of the work, may disagree about interpretation for any of the same reasons Q and R disagree and because the material texts in which they encounter the work differ. They may also, fortuitously, agree with each other if one or both have managed to ignore or "misread" the material texts where they differ. Critics X and Y, who read different copies of the work, each representing a different version, may disagree for any of the same reasons affecting Q, R, S, and T and also because the linguistic texts they are reading are different. To the extent that Q, R, S, T, X, and Y think their copy of the work *is* the work, their disagreements will seem unaccountable, irresolvable, or evidences of inadequacy in the others as critics.

It might be useful to describe the process of reception performance by adapting some terms used by I. A. Richards to describe his experiments in practical criticism in the 1920s. Several "perusals" of a text at one sitting constituted an "attack" on the work of art. Several attacks spread over a short period of time, say a week, constituted a "reading." The reader's commentary on the work—the record of her or his reading and reaction—was called a "protocol." We sometimes call interpretations of works readings, but the word is vague and overused; we should call them something else such as protocols or records of the reception performance. I think it can be said that Richards was interested in the process of interpretation of meaning, effect, and tone suggested by the words as grouped into sentences and paragraphs and that he was not concerned with the problematic nature of the material texts he and his students used. Nor was he concerned with the problematic nature of the dematerialization of the text signs for words and punctuation. That is, he was interested in what the text said, not in what the work was. This is a common strategy of literary critics to avoid the problems of authorial intentions. What I have called the reception text is in part the reader's decoding of the linguistic text as embodied in the material text at hand, but it also includes the reader's semiotic reconstruction or reading of the material text as a totality and the influence of the environment in which the reader has undertaken the reception performance. Anything the reader says or writes about his experience of the work is a protocol. The rules by which protocols are produced and judged are as numerous as there are games to be played in the *performance field*. (See summary of terms in app. B.)

We have in these three performances a key to why observations made about speech acts go awry when applied to writing. A speech act or spoken utterance is one event with three basic elements: the utterer's mental concept, the physical medium of utterance, and the listener's mental concept. These three elements always exist together in the context of time and place when and where the utterance is spoken. In written works all three of these elements exist also, but the context of time and place is fragmented, so that the writer's utterance takes place, so to speak, in the presence of an absent reader, and the reader's reception or construction of utterance takes place in the presence of an absent writer. Therefore, each utterance takes place in a context of time and place that is unknown to the other party and adventitious meanings are the highly likely result, for the bundle, or "sememic molecule," has been broken, modified, or replaced. Finally, to complicate things even more, the writer's writing is seldom seen by the reader who usually has instead the printer's printing. So a written work entails at least three separate events (performances) whereas the spoken work is one event.[36] Experienced writers are, of course, aware of this and compensate by a multitude of strategies. That is one reason why it is normal to think of writing as more formal and requiring more care than spoken communication. There are also many other reasons that written language must be made clearer, among them the fact that punctuation is a coarse substitute for intonation and gesture.

V. HERMENEUTICS OR THEORY

The terms and definitions provided thus far represent a "structuring of reality" that cannot be "true" but can perhaps be useful. It can be used in two fundamentally different ways that correspond to hermeneutics and literary critical theory. Photography again provides a good though not perfect analogy, since photographs can also be treated in these two ways. One could say that the material text is not the work, but, like a photograph, it represents the work, so that a person contemplating the material text (photograph) can create a mental construct corresponding to that which was photographed. There are, in this view of the matter, two reception images: one of the photograph, or material text itself, and another of that which

---

36. This formulation does not fully apply to letters from one specific writer to one specific reader (addressee) in which, at least for the first reading of the letter, the event of writing and the event reading are just two events.

was photographed, or the "created world" in the work of art.[37] Another useful analogy to emphasize this hermeneutical use of the taxonomy is musical. The material text is like the score of music; the reception performance is like the concert that created the musical event when the score is played. Thus, the documentary musical score and the musical performances it enables are separate though related referents; likewise, the material text and the reception performances it enables are separate though related. Reception performances actually have two distinguishable parts: the first is the (mental) construction of a reception text, the second is the interpretation of and response to it.[38] In the analogy with music, constructing the reception text is like an orchestra playing the music. Response to the reception text is analogous to listening to and responding to the played music. The reader is orchestra and audience rolled into one for a literary work. This distinction is readily seen as applicable to drama. Not only is there a difference between the written text of a play and the performances onstage—both of which precede reception performance by the audience in a theater—but there are often differences between the written text for performance and the written text for publication, the latter intended to be performed as a reading (closet drama) rather than as a stage performance.[39] It is important to

---

37. Of course, the reader may conjure up a number of mental representations, including what is thought to be authorial intention, what should have been intended, what could have been intended, and what new uses or representations it could be made into. These might be whimsical or serious attempts to see the implications of differences.

38. This distinction between the construction of a reception text and its interpretation is not be confused with the spurious distinction between the editor's task of producing a text and the critic's task of interpreting it. Every editor and every critic must read (perform) the text into a reception text before responding to it. These acts are usually mixed and may be simultaneous, but my point is that all interpretation is relative to reception texts in the minds of interpreters.

39. T. H. Howard-Hill develops the implications of these differences in "Modern Textual Theories and the Editing of Plays." After cogently arguing through the distinctions in aim and function of various possible versions and after justifying the critic's interest in works of shared authority, he concludes that, with Renaissance plays, the theatrical version, completed where necessary by the editor into a theatrically satisfying work of art, is the (apparently one) legitimate goal of scholarly editing, for "to assign paramount importance to the existence of uncertainty is not a useful editorial principle. Least of all should an editor transfer to the reader the responsibility of adjudicating imperfect or conflicting evidence of authorial intentions, and never should he present the reader with a critical edition which he knows does not incorporate the author's intentions for the work" (114–15). Howard-Hill justifies this goal by defining the "writing of a book" as "a synecdoche: the full authorial intention is to write a work, a novel, a play, a poem," which he sees as very different from the intention to write an edition of a work—but this is to slough over the distinctions in the meaning and effects of intention into which so much scholarly attention has been invested by conflating the term into a single rather vague meaning. Howard-Hill is committed to the implications

note that readers' responses are not to the work as a preexisting conceptual entity referred to as "the work itself" but to the reception text, a product of the reader's own skill and imagining. The quality of the reception text depends in part on the material text used as a basis and in part on the skill and quality of its rendition as performance; halting or inattentive readers are not likely to perform technically "good" reception texts, but this will not keep them from responding to them.

This taxonomy, then, shows not only how interpretation or other protocols depending on a specific material text to reconstruct a work might differ from other protocols depending on other material texts with the same title, but it shows how interpretations of the same material text by two persons or by the same person on two different occasions might also be different. Each experience of the work is based on a separately constructed reception text in a separate reception performance using a particular (and partial) representation of the work.

The second way of looking at this taxonomy is analogous to literary critical theory, focusing attention on the phenomenon of works embodied in material texts rather than focusing on the interpretation of those texts. In the analogy with photography it is an examination of the photograph as photograph and photography as a process rather than the photograph as representation of something else. The photograph becomes, in a way, an end in itself, with its own meaning and ways of meaning, regardless of any correspondence between itself and some other object or objects toward which the camera was aimed when the exposure was made. The critic's attention might be focused on technique, composition, texture, and any number of other things relevant to the photograph as object and as a result of process, all of which are unconcerned with "realism" or accuracy of representation. In photography each newly developed picture from a single negative is a material object that may be considered as a separate work; viewers of more than one copy might comment on the differences and prefer one to another for various technical and aesthetic reasons. We can use this taxonomy, therefore, to illuminate a variety of interests relating to process rather than to interpretation.

---

of his statement that "the product of a theory that interprets authorial intention primarily on the level of the document rather than on the level of the work is unacceptable for drama and perhaps, if it were my charge to examine the proposition here, unacceptable for poems and novels also" (90). See section 7.B(2) for comments on the way the four unities are used to determine versions—here Howard-Hill uses them to determine the work. One can, of course, use with gratitude Howard-Hill's "theatrical" text for what it is (a representation of the theatrical version) without necessarily agreeing either that it is *the* work or even that it is the best version of the work.

Literary critical theory has focused its attention primarily, though not exclusively, on the portion of this taxonomy indicated by the terms *linguistic text, creative performance,* and *reception performance.* These correspond to the West, North, and East in the map of related interests described earlier. Literary critical theory has tended to neglect the portions indicated by versions, material texts, and production performance. These correspond to the South and, astonishingly, the center of the map. (See fig. 1). Marxist criticism has paid attention to material texts and production performance but has tended to neglect or downplay creative performance and the mental constructs of works and versions. Textual criticism, until the late 1980s, focused primarily on linguistic texts and creative performances and tended to neglect or de-emphasize production performance and reception performance. To the extent that textual critics neglect reception performance, they turn a blind eye to the role of their own reception performance in "reconstructing" authorial intention. More recently, textual critics emphasizing production processes as aspects of a "social contract" have unjustly denigrated intention.

VI. CONTEXTS AND CONVENTIONS

This taxonomy is rounded out with three more terms to indicate the relevance of contexts and conventions to concepts of text: *material base, social context,* and *performance field.*

The *material base* is the world of sense data to which biological authors and actual readers and material texts (manuscript, book, etc.) belong. The material base includes all the raw materials of historicism. The term was used by J. Hillis Miller to refer not only to the book and earth and cities and to agricultural and industrial products, but he extended it to include institutions, conventions, and mores. He does so to present the view that there can be a visceral (i.e., physical) connection between "a people" and "the land" that is part of the textual complex.[40] Note that the material base is the "world" that the book and reader are a part of, not the world to which the work could be said to refer or to portray. Both of these worlds are, according to the "beliefs of the time" with which I began this discussion, constructs or structured "texts of reality," but the "world the work refers to" is one construction removed from the material base.

Social context is my preferred term for the complex of institutions, conventions, and mores whose expectations and habits are reflected in the ma-

---

40. See particularly Miller's "Presidential Address 1986."

terial text and which form the extended field of inquiry, along with the material base, for new historicism. In particular with regard to texts it should be noted that these conventions include relations and contracts and expectations between author and typists; author and publisher; publisher and editor, compositor, printer, binder, bookseller; and between author, publisher, bookseller, and reader. I separate the social contexts from the material base because, as Thomas Carlyle pointed out in *Sartor Resartus* with more panache than originality, institutions, skills, and conventions are aeriform: they are constructs, not found objects. The principles of relativity and structuralism tell us that "found objects" are also constructs, but that insight does not smooth out the distinction between material constructs and social constructs.

The *performance field* is where the performance text is "played" according to the rules of the reader's particular game of textual interaction and further limited by the performer's capabilities and resources. This is a term suggested by Roland Barthes's definition of *text,* which he distinguishes from *work* (by which he means book or material text) but which he does not distinguish from *linguistic text* or *performance text*. Performance field is Barthes's field of play, though every reader performs or plays by the rules of his or her own league.

VII. PROBLEMS WITH CONCEPTS OF VERSIONS

A. One Version or Several?

Earlier I passed rather quickly over two crucial but complicated issues raised along the way to which I promised to return. The first was the question of how one determines whether an inscribed text accurately reflects the work it was meant to represent. The second, even more complex, had to do with determining when a developing version had coalesced as a finished form as well as when a new, differing version can be distinguished as a separate entity.

Textual criticism from earliest times has been primarily concerned with the first of these problems; one might say its history has been one of obsession with the problem of textual corruption. I am not going to try to provide a primer on the subject here. What I said was that when two copies of a work, both bearing the same title and purporting to be the same work, contain variant linguistic texts, one explanation could be that one or both texts misrepresent the work. That is, if the work was a single thing, then at least one of the variant texts had to be wrong. The point was that a work could be misrepresented by a copy of it. And it follows, therefore, that the work might be misrepresented by every copy of it. From this observation we must conclude that the work and the copies of the work are separate entities. It has been the business of textual criticism to do what it could about such misrepresentations. I will say no more here about how that can be done except to note that the textual critic's concept of authority for the work is central to the task.[41]

The other explanation offered for textual variation between copies of a work was that the work might exist in two versions, each represented by one of the variant copies, each of which could be correct. Now it is a commonplace that authors revise their works, and mere revision has seldom been taken as proof that a separate version of the work exists. But if variant forms of the work are legitimate (i.e., not the result of corruption or inattention), and if reader X disagrees with reader Y because they are not reading identical texts, then something significant has occurred, which impels us to think that the concept of versions of a work might be useful.

But for several reasons the problem of versions is not simple. Literary works of art occur in linear and single form in documents. Variant texts, therefore, are difficult to present and assimilate; they are not easily experienced simultaneously or side by side. Thus, most reading experiences are restricted to interaction with one material text representing better or worse one version of the work. Publishers are committed to perpetuating this form of experience and resist multiple text editions. Perhaps that is why there has been a tendency to consider revisions as a continuation of creative efforts to improve the work. The process is said to be over only when the last revision is made—and even then the process might have just stopped unfinished. This is a fundamental principle for "final intention" editions. James McLaverty calls this a "Whig" interpretation of revision, which often disregards meaning and effect in favor of a predisposition to credit revision with improvement ("Identity and Function"). The Whig view is convenient, for it maintains that the work is singular and revisions are all part of a grand design toward which the author works from beginning to end. Variant texts, according to this view, either contain errors or represent incomplete revision. With this view it would be considered a

---

41. More on this subject is in my *Scholarly Editing in the Computer Age*. See also G. Thomas Tanselle's *Textual Criticism since Greg: A Chronicle, 1950–1985*, which provides a sensible evaluative guide to much theoretical and practical writing on editing; and F. T. Bowers, "Regularization and Normalization in Modern Critical Texts." Differing rather sharply with Bowers and Tanselle is Jerome McGann, *A Critique of Modern Textual Criticism*.

reading utopia if all material texts in circulation were accurate renditions of the final intention text—a utopia of logocentrism.[42]

It is tempting to dismiss such views of the work as oversimplifications, but not only do such views characterize most readers' habitual attitudes toward the texts they use; there are also powerful influences in our culture, at least in the present, to accept and even to enforce such a view. The alternatives might be more honest or more sophisticated or more intellectually rigorous, but is it art? Is it the real thing? These are questions about authority and authenticity. In painting the questions are: is it a copy? is it a fake? In literature one hardly ever thinks of a fake novel. But we can say of a poem that it is "only a copy, and not a very good one at that," by which we probably mean that its authority has been compromised through textual variation from "unauthorized" sources.[43] Authority is not found *in* works but is attributed to them according to how the user defines authority. There are currently four common definitions of *authority,* some with a marvelous variety of subdivisions that feed astonishing controversies about which is the proper work of art and what is the proper goal of editing. Authority is a system of valuations relating to the work for the purpose of distinguishing between what is the work and what is not the work.[44] In the hands of Whigs—those who want the work to be one identifiable, real thing—authority is used to discountenance all versions but the "true one." Exceptions are sometimes made for works that have two or even more "true versions," such as Wordsworth's *Prelude* or Marianne Moore's "Poetry," but these are quite exceptional cases. Anyone who admits the possibility of more than one version, however, needs concepts other than authority to

---

42. A variant form of Whiggism is identified as "primitivism" by Jack Stillinger in "Textual Primitivism and the Editing of Wordsworth," in which he mounts considerable evidence to debunk the prevailing editorial attitude that every revision postdating Wordsworth's first complete version is an evidence of the poet's deterioration and growing heterodoxy. Unlike T. H. Howard-Hill, who opts for a logically superior text as the aim of editing, Stillinger concludes that Wordsworth's poems should be produced in editions of every version. He does not, however, offer a guide for such a proliferation of texts, since his focus is on the Whiggery (my word, not his) of current reductive editions and the determining and limiting effect they have on our experience of Wordsworth's works. Stillinger develops similar ideas in *Coleridge and Textual Instability,* which I address in some detail in chapter 8 of the third edition of *Scholarly Editing*.

43. I have discussed the question of authority in *Scholarly Editing in the Computer Age,* pt. 1, particularly pp. 9–14; and in chapter 5 of the present work.

44. Authority can be bibliographic, authorial, documentary, sociological, or aesthetic, depending on whether greater value was placed on the iconic page, the author, the document, the social contract of production, or the "aesthetic integrity of the work itself" (*Scholarly Editing,* 3d ed., 15–27).

distinguish them. It stands to reason, that, if two people disagree on the definition or application of the concept of authority, they will not be able to agree about version. Version, like authority, is not so much found in the textual material as it is put there. The ways in which versions are identified, then, become an important matter to discover.

B. Structuring Multiple Versions

"Post-Whig" ways of gauging the significance (i.e., meaning and effect and, thus, importance) of revision involve a concept of versions identified or delimited with reference to one or more of "four unities": time, content, function, and material. The main point here is that a concept of versions requires a way to identify something that can be "perceived" only through potentially misleading physical representations of it. A concept of version has to be able to identify version by distinguishing it both from other versions of the work and from the physical manifestations of it, which might be corrupt or which might actually mix text from more than one version. It must also be able to distinguish between texts that differ because they represent different versions and texts that differ merely because one or both contain errors. Unlike any of the distinctions between terms referring to the forms of texts (conceptual, linguistic, semiotic, material, and reception texts), decisions about what constitutes a version are matters of judgment and will depend entirely on the relative weight that the judge places on one or more of four unities in making that judgment.

1. Utterances   Before discussing the four unities and how they have been used to identify versions, we need to look again at the concept of *utterance,* a term borrowed from speech act theory and literary theory.[45] The term is a problem, however, because it has been defined in several ways and applied to the acts of persons other than the author. *Utterance* can be the act of formulating the conception of the work we call a version into a linguistic text. If we define it so, however, we come very close to saying that each utterance is a work of art, and we might hesitate to accept this idea. *Utterance* can also be defined as the act of making a version available or making it public. Here again several acts can be referred to by the term. Making a version available might be done by writing it down or by giving it to a typist or by submitting it to a publisher or by reading and approving

---

45. The appropriation of this term by textual criticism was first placed in its larger context, I believe, by G. Thomas Tanselle in "The Editorial Problem of Final Intentions" 309–53. McLaverty used it to good effect in "Identity and Utterance."

final proofs or by publishing the printed book. Each of these acts might be thought of as a moment of utterance that gives the linguistic text involved status as representing a distinct version. Further, utterance can be defined as what the author said or wrote, what the production process produced and published, or what the reader heard or read.

In order for *utterance* to be a useful term we must not only distinguish it from *version* and our other terms but also show how it is helpful in describing or organizing them. We might say that version is the aim of utterance but that an utterance might not succeed or might only partially succeed in its aim. But utterance is not merely the production of a material text that might or might not accurately represent a version. Utterance not only refers to the performances of works but also to the circumstances, the contexts of those actions that influence and contain (i.e., keep from running wild) the meanings and help indicate what meanings are operable. This is a relatively simple concept in speech, as I have already noted, in which the speaker and listener and circumstance are all together interacting at the moment of speech. But with written or recorded language the utterances of the author, of the various members of the production crew, and of the reader are each separated in time and circumstances so that meaning at every stage in the life of the written word is influenced by different milieux. It is not absurd, therefore, to conceive not only of creative versions resulting from authorial acts (authorial utterances) but also of production versions (publication utterances) and reception versions (reader utterances). Now this would be complicated enough if the work were one thing that could be rationalized into one universal text out of this proliferations of "versions" (which would not be true versions but simple imperfections). But, in fact, there is no agreement among scholars or artists, for that matter, about what one thing the work is or ought to be (i.e., there is no universal definition of authority). Each person has a notion about what it ought to be; the possibilities are quite numerous. Some concept of authority (to identify the authentic elements of the work) and the four unities (to distinguish versions of the work) are the means by which readers impose order on this cacophony of utterances. That is, how an individual student of the work understands versions and how one reacts to material text X in hand will depend on the specific utterance selected and defined for use. And that selection and definition depends on the values given to the four unities: content, time, function, and material. Needless to say, these values are usually selected and applied without conscious thought—in which case the material text becomes transparent, and the only "text" that matters is purely and simply the reception text in the reader's performance field.

2. Unities as Structural Glue   The unity of content is the place to begin.[46]
It is because the content, particularly the linguistic texts, of copy X and that
of copy Y were not identical that this discussion began. If they had been
identical, there would appear to be no problem. The idea that one copy is
accurate and the other inaccurate does not explain cases of revision. The
idea that one copy represents an early incomplete stage of the work and the
other represents a completed or improved stage does not explain cases in
which the revisions appear to mean contradictory things or to have palpably different but individually satisfying effects. But the problem here is to
calculate first whether the content had a sufficient stability as an "entity" to
be called a version and, next, to calculate how much of a change or what
kind of change in content is required before a *different* version, rather than
an *improved* version, results. The most radical answer to this question was
offered by Hans Zeller, when he described the work as a network of relationships between its parts. He reasoned that any change in any part would
change the nature of the network, and, so, every textual change produces,
logically, a changed work ("New Approach"). There is an empirical attrac-
tiveness in this view because it equates the work with the copy of the work;
each variant copy is a new work, but there is an unsatisfying or disturbing
implication in this view because it makes editing a work a nearly impossible
task. A scholarly edition would have to incorporate whole texts of every
authoritative source. G. Thomas Tanselle offers a compromise through his
distinction between "horizontal and vertical" revision. Horizontal changes
merely improve a presentation or intention already achieved more or less
well in the original text; vertical changes alter the intention by changing the
meaning or direction of the work ("Editorial Problem," 334–40). In order
to gauge the type of change, Tanselle uses also the unity of function, so
that not all changes in content signal changes in version. He suggests also
that differences in the time of revision might be a useful factor, but he does
not anticipate the case of an accumulation of "horizontal" improvements
having a "vertical" effect.[47]

The unity of time derives from the idea that the person changes with
time so that, if an effort of creation is temporally separated from an effort
of revision, it is likely or at least possible that the revision effort will reflect

---

46. Content here refers to the makeup of the linguistic text. The word *content* might
suggest to some the substantive existence of the book or printed document. That concept will
be taken up under the unity of material.

47. A particular case is Samuel Richardson's *Pamela,* in which subsequent editions
steadily improved Pamela's grammar till by 1800 she had lost most of the lexical roots of her
rural past. See T. C. Duncan Eaves and Ben Kimpel, "Richardson's Revisions of 'Pamela.'"

changes in the person and thus follow a new line of inspiration rather than that which informed the first. But the problem here is how to calculate how much time must elapse between engagements with the text for the lapse of time to be deemed significant and the resulting effort to be seen as a separate version.[48] Among modern textual critics the most radical view of version that depends on the unity of time is that presented by Hershel Parker in *Flawed Texts and Verbal Icons,* in which he argues from a psychological model of creativity that authors lose their authority over a work after a certain period and that revision often not only violates the creativity of the original effort but can end in confusion, which might make a text unreadable.[49] A good deal of my own 1984 recommendation concerning identification of versions depends on the unity of time. I would no longer rely so heavily on this one aspect. Even for an editor who is concerned with presenting only one somehow "best" version of the work, the unity of time is sometimes used to reject undesirable authorial revisions made later in time on the grounds that the passage of time had deprived the author of the inspiration (or at least continuity of thought or purpose) that informed the work now being revised without inspiration or along new lines.

The unity of function relates to the purpose for which the work is designed. Is it for a magazine; is it a chapter in a book; is it a play adaptation, a translation, a revised edition aimed at a new market? Each new function constitutes the potential for a new version. Revisions undertaken to adapt the work to a new function should not, according to this unity, be confused with revisions undertaken to enhance the success of the same function served by the unrevised text. This criterion requires that the revision be for a different purpose, not just a better fulfillment of an old purpose. Fredson Bowers has written considerably about this aspect of the identity of versions, but in practice Bowers has tended to see new functions as superseding old functions (as long as they are authorial), so that, while he admits that the previous versions have authority, he tends to see new versions as having "superior authority."[50] This is an example of what

---

48. A significant lapse of time may be the duration of a "lightning flash of inspiration" that alters a whole concept or the time it takes for the "burning coal of inspiration to flame, flicker, and die" or the time it takes to "build the cathedral of art from foundation to capstone." The metaphors one uses for art often reflect, or perhaps even determine, what value one places on the unities.

49. See particularly the chapter on Mark Twain.

50. See his essays "Multiple Authority: New Problems and Concepts of Copy-Text"; and "Remarks on Eclectic Texts." Bowers was not wedded to this tendency, as he showed in his

McLaverty calls the Whig interpretation of revision, the idea that revisions are better because it is absurd to think that an author would deliberately revise a work to make it worse.

The unity of material relates to production efforts. In this concept the word *material* means the physical object or document that bears the linguistic text. It equates, in effect, the concept of version of the work with the material text. The material text is, after all, the place where all the performances and all the component aspects of a work are brought together. The creative performance resulting in a linguistic text is united with the production performance, resulting in a material text, which is where the reception performance must begin. The material text can be seen then as a social, economic, and artistic unit and is the entity necessary for the full functioning of literary art. The primary proponents of this point of view are Jerome McGann and D. F. McKenzie.[51] The most obvious shortcoming of this position seems to be its rigidity, its rather helpless acceptance of determinacy in the material text. There is a grand sense of coalescence in the view, but the linguistic text involved in many cases will strike some readers as having been overdetermined or perhaps overpackaged. Production processes notoriously tamper with a linguistic text in ways both beneficial and detrimental to it as a representation of the essayed version. And it does not sit well with some people that the economic necessities and accidents of production performances should be allowed to shape (sometimes to shape out of existence) the subtleties of the creative performance.

VIII. THE READER AS AUTHOR

The conflicting claims of these four unities have been forcefully and amusingly presented in James McLaverty's rehearsal of the old analogy of Theseus's ship, except that the distinction between content and material is fudged ("Identity and Utterance"). Suppose that Theseus sets sail, says McLaverty, in a ship that after a while undergoes repairs. Say further that the ship eventually is so repaired as to have had all its material parts replaced. Is it still the same ship? The unity of function would say yes, but the unities of content, material, and time would say no. Suppose further

---

treatment of two versions of William James's reminiscences of Thomas Davidson (Fredson Bowers, "Authorial Intention and Editorial Problems"). I respond in some detail to Bowers's formulations in chapter 7.

51. See cited works by McGann and McKenzie. I have reviewed the historical development and arguments for this view in chapter 5. Jack Stillinger's significant variation on this theme is rehearsed in chapter 8 of *Scholarly Editing,* 3d ed.

that someone gathered up the discarded parts of Theseus's ship and reconstructed the original ship; would the old reconstructed ship be Theseus's ship or the new repaired one? The unity of function, if considered in the light of continuity, would say the repaired one was the ship, but in the light of identity of function it would say the old reconstructed ship had as good a claim. The unity of material would support the old ship's claim, while the unity of time would insist that three versions of Theseus's ship existed: the old one that had been Theseus's ship but which no longer exists; the repaired one Theseus now sails; and the reconstructed one that is not identical with the original ship though made of the same materials in the same configuration.[52] What happens if Theseus sells his ship and it becomes a cargo boat? Or what if a new owner also named Theseus uses it for the same purpose it originally served? Is that possible? Etc.

The main difficulty with the analogy is that in the case of the ship the material being is the ship, while in the case of literary works the physical documents, the material text, are but a representation of the work. If Theseus were to say, "No, that ship reconstructed from old material is *not* my ship," we would believe him only if we vested authority for the naming of the ship in Theseus (the author, as it were). The material text—whether it is the author's or the publisher's, whether it represents version 1 or n, whether it is accurate or corrupt—is a necessary representation without which the work cannot be experienced, but it is not identical with the work, for no *particular* copy of the work is needed for the work to be experienced.

We see in this way of putting the problem the beginnings of an answer to the question "What difference does it make to a deconstructive reading of the work which text is used?" For we see that the structure of the work (that which the reader takes to be the work) depends upon the structure of the material text (the linguistic text in semiotic form contained in a particular document). And we see further that the material text is not one unproblematic transparent "voice" but, rather, the "spoor" so to speak of a multitude of speakers working at various times and places, combining their efforts in the material text. Which of these voices is to be centered in order that it may be decentered? Which self is to be focused on as self-subverting? The voice that is foregrounded by one particular material text may not be

---

52. The most obvious difference between Theseus's original ship and the reconstructed ship made from the identical materials is not one of time but of production; the original ship was not a reconstruction or restoration, and the restored ship is not an original construction. This difference can be seen as one in function, or it may point to the need to expand the four unities by adding other useful criteria.

the same as that foregrounded in another. A deconstructive reader might not care for one reading more than another; indeed, a deconstructionist could not do so *and* remain true to deconstructive principles. Nevertheless, everyone's understanding of the process of constructing meaning for a given text will depend to some extent on the particular material text he or she is exposed to. One can see, therefore, that a concept of authority underlies the way in which the unities are employed to identify a voice or a text for the work by identifying an utterance.

McLaverty, following the lead of James Thorpe (*Principles*) and Jerome McGann (*A Critique*), places coalescence, or utterance, of the work at publication, referring to stages of composition as moments of "pre-utterance." He is led to this, I believe, by the analogy of Theseus's ship. The parts of the boat removed and replaced are no longer the boat because they do not function as boat. And the boat does not function as boat until it is completed and launched. I suppose with boats one knows if they function by putting them in the water. But works of literary art are not boats. The question of coalescence of a work as a version is a matter of opinion and judgment. Versions are not facts to be discovered about works; they are, rather, concepts created and put there by readers as a means of ordering (or as justification for valuing) textual variants. To say that an editor who had edited from the manuscripts a prepublication version (such as Hans Gabler's edition of Joyce's *Ulysses*) has prepared a pre-utterance text is to evaluate the work by a particular conjunction of the four unities and condemn it a priori. One can do that, but it is not a purpose of this taxonomy to encourage such judgments. Rather its purpose is to describe more accurately what judgments are being and can be made concerning the identity of copies of a work. Perhaps the most useful way to use the term *utterance* is to say that each utterance has its intentions and its "social life" (i.e., the purpose for which it was released and the context, moment, and form in which it was designed and launched). Regardless of what decisions are made about the identity of a version, when that tenuous issue is settled there remains the original question concerning works and versions: how accurately does the material text represent the version or work? Are there errors in the text?

All of this points, it seems to me, to an overwhelming conclusion concerning the concepts of works and versions—a conclusion that is consonant with the three fundamental propositions of this study. The concept of work and, even more so, the concept of version depend on reception performance just as much as on creative performance. If the reader must decide whether a version is in fact a version, its functional existence is determined by the reader. Creative performances, the idea of the work as an utterance of the author, and the idea of intended meanings are all reader constructs. All the reader has is the material texts and whatever information about their provenance and alternative embodiments that have been provided or scrounged up. The term *work* helps the reader separate this mass of material from other masses relating to other works; the term *version* helps one sort through this mass of material. One does so by classifying material texts according to the structure of versioning that, to each person's perception, best accounts for the materials at hand. In short the reader becomes the "functional authority" for the work and its versions. It would seem, therefore, that ideally the reader should have ready access to the evidence that would fully inform the necessary decisions—hence, the importance of scholarly editions that foreground rather than submerge the evidence for versions. T. H. Howard-Hill, contending that "uncertainty is a condition of mind and is not inherent in circumstances," recommends that "editors move with confidence and resolution like Tamburlaine" not like "Hamlets, shillying and shallying between this and that" ("Textual Theories," 113). But if in the grip of such resolve an editor unwittingly stands in for all readers, making the decisions and producing a single reading text that purports to have reduced the work to a book (the text that *is* the work), that editor has oversimplified and, therefore, misrepresented the work, not refined and purified it.

IX. CONCLUSIONS

This exercise in naming leads, I believe, to a number of conclusions about literary works of art.

One is that the word *work* conveys both a singular and a plural meaning. A work is one thing: all the versions of Henry James's *Roderick Hudson* are subsumed under this one title. Simultaneously, a work is a thing of internal diversity. It exists wherever a copy of the work exists. Each copy is a more or less accurate representation of one version of the work.[53]

Another conclusion is that attempts to repair or restore original or pure texts of a work or to revise and improve them tend to proliferate texts rather than to refine them. If one thinks of proliferating refined copies, one

---

53. A single copy might represent a mixture of readings from more than one version. Such a copy is said to be eclectic or sophisticated, depending on whether one approves or disapproves of the mixture.

must remember not only that the "unrefined" copies have not been changed but that, by the unities of material, time, and perhaps function, the refined copies represent new and therefore different material texts, complete with all that this entails.

Another conclusion is that the crucial act in relation to a work of literary art is not writing or publishing or editing it but reading it. Of course, without the first of these there will be no reading, but without a reading the preliminary acts will seem incomplete or lack fulfillment. Several observations about reading arise from this taxonomy. First, to read material text X is to decode a work (i.e., that which is implied by its various versions) from interaction with only one of its many static forms. Reading, therefore, is always a partial (incomplete) interaction with the work. Second, if material text X is taken as a transparent window on the work, there is no question asked about versions or about errors. Third, if material text X is taken as the result of a single, prolonged production effort, subject only to human error, there is no question asked about versions, just about accuracy. Fourth, if material text X is taken "for what it is"—one of many representations of a version of a work—there are questions of both accuracy and version. Questions of version include questions about the agents of change (author, editor, etc.) and about time, function or motive, and material. Material texts are not, in other words, transparent.

Since editing and publishing tend to increase the number of copies of a work, not just in numbers but in variant forms, it seems useful to devise a graphic system to identify and categorize the material texts that represent the work (see fig. 3). Thus, when person X reads and remarks upon material text X (MTx) and person Y evaluates those remarks in relation to material text Y (MTy), difficulties arise from several false assumptions: that both MTx and MTy contain the same linguistic text, that both are equivalent material texts, that a linguistic text as embodied in a document is a full rather than partial representation of the work, and that the work is represented adequately and equally well by any material text (or at least by MTx and MTy). Persons X and Y may disagree about the work because they are not discussing a work but, instead, two unlike manifestations of the work. If, however, X and Y understood the relation between the material text in hand and the work, they might temper their judgments and remarks about it in the light of that understanding. Finally, if X and Y understand how each is developing a sense of version by applying various mixes of the four unities, they might at least disagree with clarity about the issues in dispute.

For example, in the disputes between those who say the work of art is a social product finding its "true" form in the material text and those who consider the production process as unfortunately corrupting—but why be abstract? In the disparate views represented by Jerome McGann and Hershel Parker about the moment of coalescence for a work, McGann placing it in the material text and Parker placing it in the linguistic text at the moment of greatest creative control by the author, we have, I think, a disagreement that becomes clarified and a bit nonsensical. While many people have a gut feeling that "authorial authority" or creative performance, is more interesting than "production authority," or production performance, the plain facts are that authors do some things badly and production does some things well.[54] If we take the view that the inscription that the author is finally satisfied to relinquish to a publisher is the closest representation of a version, we are likely to take it as the basis for a new edition. But authors often show or relinquish manuscripts they know will be or must be changed. Would we be willing to say that the essayed version as embodied in the printer's copy (author's fair copy) is a form of the work that the critic can use as the basis for a "reading" of the work? Does the scholarly editor have a production performance task parallel to that given the work by its original publisher? It has seemed wise to say that the materials of the editorial project will dictate which answer is the most appropriate, but if that were true there would be no disputes. Disputes arise not only because, for example, McGann worked on Byron (who gratefully left the details of punctuation to those who cared and knew about such things) and Parker worked on Twain (who claimed to have telegraphed instructions to have a compositor shot for tampering with his punctuation), but because they define version and work by differing valuations of authority and of the unities. I suppose the final irony is that any edition Parker would produce would be, after all, a new production performance and that any edition McGann produced would undoubtedly be read by many as establishing the author's intentions. In short the problem is not one of editor's shillying and shallying over uncertainties in their minds but, first, of a cacophony of voices "in" written texts to be selected from and, second, a world of readers who habitually treat books as if they fully represented the one voice that matters (each reader, of course, identifying that voice as seems right in his or her own eyes).

Another conclusion that might be drawn, tentatively at least, is that the idea of "conveying meaning" might be a misleading way to think about

---

54. Actually, these "facts" are no plainer than any other. The *judgment* of many people is that authors do some things badly and therefore need typists, editors, and publishers to help them; likewise, the judgment of many people is that these helpers do sometimes overstep their functions or perform them badly.

how texts function. The processes of encoding meaning (by authoring) and repackaging the coding (by publishing) and decoding (by reading) are perhaps too complex and fraught with "noise" to allow for "conveying," and our experience is rife with instances of meaning being apparently misconveyed (*misconstrued* is a more accurate and more frequent term, as it should be) either by accident or by deliberate appropriation. This taxonomy suggests that texts influence, rather than control, reception performance. All the work of creative performance and production performance is ostensibly geared toward influencing reception performance.[55] The only chance that an author has to influence the reception performance is to so arrange the linguistic text that it will have the best chance possible of influencing the reading and thus be said to have been understood rather than to have been misconstrued. The reception performance is, however, influenced not only by the linguistic text but by a great deal besides, much of which is subconscious and fortuitous. When the reader has produced a reception text, its coherence is usually considered satisfactory proof that the performance has succeeded. Dissatisfaction with that coherence can only come when a second reading or someone else's description of a reading appears more satisfyingly coherent. There is, of course, no way to verify any correspondence between reception performance and creative performance. It should be observed, therefore, that every reception performance is not only partial because it is an incomplete engagement with the evidences for the work but because it is biased (not impartial) by the reader's human limitations and conditions.

All of this seems to confirm a conclusion bruited about among literary theorists: that the community of scholarship (or, in any community of readers, the sense of cultural heritage and values) derives its power and cohesiveness from arbitrary agreements to use certain conventions as standards of behavior regarding the interpretation of works and the assessment of the relevance of history and perceived hegemonic structures in commentaries upon literary works. All of these conventions and standards are convenient constructs, not natural truths, and are deemed convenient as long as we agree to find them so. I no longer find it convenient to consider

---

55. That statement should be qualified by the possibility that some—and, unfortunately, perhaps all—production performance is geared toward influencing the consumer to *buy* rather than the reader to *comprehend*. But the surface intention of copyediting, type design, proofreading, and format and binding design is to "help the reader" apprehend the work. That the covert intention of production actually works is verified in every book purchased and shelved unread.

the material text an original, stable, or transparent sign source for an entity called the literary work of art.

APPENDIX A

Occasionally, textual critics have referred to theories from related disciplines that seem suggestive as clearer explanations of some aspect of textual criticism or of some problem relevant to editorial practice. The following is intended as a tentative "commentary" on two of them, J. L. Austin and Michael Hancher.

J. L. AUSTIN

The following remarks arise from a reading of J. L. Austin's *How to Do Things with Words*. The most frequent references by textual critics to Austin's theories are to the terms *illocution, perlocution,* and *locution*. These are thought to correspond to intention and execution, for illocution (the way an utterance is used—as warning, advice, etc.) and perlocution (the effect aimed at by the utterance—as persuading one to respond appropriately) are thought of as the intended force and meaning of the locution (the whole act of uttering something).

There are several problems with this appropriation of Austin's ideas. Austin writes of "constative utterances," which are statements that can be tested as logically or factually true or false, and he distinguishes them from "performative utterances," which are not true or false but by which or in which the speaker does something such as warn, advise, threaten, marry, or contract; that is, the speaker does something besides just "make an utterance" (which could be said of constative statements also). Just as constative statements can be true or false, the effect of performative utterances might be "happy" or "unhappy" depending on a number of factors, including the sincerity of the speaker, his or her right to do the performative act, and the success of the utterance within the circumstances attending it.

One should note that most of Austin's remarks are particularly apropos of spoken, rather than written, utterances, which he says are "not tethered to their origin" as speech is. He admits written utterances if they are signed. This would seem to admit books which bear the author's name; indeed they nearly always bear the publisher's name, and sometimes that of the printer, book binder, and occasionally, on a sticker inside the cover, that of the bookseller. But it is difficult to apply Austin's categories to fiction because, for one thing, as an utterance fiction is usually multi-voiced; not only are the agents mentioned above as having their names on the book in a sense the utterers of the work as a whole, there are the voices of the narrator (or narrators) and that of each character in the book. Austin's categories seem more apropos when applied to the "speech acts" of a character than when applied to the script acts of the author.

In addition, a book, a poem, a novel, is in a way not a single utterance but a string of utterances. Austin's categories apply to sentences, not to whole paragraphs. Second, though Austin develops the idea of performative utterances very interestingly, he sees them as but one kind of utterance in a range of possible kinds of utterances—"constative utterances" being one of them. Third, in developing the idea of performative utterances, Austin explains their occasional failure to succeed by listing a variety of "infelicities" which cause the utterance to "misfire" or to be "abused." Among the "abuses" of performative utterances are "insincerities" such as jokes and lying. He considers a speaker's authority and sincerity as essential elements for "happy" performative statements. That is to say, if the performative utterance is given with any other than its "sincere" surface intention, it fails. Irony and parody, therefore, have no place in his scheme. Obviously, if Austin's scheme is to be applied to fiction or poetry, a whole range of new types of "felicities" would have to elaborated, for there is no room in Austin's theory for an ironic utterance that succeeds in spite of itself by "intentionally" subverting its surface meaning, not in order to lie but, rather, to convey happily a subsurface meaning that is expected to be understood. Austin himself considered fiction and poetry an "etiolated use of language."

Austin seems, therefore, an oddly weak reed to lean on in explaining the problems of textual criticism. His theories apply to single sentences uttered in spoken form. And he restricts his interests to certain types of sentences that exclude the majority of uses we associate with literary texts. Nevertheless, Austin's categories have been picked up and elaborated with some success for use with literature, in particular by Richard Ohmann, who modifies Austin's categories for analysis of jokes, irony, and fictions as happy acts; by John Searle, who considerably extends Austin's notion of varieties of illocutionary modes and who emphasizes the importance of context in understanding the "functional" referentialness of words when that deviates from the "normal or expected" references; and by Quentin Skinner, who develops the idea of locutions as functional within circumstances and through conventions in such a way that a theory of script acts could be developed, except that he tends to treat the medium (sound waves and written texts) as transparent vehicles.[56] Paul Hernadi drops Austin's divisions into constative and performative utterances, adds the terms *prelocutionary* (why the speaker decides to make the utterance) and *postlocutionary* (what reaction or outcome eventuates in the listener and reader), and divides perlocution and illocution into originating and receiving counterparts, so that the text points back to authorial prelocutionary input, perlocutionary intention, and illocutionary force and at the same time provides the basis for the reader's illocutionary uptake, perlocutionary impact, and postlocutionary outcome (Hernadi 103–5). This use of Austin's terms is somewhat loose, but it applies better to literary utterances than Austin's original schema, which was both more precise and more rigid.

MICHAEL HANCHER

The most frequent references to Hancher are to "Three Kinds of Intention" (*Modern Language Notes* 87 [1972]: 827–51). Hancher's three kinds of intention correspond roughly to Austin's analysis of performative utterances, except that Hancher applies his theories directly to literary texts. His terms are *active, programmatic,"* and *final*.

By *active intention* Hancher means "the act of meaning-something-by-the-finished-text." Here he subsumes Austin's idea of locution, which corresponds roughly with "the-finished-text" and the idea of content or subject, "meaning-something." But it is not entirely clear whether Hancher is defining *meaning* in any other than the ordinary general sense of the word, which Austin has done a much better job of subdividing into types of meaning.

By *programmatic intention* Hancher refers to the attempt to have a certain effect or elicit a certain response. Here Hancher incorporates what Austin calls perlocution and considers happy if it has the desired or intended effect. Hancher does not measure the "happiness" of programmatic intentions by their success, but he suggests that the motive power of "active intentions" might run counter to the motive power of "programmatic" intentions—as when the active intention to describe a scene with honesty and detail might run counter to a programmatic intention to satisfy the censors.

---

56. Skinner's distinctions, or very similar ones, have made their way into Wendell Harris's very useful book *Interpretive Acts: In Search of Meaning* (Oxford: Clarendon, 1988), though Skinner is not mentioned.

By *final intention* Hancher means the author's intention, by the finished product, to cause a reaction or to make something happen.

It will be noted that these schemata treat the linguistic text as a totally transparent entity; that is, all the analysis is expended on intention to mean something and to cause effects on readers. They do not consider the material text as a focus or object of intention itself. They do not describe the author's intention to write a paragraph or spell a word or use a point of punctuation. The technical construction of the text is not seen as problematic. The result is that little attention is given to the particular characteristics of the material text in hand being subjected to analysis. Further, none consider the work of book designers (type fonts, page formats, density of lines, width of margins, quality of paper and binding) or of price and methods of marketing and distribution as intentions of production performances or as influences on the total "perlocutionary impact" of works.

APPENDIX B

DEFINITION OF TERMS

Text as Matter

material text. The union of *linguistic text* and *document:* a *sign sequence* held in a medium of display. The material text has "meanings" additional to, and perhaps complementary to, the linguistic text.

document. The material medium of display (paper, ink, etc.).

protocol. A written or otherwise verbalized response to and commentary on a work.

Text as Concepts

work. That which is manifested in and implied by the material and linguistic forms of texts thought to be variant forms of a single literary entity. The term work incorporates concepts of versions (ideations) that are made concrete or material by a production performance and then reconceptualized by reception performance. Each performance—whether by author, producer, or reader—accesses the work in some partial form.

versions. Conceptual forms of the work sufficiently different from one another so that each seems to require separate treatment. *Versions* is a concept by which variant material texts (such as manuscripts, drafts, proofs, first editions, revised editions, etc.) can be classified as representative of:

potential versions: abstract conceptual texts in the mind of an author;
developing versions: abstract conceptual texts as evidenced by trial
    drafts in some material form;
essayed versions: finished (at least temporarily) versions as evidenced
    in completed manuscripts or revised texts.

linguistic text. A sign sequence (sounds or letters and punctuation or
other symbolic forms) representative of a version whether conceptual,
semiotic, or displayed in a document.

reception text. The performed text conceptualized by the reader in the act
of reading; the decoded material text.

conceptual text. Any text that is "handled" in the mind or contemplated
by a person. Conceptual texts are the only kind that can be experienced,
though material texts are the shareable forms of texts, being evidences of
authorial and production conceptual texts and the place where reception
texts begin.

semiotic text. The signs as signs used to represent any given linguistic text
as version.

Text as Actions

speech act. The whole event of creation, production, and reception of a
communication at a specified time and place.

script act. The complex, never closed, serial event encompassing the cre-
ations, productions, and receptions at any and all places and times in
which a written work is created, produced, and received.

utterance. A whole speech act or a coherent selection of "speaker,"
medium, hearer, time(s), and place(s) employed with regard to a script
act within which "an understanding" of the work is achieved.

creative performance. The authorial development of essayed versions resulting in linguistic texts as found in manuscripts and in other authorially
revised texts. A creative performance that stopped short of recording a
version remains inaccessible to anyone except, perhaps, the author who
can remember what it was.

production performance. The scribal and publication development of
material texts resulting in typists' copies, proofs, and printed books.

reception performance. The development of a conceptualized reception
text in the act of reading.

Texts as Units

The integrity of Texts as Units is defined by the following.

time. The work as it existed at some significant time.

content. The work as represented by one linguistic text as opposed to variants of it.

function. The work as designed for a particular purpose or appearance.

material. The work as embodied in one or another particular physical format.

Textual Contexts

material base. The world of sense data to which the material text (manuscript, book, etc.) belongs.

social context. the complex of institutions, conventions, and mores whose expectations and habits are reflected in the material text.

performance field. An ambiguously conceived abstraction that provides the illusion of stability, or a "locus of meaning." It is where the text is "played" according to the rules of the reader's particular game of textual interaction and limited by the performer's capabilities and resources. The "game" metaphor here accounts in a different way for the "play," or looseness, in the "machine" model of interpretation, in which play is equivalent to tolerance, a concept about how much variation in interpretation is allowable before communication "breaks down."

Chapter 4

Texts, Cultures, Mediums, and Performances: *The French Lieutenant's Woman*

This story I am telling is all imagination. These characters I create never existed outside my own mind. If I have pretended until now to know my characters' minds and innermost thoughts, it is because I am writing in (just as I have assumed some of the vocabulary and "voice" of) a convention universally accepted at the time of my story: that the novelist stands next to God. He may not know all, yet he tries to pretend that he does. But I live in the age of Alain Robbe-Grillet and Roland Barthes; if this is a novel, it cannot be a novel in the modern sense of the word.

—John Fowles, *The French Lieutenant's Woman*

Authoring, manufacturing, and reading performances are seen more clearly if we keep in mind a distinction between the products of these performances and the uses to which they are put. John Searle insists on this distinction when he explains the difference between *sentence* and *utterance*. Sentence is the formal structure of the words and their relation. Sentence can be recorded as a series of words; sentence is iterable. Utterance, on the other hand, is the intended meaning in the use of sentence. The same sentence can be used on separate occasions to mean different things. The particular use of sentence on an occasion in a specifiable setting is utterance; utterance is not iterable. Another way Searle puts this is to distinguish sentence meaning from speaker meaning in which speakers can use a sentence to convey understanding indirectly, metaphorically, ironically, etc. Sentence, not utterance, is what is recorded literally in written texts. Utterance is reduced to sentence in written works.[1]

A fundamental, and relevant, tenet of communication theory is that meaning (speaker meaning or utterance) takes place in a context of presupposition that forms an unstated but operative background to texts. Texts cannot incorporate all this presupposed background, though attempts to do so are probably motivated by a desire to prevent misunderstanding. Few texts manage to prevent all misunderstanding.

It is in relation to these concepts of communication that the four elements of my title—texts, cultures, mediums, and performances—reveal their significance in authoring, editing, manufacturing, and consuming texts. At the risk of some tedium but in the hope of heading off misunderstanding, I summarize the range of references encompassed by these crucial terms:

The word *text* as in "The text of the novel," indicates many things, among them:

1. the sequence of words that constitute the novel as it appears in a particular publication, like the first edition, or in a manuscript;
2. the novel as the author conceived it and inscribed it;
3. the novel as its editors, compositors, and printers conceived it and manufactured it;
4. the novel as reviewers and readers perceived it in the act of performing their readings of it; and
5. the novel as former readers remember it and reshape it to themselves through memory and through interactions with written or visual commentaries.

In relation to John Fowles's novel *cultures* can refer to:

1. Victorian times (specifically the late 1860s);
2. John Fowles's reconstruction of that time (and the similar reconstructions by other students of Victorian history);

---

1. Searle's ideas were presented in a conference paper at the University of Alabama in 1990. James McLaverty's otherwise very precise and provocative essay "Issues of Identity and Utterance" notes that utterance is an event in time rather than an object in space, but he fails to distinguish utterance from object in the way Searle distinguishes utterance from sentence. The result is that McLaverty, by a logic that totally escapes me, declares "pre-utterance" forms of the text to be outside the work, not a part of it. And he ties his notions of editorial duty entirely to documentary stages of sentence rather than to intentional stages of utterance.

3. English culture of the late 1960s, when Fowles was writing and publishing the novel;
4. American culture at the same time; and
5. English and American cultures of the 1990s.

The term *mediums* includes:

1. the novel in manuscript form including revisions;
2. the printed novel in a variety of forms including paperbacks;
3. screenplays in manuscript, typescript, or published form;
4. movies and videos; and
5. reviews, articles, or even conversations about the work.

The term *performances* indicates a variety of acts:

1. the authoring acts of conceiving and inscribing the novel or reconceiving and inscribing the story as screenplay;[2]
2. the manufacturing acts of making the printed or film mediums; and
3. the reception performances of reading the novel or watching the movie.

One basic observation about these concepts and materials is that the physical objects usually referred to as *The French Lieutenant's Woman*, the books and movies, *seem* to have a stable existence that persists through time without change—except perhaps for physical deterioration.

Another basic observation is that culture is a dynamic to which historical snapshots such as histories or historical novels seem to give (spurious) coherence. Most authors and readers would be hard-pressed to give a picture both coherent and accurate of their own culture, let alone that of another person or another time. It seems now to go without saying that any (re)construction of a (past) milieu is driven by a (present) milieu; we cannot escape the influences of our own point of view when examining the point of view of any text.

---

2. A good case can be made for the idea that the screenplay, or any other adaptation of the novel, is not an authoring performance but is, instead, a reception performance. Screenplays do not have to be parodies in order to be viewed as an indirect and sophisticated form of criticism. The novel is 447 pages in the London, World Books edition, while the screenplay is less than a third that long. Verbally, the movie is probably only a tenth as long. Critical articles, like the screenplay and movie, do not pretend to account for the whole novel; selected themes and actions to dramatize them are focused on at the expense of others.

A third observation is that each performance of a work (whether authoring, manufacturing, or reading) is an act or event. The product of these acts is in some sense merely a record of an event's having taken place. Events take place in time and steadily recede into history. One cannot write, manufacture, or read the same book or watch the same movie twice. Each performance is a new event.

These are simple and obvious observations made numerous times by others in the current climate of attack on definitive editions and established texts that, if done right, will never have to be done again. I will not argue here that definitive editions are impossible; that horse is dead. Instead, I'd like to demonstrate the consequences of accepting these observations as givens and ask what I think is the next question: can a novel, can literary works, be communicative acts? Can a novel be the vehicle for communicating a set of ideas, emotions, questions, statements, speculations, or other significations by an author (or authors) to an audience? There are several familiar ways to say no. No, it is not a communication or message, because the author's actual ideas, emotions, states of mind, or intentions concerning the work produced must be set aside since the text (not the intentions for the text) is now all that is available to the reader. Or, no, it is not a communication, because the reader has an agenda more immediately pressing or interesting than whatever the author may have intended. Or, no, because the author's notion of what was being communicated may be considered a mere occasion for the actions leading to the production of the work, for which the reader is at liberty to explore a range of possible meanings rather than to try, futilely, to find the unlocatable and far from determinate authorial meaning. Or, no, the text of a work is an object that evokes response, not a communication that conveys particular meaning or intentionality demanding a particular response. It may be easier to see this last possibility with music and with certain kinds of sculpture and painting than with literary works because frequently with these nonverbal forms of art many people are comfortable with the notion that nothing specific beyond the visual or aural is being communicated. With works in words, on the other hand, there is usually a temptation to seek, however forlorn the attempt may appear to some, what the author meant, rather than to concentrate contentedly on whatever the work evokes or provokes in the viewer.

The most convincing way to say, "No, a work of art is not an act of communication like a conversation or speech," might be to say that authors of written literary works of art usually try very hard to create texts that are freestanding, that have internal integrity, that have sufficient internal coherence and useful redundancy to succeed independent of external context. This argument concludes that it is okay if the author is dead; it is okay if the bibliographic code is altered; it is okay if the reader does not share the author's culture or belong to the "intended" interpretive community. The work stands independently of these external contexts. But I wish for now to set aside those arguments and their implications to editorial concerns in order to focus on questions about literary works of art as communicative acts, the interpretation of which depends to some exent on presupposed or otherwise supplied external contexts.

The controversy over whether a reader should try to extract from a work what the author put into it or should rule speculations of that sort out of court is sufficiently well known that it does not require elaboration here. Much of that controversy gains perspective when one puts aside the attempt to legislate or decide *what* a work of art is and asks, instead, what kind of questions are being asked about the work and what assumptions are being made about the work by the approach taken. Some questions are appropriate to ask of the work of art as an authorial utterance with intentionality. Others are appropriate for the work as text or sign or sentence. Others are appropriate for the work as a reader creation with a history of readership exceeding in importance the events of generation and production. John Searle points out with some justice that reader response or interpretation relative to the author's intentions falls into three categories: failure to understand, misunderstanding, and understanding. Epistemology teaches us that readers cannot know for sure which of the first two of these their interpretation fits.[3] But communication theory helps us see how to test interpretations and how to know what questions are being asked.

Without implying that these are the only questions or the only approach worth taking, I explore some of the consequences involved if one treats a literary work as a communicative act. Communicative acts take place at some time; they are temporal; they are events in which a communicator generates signs through some medium and in which a recipient attends to signs in some medium and experiences the communicative act. In oral communicative acts speaker, medium, and listener usually converge in a historical moment. In such cases there is often a sense by both speaker and listener of familiarity or even control over the context of presuppositions that forms the unspoken background of text. In written communications, on the other hand, disjunctions occur that violate this historical cocoon

---

3. I return to this set of distinctions in chapter 9.

uniting speaker, medium, and recipient. Failure to take these disjunctions seriously, failure to try to compensate for them, leads to a false telescoping of time and place that confuses the operative contexts of presupposition. In a literary work the apparent but not real telescoping of the various historical moments represented by authoring, production, distribution, and reading into a single event as a single communicative act, apparently contained in or represented by a stable physical printed paper, introduces the possibility for reduction and distortion of what the problem of communication is. When one adds to the complexities that attend most written communications the further complexities of historical fiction set in one epoch but written for an audience of another epoch, and read ultimately by audiences from subsequent epochs, the idea of a literary work of art as a communicative act becomes very complex. It is an interesting complexity to unravel: important to the range of appropriate interpretations made possible by the basic approach and important because of the responsibilities of editors and teachers in assembling and presenting the work to students and other readers.

The case of John Fowles's *The French Lieutenant's Woman* illustrates the complexity of communicative acts and will serve to revisit the added problem of textual instability. A bibliographical summary of *The French Lieutenant's Woman* states that the novel was first published in 1969 in London by Jonathan Cape and in Boston by Little, Brown. Both editions were reprinted many times, including a Taiwanese piracy of Little, Brown. Other editions and reprints were produced by Franklin Press, International Collectors Library, and a large-type edition by Associated Reprinting Company in Buffalo. Paperbacks by Triad Granada (Panther) and Hodder and Stoughton in England and by New American Library in America have also been reprinted frequently. Translations, including Portuguese, German, Russian, Danish, Finnish, Norwegian, Italian, Chinese, Hungarian, Spanish, and Polish round out the book versions of the work (Olshen). The manuscript, at the University of Tulsa, has been described by David Leon Higdon and Elizabeth Mansfield.

Given D. F. McKenzie's definition of bibliography,[4] this summary of the novel's print history would go on to say that Harold Pinter created a movie script, published as *The Screenplay of the French Lieutenant's Woman* with a foreword by John Fowles (London: Jonathan Cape, 1981), and that Karel Reisz directed a movie version based on Pinter's screenplay, edited by

---

4. "Bibliography is the discipline that studies texts as recorded forms, and the processes of their transmission, including their production and reception" (McKenzie, *Bibliography*, 4).

John Fowles, produced by Leon Clore, manufactured at Twickenham Studios in England, and released by Twentieth-Century Fox and United Artists in 1981. A video version distributed by CBS/FOX Video became available in 1983. It is interesting, though not crucial to our concern with this adaptation and performance of the story, that the author had an important controlling role in developing the movie version. Discussions of the novel and movie adaptation filled the reviews, journal articles, and dissertations, theses, and student papers uncountable and untraceable.

The bibliographical record is often taken at face value as a record of compositional activity. We refer to John Fowles as the author of the novel. And, though most of us know better, we often assume we are reading what the author wrote; in any case, we frequently act as if there were no textual discrepancy between what the author wrote and what we read. In spite of the bibliographies we seldom refer to *The French Lieutenant's Woman* as Jonathan Cape's or Little, Brown's or the New American Library's novel. This fact suggests that we do not pay much attention to the novel as the brain child of publishers or even as entrepreneurial enterprises in a market economy. And yet it is that which the bibliographies are a primary record of, not of authorial activity or intention. We do a much better job of distinguishing these matters for movies where we speak of Harold Pinter's screenplay and Karel Reisz's movie. Perhaps we go too far when we say it is Meryl Streep's movie, but maybe that betrays an intuitive recognition of the multiple voices and multiple events that constitute the movie version of *The French Lieutenant's Woman*.

The bibliographical summary (i.e., the record of physical products called *The French Lieutenant's Woman*) suggests a third activity more difficult to document than the authorial history or the entrepreneurial or publication history. (Incidentally, the word *document* used as a verb indicates one of the problems relevant to this subject, for it suggests that documents form records of actualities and provide stability to events or to memories of them. The concomitant suggestion is that that which is undocumented or, worse, undocumentable has less claim to attention or credence as "actual.") Though less documented, this parallel to the bibliographical summary is, however, quite easy to infer. It is simply that the books produced—the various editions and reprintings—and the movies and videos produced were read or seen. That is, the bibliographical record implies a history of audience interactions. This point is so obvious it usually goes without saying. Yet this activity is of utmost importance to our enterprise, for the written records of reception—the reviews and even the adaptations—are records of readerly performances of the work, not records of the work itself.

These parallel histories of the text "documented" by physical entities titled *The French Lieutenant's Woman* raise four interesting questions concerning literary criticism. Are references to the work in critical writings references to one thing, to many things, or to one of many? Are such references to physical objects or to events? Are they references to intention-laden communicative acts or to autonomous occasions for response? And what relevance to our concept of the novel is our experience of the movie version? As a term or as a label, *The French Lieutenant's Woman* is too vague to identify any particular manifestation of the work. This is important to remember because of the frequency with which the title is used in reference to a copy of the work as if it *were* the work. Any particular manifestation of the work is only one thing in a range of things of the same name. To accept the notion that the novel (or movie) is a communicative act entails referring to it as an event or, more accurately, as a series of many events.

And yet there is a sense in which all copies of the novel represent a single thing we call *The French Lieutenant's Woman* and which we claim to share in common even when some of us read the first English edition and others a U.S. paperback. There is a sense in which the movie version is also *The French Lieutenant's Woman* in another form. The question of translations suggests a similar sense in which, though every word has changed to some other word, the translation is yet somehow *The French Lieutenant's Woman*. Perhaps we need to follow George Steiner's lead in recognizing somehow the "real presence" of this work that becomes substantiated to us in a variety of mediums and performances like communion. I am inadequate to the task, but I see in the concept an attractive but ultimately futile way to explain the oneness of *The French Lieutenant's Woman* in spite of its variableness and instability. These complexities can be sorted into subsets of complexity. The one I wish particularly to focus attention on is the temporal, history-bound "eventness" of text production and text reception as communicative acts and on the implications of this temporality to interpretation.

I focus on two episodes or issues in the work: Mrs. Poulteney's imagined visit to the upper reaches of her house one night where she might have discovered Sarah Woodruff and Millie asleep in each other's arms; and Charles Simpson's interview with Mr. Freeman, his intended father-in-law, concerning Charles's future in the trade.

One reason to focus on these episodes (and one could list many more with a similar attraction) is that the narrator of the novel, a reasonable facsimile of the supposedly intrusive storyteller of Victorian baggy monsters, finds it repeatedly necessary, in 1969, to explain the novel's actions in terms of social, economic, and medical knowledge and beliefs of 1867. It seemed necessary in the novel to explain that Darwin's theories were still assumed by most people (in 1867) to be a bad joke, that to work in "trade" was viewed with tentative pride by the middle classes and with disdain by the upper, that the leisure class was cursed with an excess of time (while in 1969 even novel readers seem universally cursed with insufficient time), that tans were infra dig for both men and women of Charles and Ernestina's social class, that universal male suffrage in England was not granted until 1867, that a proper woman's place remained domestic, demure, and nonvoting, and that the pervasive religious life of Victorians was punctuated at its poles by specific forms of ceremony and disbelief, represented by the secret, High Church leanings of the Exeter priest who offered Charles the services of a confessional and by the agnostic scientism of Dr. Grogan, who substituted the *Origin of Species* for the Bible upon which to swear an oath.

John Fowles's access (as is our own) to the knowledge and beliefs of 1869 is limited to what can be reconstructed from wide reading, museum visits, and an active imagination. Fowles's assumptions about his 1960s audience—their ignorance of Victorian life, their values, their acceptance of sex without fear or marriage, of religion without conviction, of science with conviction, and of the intrinsic and civic equality of men and women—were firsthand knowledge to him and guided his choice of things to explain and ways of explaining them. But we have reached a significant remove from the late 1960s, and Fowles's explanations for a twentieth-century audience begin to sound quaint if not alien. We still have access to the sensibilities of the 1960s from wide reading, television documentaries, active imaginations, and, for some of us, memories, but more and more our students find the 1960s as foreign as the 1860s.

It is notable that these historical explanations are largely omitted from the movie version, in which they are dramatized by the jarring juxtaposition of scenes of characters allegedly Victorian and scenes of actors allegedly modern, and in which clothes, manners, accents, attitudes, beliefs, sexual behavior, and forms of politeness are paralleled and contrasted—indeed, choreographed—to make historical explanations unnecessary. A remarkable exception occurs early in the movie, when Anna reads out a statistical account of prostitutes and brothels in 1857 London that Mike turns into a joke.

In the novel, when Mrs. Poulteney might have gazed at two of her female employees, Sarah and Millie, sleeping in each other's arms, she is allowed one of her very few gentle acts: to close the door softly so as not to disturb the sleeping pair. And the narrator finds himself having to account for her gentleness to a reading public that, according to him, knew much more about lesbian behavior than Mrs. Poulteney or any of her ilk had ever experienced or even imagined. The narrator's explanation of Mrs. Poulteney's reaction is couched in terms apparently meant to address and prevent the potential snickers of a 1969 audience. That audience, though knowledgeable, would for the most part have been assumed by Fowles to be morally opposed to lesbianism. The prudes of 1969 would need to understand why the prudes of 1867 were not upset by the scene. Of course, the prudes of the 1990s may wonder the same thing, but the audience of the 1990s has a much larger contingent of folks who would tolerate, condone, approve, or encourage lesbian behavior. How will Children of the Rainbow react to Fowles's narrator? Such modern readers, in misunderstanding the nature of Sarah and Millie's 1867 embrace, might also be offended by the 1969 explanation of their "innocence," given as if to palliate aberrant behavior. Thus, an annotator or teacher of the novel today might find it necessary or tempting to provide the communicative context of the narrator's explanation in 1969 in order to deflect quite understandable 1990s reader responses that misconstrue the 1969 communicative event.

Deflect and *misconstrue* may be the wrong words to use here. They suggest that the 1990s reader might be wrong to be offended by the narrator's apparent assumption that most readers would be quick to label the two servants as lesbian and to be puzzled by Mrs. Poulteney's failure to be shocked. Quite the contrary. The assumption I am counting on is that the novel is a series of communicative acts that must be seen as a series of events with a developing sequence of contexts for the performances that these events are. The layering of social contexts, from Fowles's reconstruction of 1867 attitudes through his own perception of the views of his day and down to the shift in those views taken by many modern readers, combine to enrich and give perspective to that modern attitude. Of course, some readers might find it more immediately satisfying to write off, with indignation, the novel as the product of a male chauvinist prude. Righteous indignation occasionally thrives on ignorance and denial, but I maintain that one's disapproval cuts with a finer edge when it is directed from a position of knowledge rather than ignorance, regardless of how righteous.

One could object that Fowles was no prude, for many commentators have noted or claimed that this novel, as well as much other work by Fowles, is aimed at the "depuritanization of sex" (Conradi 41) or that it is devoted to the "myth of the overthrow of 'Victorianism,' entailing the ritual exorcism of Duty and Work and Chastity" (Brantlinger 340). Yet free heterosexual love and other rebellions against authority and tradition that were frequently celebrated in the popular culture of the 1960s ring with a different sound in the 1990s, when the freedom to be sexually active includes the freedom to be gay or lesbian and when that freedom, along with the freedom to use drugs, is "limited," not celebrated, by the fear of AIDS. These new perspectives—granted not universally subscribed to—make the new reader in the 1990s something of a foreigner both to the 1860s world of Mrs. Poulteney and to that of her 1960s apologist, John Fowles.

One might note that the scene with Sarah and Millie in each other's arms did not make it into the movie in 1981. There is no instance to parallel it either. Mrs. Poulteney in the movie has no scene betraying the existence of approval for anything that would have to be explained to a modern audience. Nor is she consigned to hell in the movie as she is in Charles's dream ending to his life's story in the book as he dozes on the train to meet his actual fate in Exeter. Is that because the screenwriter found that kind of double-world experience impossible to portray and explain in a movie? Is it because the director and producer even in 1981 were afraid of adverse public reaction detrimental to income if they undertook a risky attempt at complexity in a character that could safely be kept a simple stereotype? These are the kinds of questions that tantalize the reader/viewer who tries to see the work as a series of communicative events.

Sexuality is not the only field of dislocation between the setting, the narrating, and the reading of this book. Charles's two visits to Mr. Freeman in the book, the first to ask for Ernestina's hand in marriage and the second to explain that his financial expectations were reduced and his anticipated title placed in jeopardy by his uncle's marriage, are telescoped into one visit in the movie, which eliminated all references to the uncle. In the book the second visit is the only one dramatized. It takes place in the Freeman mansion overlooking Hyde Park; the home's primary function was to assert the gentility of this captain of industry—who, incidentally, is a mere merchant, a retailer of goods, not a producer. This backdrop for Mr. Freeman's suggestion that Charles consider entering the generalship, the commander post, in trade puts mercantilism in its best possible light, and yet it appalls Charles, whose shocked reaction is mishandled in yet another of his typically weak responses to the challenges in his life. The scene is followed by a chapter in which Charles wanders on foot into the economically underprivileged but apparently happy haunts of the London poor and in which he confronts the Freeman emporium, where in solitude his gut reaction finally generates a rejection of Freeman's proposal. Fowles thus conveys a complex and accurate picture of the upper-class's simultaneous fascination with mercantile money, abhorrence of trade, and fear of extinction in the face of industrial progress. Charles retreats to milk and punch, but the modern reader is left to sort out whether the class structure of Victorian England is the dinosaur on the edge of extinction or whether class structures in the 1960s and 1990s in England and the United States still maintain the breed of clean-handed dilettantes represented by Charles. Readers in any age might have no trouble at all "relating to" sentences like these: "Death is not in the nature of things; it is the nature of things. But what dies is the form. The matter is immortal" (286). Yet, a student in the 1990s may wonder at the quaintness of another sentence on the same page concerning the "modern computer scientist deaf to the screams of the tender humanists who begin to discern their own redundancy"; for the battles between T. H. Huxley and Matthew Arnold or between C. P. Snow and F. R. Leavis or between the tender humanists of the 1960s and the hard computer scientists seem in the post-Reagan, post-Thatcher era to be as lively as ever. Humanists are among the most avid computer users on the planet.

In the movie Charles's one dramatized visit to Mr. Freeman is to ask for Ernestina's hand in marriage. It takes place in Mr. Freeman's warehouse office, access to which must be the back streets filmed in reasonable imitation of Gustave Doré's illustrations of industrial London. We do not see the elegant and clean Oxford Street front of the Freeman emporium. Instead, in the midst of the noise and turmoil of trade warehouses Freeman both approves of the marriage and invites Charles to consider joining the firm. There is much less examination of motives for either man, but the inappropriateness of Charles for industry and the gulf between tradesman and gentleman is abundantly clear. Anyone familiar with Matthew Arnold's descriptions of Philistines and Barbarians would recognize the narrowness of Mr. Freeman and the wastefulness of Charles. But do students of the 1990s recognize Arnold's categories? And when they do, should they or do they participate in Arnold's or Fowles's attitudes toward them?

Again, the difference in medium dictates differences in reading skills for the audiences. The movie leaves rather a lot unsaid, but the discerning viewer is informed, nonetheless. My argument would be that the more the reader/viewer is able to discriminate between the sets of performances that are being layered in the work and the more that discrimination exposes the contexts of presupposition that are, were, or would have been operative in the various communicative acts being observed, then the sharper will be the reader/viewer's intuition and the richer will be the readerly performance.

It is worth noting, however, that many critics already disagree. Glen Mazis, for example, reads both the novel and the movie as an indictment of the "present age's" lack of historical context, which vitiates the vitality of the sexual encounters portrayed by Mike and Anna. He seems to think that the telescoping of time that the past, the enactment of the past, and the present provides is a confusion that points the reader/viewer "to that deeper sense of ambiguity which accompanies the discovery of one's present possibilities through a sudden shift to the past when that shift is created through commemoration" (Mazis 308). In other words, Mazis is interested in having the film "work" on the viewer transparently to achieve the film's "desired" (therapeutic?) effect by rapid and confusing dislocations of time and of selves. Mazis's approach seems enhanced by Anna's two sudden shifts into Sarah (one at the opening of the film in which, as Anna, she checks her makeup seconds before, as Sarah, she walks the Cobb and another when the movie cuts from rehearsal to action when first Anna then Sarah "stumbles in the woods") and by Mike in the closing scene, when he reveals his confused desire for Anna as Sarah by calling out Sarah's name "after the departing Anna" (Mazis 309). In this view the reader participates in the medium's and the characters' merging of temporal worlds in an enrichment of the present historicized. I would argue, instead, that in these scenes of obvious convergence an alert viewer catches the message of *potential* confusion of time and identity through recognizing the "fakes" and "mistakes"— not through being confused by them. One notes, for example, that in the final party scene both Mike and Anna still wear parts of their costumes as Charles and Sarah, making them visibly fake mergings of their double roles as Sarah/Anna and Charles/Mike. Yet I acknowledge that it is not difficult to be confused; it is tempting to telescope rather than discriminate among the communicative acts layered in both movie and book.

Tony Whall, for example, considers the film a failure fundamentally because the novel is "'about' personal liberation," while the film is about "love, not liberty."[5] Whall does have a point in that the novel is far richer

---

5. Whall, 76, 78. Susan Lorsch blames Pinter's screenplay, not Reizs's movie, for providing too much certainty in the endings. By giving Charles and Sarah a conclusive happy ending and Mike and Anna a conclusive unhappy ending, the screenplay does what the novel refuses to do: exercise freedom on behalf of a character (Lorsch, "Pinter Fails Fowles"). I see the point but disagree on several grounds: Anna's ending is not as unhappy as Mike's and repre-

and more explicit than the film, but he grossly mistakes the film, which he claims reduces the complexity of the novel to a mere love story with a clever but largely pointless counter story in Mike and Anna, whose casual sex reveals the paucity of modern life. He further claims that the movie "disregards the function of the novel's narrative point of view" (80–81). But the novel is about more than liberty, and the movie captures much more than a love story. The book's concentration on itself as a book is paralleled by the movie's focus on itself as film. The book's preoccupation with the dislocation of past and present is choreographed in the movie's paralleling and juxtaposing scenes of past and present. The book's denial of epistemological certainty is paralleled in the movie's slippage from one illusion of reality to another illusion of reality. (What moviegoer ever fails to see Meryl Streep and Jeremy Irons pretending to be the "real" Mike and Anna acting out the "illusion of realities" of Sarah and Charles?) The book's preoccupation with identity and self are paralleled in the movie's portrayal of a double progression in Charles and Mike, who both begin by playing at falling in love with beautiful but strangely aloof and thoroughly modern women and end head over heels in love in earnest with images of unreality that they have constructed out of the flesh-and-blood women—except that, of course, neither novel nor movie is "documentary"; all is imagination.

Whall, it seems to me, fails to note that liberty in the novel is a playing out of the "hazard" Fowles considers endemic to the universe (see *The Aristos* and *The Magus,* particularly the revised version). It is possible also to misread the movie by failing to recognize what goes on in Anna's mind as she checks her makeup in her final scene in the Windemere house; is she perhaps making sure she is still Anna and checking her final choice—freedom from Sarah and Charles and Mike? Likewise, one can easily fail to read Mike's mind as he realizes that he has idiotically confused Sarah and Anna there in the final window. Does he realize the structured, imagined, misimagined world of the ego-driven self? Has he in that moment accepted finally the responsibility of the Aristo? I say it is easy to fail here because, unlike the novel, with its loquacious guiding narrator, the film relies exclusively on facial expression and action to convey thoughts. Perhaps

---

sents her choice; Sarah's ending is precipitated by herself in the movie (not by the interfering Sam, as in the book); and Mike's epiphany of self-revelation in the final scene surely frees him, at least potentially, from the egocentrism that has driven his entire life. Peter Conradi provides a much more balanced and insightful account of the relations between novel, screenplay, and film. All these examinations of the screen adaptation of the novel suggest, however, that adaptation may more profitably be seen as a form of criticism than as a reimbodiment of "the work."

Whall just isn't a good phrenologist and physiognomist, lost sciences of the Victorian era.

Another way to view the cultural juxtapositions in this work or series of works is suggested by David Higdon, who finds in the story's three endings the narrative technique and philosophical inclinations of three ages. The imagined ending in which Charles marries Ernestina and Mrs. Poulteney descends to her just reward, Higdon identifies as a typical Victorian, sentimental ending. The second ending, in which Charles returns to Cheyney Walk to reunite with Sarah Roughwood and his love daughter, Lalage, Higdon recognizes as an Edwardian, tolerant, romantic ending. The third ending, in which Sarah rejects Charles, Higdon sees as a "contemporary (existential)" ending. These views seem to me self-evident and require no elaboration here, but the word *contemporary,* even when Higdon used it in 1984, already needed to be understood as contemporary in the late 1960s. The novel has no historical commentary relevant to the particular financial, social, and medical conditions of the late 1980s and 1990s; it contains no poststructural ending, though we can, of course, provide poststructural readings.

These are not startling new discoveries. The points have been made many times in recent literary criticism. They can be illustrated by almost any novel or short story and probably by any poem. But in the context of the question "What are the implications of the instability of textual forms and the insights of modern literary theory on the practices of scholarly editing and on the use of texts in pedagogy?" they lead me to a simple conclusion: editors and teachers may do better to emphasize a work's dynamics than its supposed stabilities or purities. More, I believe, is gained by empowering readers, viewers, and even beginning students to discriminate the layers of contexts and performances in literary works than in hoping that ignorance and untrammeled "natural" interaction with "pure" texts will have unconscious and perhaps therapeutic entertainment value. I conclude, in other words that hiving off the past as irrelevant or unnecessary because it is inaccessible represents a radical "presentism," which is reductive and intellectually impoverishing.

Chapter 5

Social Contracts, Production Contracts, and Authority

We have after all learned a great deal about something that has turned out to be a more difficult and confusing problem than was originally thought.

—Morse Peckham

When you get me a good man made out of arguments, I will get you a good dinner with reading you the cookery-book. That's my opinion, and I think anybody's stomach will bear me out.
—Mrs. Farebrother in George Eliot, *Middlemarch*

The roots of modern textual criticism lie in classical and biblical textual scholarship, which generally speaking assumes an ur-text, most often no longer extant. The editorial task in such situations is to reconstruct this ur-text, which is usually conceived to have been single and completed. Variant readings occurring in competing modern editions of classical or biblical works usually reflect the difficulty editors have in sifting the evidence of extant derivative source texts. The differences seldom represent disagreements about the aim or purpose of editing: to recover or reconstruct the archetype, or ur-text.

When editors turned to textual criticism of modern works for which authorized texts were extant and for which even authorial materials such as manuscripts survived, the idea of an archetype, or ideal text, was not easily discarded. The comparative richness and authenticity of materials merely made it seem more likely that success could be achieved in editorial work. The concept of definitive texts seemed plausible.[1]

Generally speaking, the editorial principles evolving in the mid-twentieth century all assumed that the literary work was the product of an author whose wishes concerning the text were paramount and that the work should be edited in such a way as to produce an "established" text representing authorial intention. The purpose of critical apparatuses was to show what the editor had done to produce the established text and to show what historical authorial forms of the text had been used as a basis for establishing the new text.

The editorial discussions of the twenty years preceding 1980 did not seriously question these assumptions, concentrating instead on issues related to "final intentions" (exploring distinctions between artistic and commercial intentions and debating whether the terms *final intentions* and *last intentions* were synonymous)[2] and on issues related to the treatment of accidentals (exploring distinctions between purely formal elements and "semi-substantives" [T. Davis 63–69; Shillingsburg, "Key Issues," 3–13]).

Some potentially interesting questions were raised about fulfilling authorial expectations (as opposed to authorial intentions), but even these did not clearly challenge the underlying assumption that the work belonged to the author and that the task of the editor was to serve the author. Most of the arguments on the side of serving the reader (objections to "barbed wire" editions, encouragement to modernize editions) were dismissed as corrupting influences that pandered to popular audiences.[3] Only one "reader service" principle found general acceptance in American scholarly editing— the clear reading text, uninterrupted by footnotes or note indicators in the text. It is probable that this principle reflected more than anything else the result of belief in the established definitive text, the recovery of "pure virgin text."[4]

---

1. The range of methods and the history of editorial practice can now best be traced in David C. Greetham, ed., *Scholarly Editing: A Guide to Research.*

2. See, particularly, Tanselle's survey in "Recent Editorial Discussion and the Central Questions of Editing." Tanselle groups these ideas slightly differently, but the point he made in 1981 remains valid: that editors tended to return to these "small number of basic problems" (59). He subsequently added that, regardless of how much they have been rehearsed, there "will be no end of debates over these issues, because they are genuinely debatable; and the process of debate is the way in which each generation of editors thinks through the questions for itself" ("Historicism and Critical Editing," 45).

3. See works cited by Herbert Davis, Lewis Mumford, Peter Shaw, and Edmund Wilson. See also James Thorpe's comments on the subject in *Watching the P's & Q's.* And see the Modern Language Association's response to Wilson.

4. The CEAA pushed this principle very hard: "Whenever possible, clear text is to be

A few relatively serious but largely unsuccessful attempts were made in that period to legitimize the role of publishing and production crews in the eyes of scholarly editors. That is, there were some attempts to show that secretaries, editors, compositors, and advisors often enough gave "good" advice and that sometimes their good effects had to be carried out in spite of the author's wishes or, in the case of absent or dead authors, without any indication of the author's wishes. One of the earliest such efforts, by James Thorpe, defined the work of art as merely "potential" until it was published (*Principles*, 37–38). The effect of this definition was to acknowledge the production process both as an aid to the author in finalizing the work and as a necessary fact of life enabling works of art to be known to readers. To support the first of these propositions, Thorpe argued from specific cases in which authors received needed help for which they were grateful (131–70).[5] The second proposition received its best support from Donald Pizer in a series of objections to the editing of texts (particularly Stephen Crane's *Red Badge of Courage* by Henry Binder and the Pennsylvania edition of Dreiser's *Sister Carrie*) in which the pursuit of purely authorial forms produced a text so different from the "cultural" artifact that had been known so long that, Pizer thought, serious confusion resulted about what the "real" text was and what it meant. Philip Gaskell generated a considerable amount of press for Thorpe's basic premise in the editorial advice appended to his *New Introduction to Bibliography* and in his discussion of textual problems in *Writer to Reader*.[6] Nevertheless, these editorial arguments remained author-centric, for they argue from the belief that the production process was an extension of authorial intention and merely fulfilled expectations for improvement of the work.

---

preferred, since in many editions it can then serve the interest of both scholars and general readers" (CEAA, 8). English scholarly editions have tended to use notes at the foot of the text page, tacitly indicating a greater modesty about the established text and drawing attention more forcibly to at least some of the alternative forms of the text.

5. Thorpe quotes confessions by the following authors to the effect that they did not know or did not care about punctuation and appealed to others, including their publishers, for help with punctuation: Thomas Gray, Wordsworth, Byron, J. F. Cooper, Charlotte Brontë, Sherwood Anderson, Timothy Dexter, and W. B. Yeats (Thorpe, *Watching*, 21–23). He does not ask whether an author's plea for help in these matters is sufficient proof that the author's own system is in fact inadequate, misleading, or less preferable than the augmented or regularized punctuation received; he merely assumes it to be so. In the same year the CEAA *Statement of Editorial Principles*, assessing the same kind of evidence, and also failing to discuss this question, assumes the opposite: "what an author wrote is to be preferred in most circumstances to what a publisher or printer imposed upon that writing" (4).

6. But see Fredson Bowers's scathing review of the former, "McKerrow Revisited."

Discussion of the "critical" nature of editing did, however, dethrone the concept of definitive texts. Its most visible manifestation was in the emblem of approval designed for the CEAA-sponsored editions, which reads "An Approved Text." The point was made that the emblem did not say "*The* Approved Text." To emphasize the point the Committee on Scholarly Editions, the Modern Language Association's replacement for the CEAA, redesigned the emblem to say "An Approved Edition," a label meant to indicate approval of the editorial work rather than of the particular text itself. Yet the arguments about critical editions and about what part of them was or was not definitive did not go beyond an acknowledgment that different editors attempting to produce a text that best represented the author's intentions were confronted from time to time with inconclusive evidence and might exercise their judgment differently in those instances. When the evidence for the authority of variant textual forms is equivocal, the variants are said to be "indifferent." In such cases editors are faced with an arbitrary decision to be explained in a way similar to this note from Edgar F. Harden's edition of Thackeray's *Henry Esmond:* "Although 'was numerous' can be interpreted as a compositorial misreading or correction [of 'very handsom' which is squeezed in nearly illegibly in the margin], this edition accepts the changed reading as authorial. Similarly, it accepts the change from 'her newly adopted son' to 'the newly adopted son' as authorial" (552). There is no elaborate explanation of the reason for this decision; indeed, what would be the point? There is no overwhelming reason to choose one way or the other—only that a choice had to be made. Whatever else they might disagree about, G. Thomas Tanselle wrote, scholarly editors were in general agreement that the aim of editing was "to discover exactly what an author wrote and to determine what form of his work he wished his public to have."[7]

Most editors were well aware of the difficulties the idea of intention represents. Much of editorial debate, as well as the generation of new approaches to editing, was fueled by the problem of identifying intention and of using the concept responsibly in practical ways. Some editors have been attracted by theories that attempt to avoid the problem of intention altogether, as will be shown. But no one should conclude from Tanselle's remark about the general agreement among editors about the aim of editing (that it is to recover the author's intentions) that he was unaware of the

7. "The Editorial Problem of Final Authorial Intention" (167). He repeats this idea in "Recent Editorial Discussion and the Central Questions of Editing," in which he says that the aim of editing is "to emend the selected text so that it conforms to the author's intention" (67).

underlying problem; indeed, the article in which he wrote it remains the most thoughtful and detailed discussion of the problem yet written.[8]

In the 1980s the tenor and range of editorial discussion, which had been dominated for thirty years by Fredson Bowers and the pursuit of final authorial intentions, suddenly changed and broadened. The changes have developed in three primary methodologies for editing, but all three derive impetus from the newer critical theories and particularly from new attention to the act of reading as well as from social theories of communication. Morse Peckham had tried something similar in the early 1970s with a behavioral model of communication, but it had little influence in the editing community. The three new editorial methods had certain things in common, but the differences led to radically different editorial results. Two of the modes remained author-centric; the third was sociocentric. It is this third, the social view, that is the concern of this chapter.

Briefly, however, the first of these new editorial modes dubbed itself the "new scholarship"; its most frequent spokesman has been Hershel Parker.[9] The reading and editing principle for this approach was to see the work in the context of its creation in order to best understand what the author was trying to do and to see that effort in relationship to what the author did do—the text that was produced. Parker questioned a basic assumption of the New Critics: that works of art are unified and make sense and that the critic's job is to discover and reveal that unity and sense. Exploring examples of works in which he believed the author did not fulfill his own intentions or in which a decently fulfilled intention was marred by the author's own later revisions, Parker dethroned the text as the verbal icon. He argued that textual criticism pursued with the diligence and the methods of the new scholarship, could reveal flawed texts with "adventitious" meanings, resulting not just from corruptions imposed by editors but from the author's failure to embody a coherent intention in the produced text. While this approach was wide ranging in its search for evidence of all sorts that might have influenced the creative process and while it was equally wide ranging in its awareness of influences on reading and interpreting

8. See also Morse Peckham; James McLaverty, "Concept of Authorial Intention"; Joseph Grigely, *Textualterity;* Donald Reiman, *The Study of Modern Manuscripts;* Jack Stillinger, *Multiple Authorship and the Myth of Solitary Genius;* Hans Gabler et al., eds., *Contemporary German Editorial Theory* (particularly the essays by Zeller, Cervenka, Martens, and Scheibe); and Shillingsburg, *Scholarly Editing,* 3d ed., 29–39.

9. Parker inaugurated the name in "The 'New Scholarship': Textual Evidence and Its Implications for Criticism, Literary Theory, and Aesthetics," which was collected with a number of other essays in *Flawed Texts and Verbal Icons.*

the work, it remains an author-centered approach. As such it is primarily a refinement of the more traditional (CEAA) modes, the main difference being that it eschews final intentions per se as a touchstone for determining the authenticity or desirability of a text. Often, in the examples Parker provided initial intention is preferred to final intentions, since by the time of final intentions, Parker said, the author might have ceased the creative mode and adopted an editorial mode. Parker's arguments are interesting and important because of the thorough research and sheer quantity of detailed information he brought to bear on his analyses of the genesis of texts. Thoughtful queries about his conclusions have been raised.[10] Parker's approach does bear a similarity to the other two emerging modes in that it emphasized a concept of the author in a social continuum that includes economics, politics, the psychology of creativity, and book production. It represents, however, a refinement, not a dismissal, of an authorial concept of textual authority.

The second new editorial mode reacted strongly against the idea of a "single adequate established text" as the goal of editing. "Multiple text" editors were not really new, but much new editorial debate emanated from their point of view. It was represented by Hans Gabler, editor of Joyce's *Ulysses,* and had roots in German editorial traditions as expressed early on by Hans Zeller.[11] Its primary difference from previous editorial principles was its insistence on multiple or fluid texts. Authorial intention is recognized as less frequently monolithic than it is developing or changing—not only in a continuous progression but reaching stages of supposed completion or being transformed by conflicting or mutually exclusive intentions. In theory no particular preference is given to the final intention text, as was the stated goal of CEAA editions, or to the text best representing the author's creative involvement with the work, as advocated by Parker in

10. See, particularly, Paul Baender's review.

11. Hans Zeller, "A New Approach to the Critical Constitution of Literary Texts." Although Gabler's defenses of the Synoptic edition of *Ulysses* made the general tenor of German editorial traditions somewhat familiar in the Anglophone editorial world, the publication in 1995 of *Contemporary German Editorial Theory* has greatly increased our sense of the different directions taken by the two editorial communities. It appears now that German insistence on multiple texts focused more heavily on the series of manifestations of the text that each new document represented rather than on developing authorial intention or control. McGann, Reiman, Stillinger, and Grigely develop ideas more in tune with Zeller and other German editors than do the main proponents of multiple texts and editing "process" rather than "product": Eggert, Bornstein, Gatrell, Kramer, Shillingsburg, and West. James McLaverty, arguing from an equation between the terms *utter* and *publish,* agrees with the former group in focusing editorial attention on published forms, but his other arguments show his unswerving allegiance to authorial intention as the guiding editorial goal ("Issues").

Flawed Texts. This position insists that the editorial aim is to present the multiple authorial texts, each representative of a stage in the developing or changed intentions, in such a way that the work could be read "radially," each version in relationship to its other manifestations. (Bowers used the term radial for multiple documents deriving from a single lost source from which authority radiated—like spokes from a hub—and might be found in isolated readings the editor selected for an established text; Jerome McGann uses the term to describe the act of reading and interpreting texts in tandem. Here I use it in the latter sense.) Each authorial version of the work, it was contended, adds to the whole critical perception of what the author was doing and, therefore, of what the work meant. Further, it allowed for the view that a new authorial intention does not deprive an original or intermediate intention of any authority: it is merely different; all authorial intentions might be equally authoritative.

It is much easier to think of the multiple text concept in theory than it is to construct a multiple text edition. "Everybody knows" texts are linear, not multiple, and everyone seems to want a text to be comfortable with. Edmund Wilson, complaining of NEH- and CEAA-sponsored scholarly editions, wanted books he could carry in his pocket on a plane. Peter Shaw, complaining of diplomatic transcriptions of Emerson's journals, wanted them "just as they were" but did not say whether he wanted to check out the originals or have a photocopy. And a reviewer of my book *Scholarly Editing in the Computer Age* (1986) objected to multiple texts specifically because people would not be comfortable with them. Comfort is an important issue, but it is secondary to the central observation: that, except for unrevised texts, a single text does not *adequately* represent the work for a critical reader.

There have been several efforts to make practical multiple text editions. In Gabler's edition of *Ulysses* one can see the "synoptic text" on left-hand pages tracing the development of authorial activity through a sequence of variant texts preceding the final fair copy used to set the first edition. The synoptic text superimposes all the preceding texts on one page through an elaborate, but decipherable, coding system. On the facing page the reader sees a linear text (clear reading text) representing the final manuscript version. The reader is encouraged to read the right-hand linear page in tandem with the synoptic, or radial, left-hand page. Michael J. Warren's *Complete King Lear* reprints two basic variant texts in parallel on facing pages with further variant versions indicated in marginalia. The idea is that the editor's critical preference, if there is one, is submerged in the arrangement of competing documentary textual forms. That the linear text is a limitation that scholarly editions can, to some extent, overcome was clearly apparent from the many iterations of the idea at the 1987 meeting of the Society for Textual Scholarship in New York. The idea of multiple texts or versions is not necessarily author-centric, though initially it was supported primarily by the argument that multiple or developing authorial intentions could not be adequately represented in a single text. Jerome McGann, reviewing Gabler's edition of *Ulysses*, called for another, complementary, edition that would represent the "continuous production text" of the work parallel to Gabler's "continuous compositional text."

As different as these various approaches to editing may seem, they have certain things in common. In each the work of art is conceived of as an authorial communication normally reaching its verbal form with minimal reference to book production, which is deemed merely an enabling process owing its allegiance to the author but occasionally failing in that allegiance. Given this set of assumptions, the critic is likely to judge the interference of the publisher, editor, and printer as legitimate only if it does not violate authorial intention or authorial practice. The production crew, from publisher to binder, is entrusted with translating the author's manuscript into print—or, in more characteristic terms, entrusted with enabling the author's communication to be seen by many in the form of a printed book. The production process is necessary but is always on notice that it may fail its handmaiden role.

The third approach was sociological. Its initial spokesmen were Jerome McGann and D. F. McKenzie, whose writings on the subject generated a good deal of excitement and confusion. The idea that authors live, breathe, and have artistic being in a social complex that includes more than the words surviving on pages of manuscripts and printed books was not new. Most editors consider themselves historical researchers—it goes with being a textual critic. It was the arguments concerning a social contract, not new evidence, that made the theory worth considering. But the confusion of argument should have been, but was not, a major block to its influence.

There were five and possibly six distinct arguments involved in the sociological approach. The first three were old and ultimately irrelevant, if not contradictory; for years they failed to influence the mainstream of scholarly editing. The fourth and fifth grew out of critical theory and are sophisticated and worthy of attention regardless of whether one adopts the conclusions of their proponents. Most discussions of social texts, including the first three, focused on the role of the production process in creating the work of art, but the concept is not limited to that subject, as the fourth and fifth arguments will demonstrate.

It is helpful to begin with another look at the basic arguments offered by Thorpe, Gaskell, and Pizer to legitimize the production process, for the first three arguments are really theirs. The first line of reason focuses on the idea that the production process is a necessary and desirable finishing process in which the author turns to the publisher for help—and usually gets it. The argument is supported with examples of felicitous collaborations, all tending to show that the normal process of book production is a happy one.[12] The conclusion of this argument is that, normally, the printed text is preferred as copy-text, and, normally, the editor restores "pre-copy-text" forms only when demonstrable errors marred the process. Notice, however, that the justification in this argument is based on a critical assessment of the effect of changes. Regardless of whether the editor acknowledges it, such assessments depend on the aesthetic principles of the critic/editor. This is true even when editors set aside their own preferences and pursue what they take to have been the author's preferences. A basic premise of this argument is that the author's intention is only tentatively or provisionally recorded in the manuscript and that the collective experience and judgment of publishers and editors help fulfill the author's intentions; thus, authorial intention and editorial judgment combine for a better end product.

The counterargument, that editorial interference is detrimental introducing corruptions, is often laced with examples of the silly results of production errors or angry remarks by disgruntled authors.[13] This argument leads to Greg's rationale of copy-text, so that authorial forms will be

---

12. These include Charlotte Brontë's letter of thanks to George Smith for taking care of the punctuation of *Jane Eyre* (C. Brontë complained of Thomas Newby's very shoddy handling of the punctuation of *Wuthering Heights* two months later; both letters are discussed in Bruce Harkness's review of *Jane Eyre* and in Ian Jack and Margaret Smith's response). Byron apparently received significant and appreciated help from his publisher, John Murray. Other help in the form of editorial advice is educed either in favor of good working relations or against, depending on the writer's evaluation of the results: Maxwell Perkins's influence on Hemingway and Wolfe, George Meredith's influence on Thomas Hardy, Bulwer Lytton's influence on the ending of *Great Expectations*, Dickens's influence on Elizabeth Gaskell—Meredith and Dickens in these cases working as publishers.

13. These include John Dryden's remark, "The Printer is a beast and understands nothing I can say to him of correcting the press"; Tennyson's milder remark to his publisher, "I think it would be better to send me proof twice over—I should like the text to be as correct as possible"; and Mark Twain's remark to W. D. Howells concerning a proofreader improving his punctuation, that he knew "more about punctuation in two minutes than any damned bastard

more likely to survive without these production-level "corruptions." Later printed forms are adopted only where they are demonstrably authorial or are plausible corrections of manuscript errors. Though many editors would want to deny it, the basis for this counterargument is also a critical assessment of the effect of production crews (proofreaders, editors, compositors, and/or other persons who help or hinder in the production of the published work). Scholarly editors who recognize the critical bases for judgment tend to say that rules cannot be made and that each textual situation should be judged on its own merits; after all, they say, what is critical editing if it is not critical?

A second argument for social texts, one used by both Donald Pizer and Jerome McGann, is very different because its logic denies the relevance of either authorial intention or critical judgment. The argument is that production and the resulting book are a part of history, which has integrity of its own regardless of the author's or the readers' assessment of its success. Thus, the fact that William Faulkner's *Sartoris* was published as it was becomes more important than might be the work that was to have been *Flags in the Dust*. In that particular case the enormous difference between the version Faulkner submitted to the publisher and the version Random House published, combined with the changed title, makes it easy to consider the two forms as completely different works, for which it is silly to ask, "Which is the real X——?" But when the difference is not so great and the name remains the same, as with Crane's *Red Badge of Courage* or Dreiser's *Sister Carrie,* the historical product, the first edition, has a validity or status that seems to some people to be threatened by editorial efforts to undo or redo the work of the original publication process—hence, the argument for the historical integrity of the first edition. In this argument many will recognize what has often been called documentary integrity. Historical integrity and documentary integrity need not, however, be the same thing. Tanselle, for example, describes the work of eclectic critical editors as historical, though they do not confine themselves to the readings of any single document. In addition, one might distinguish between the integrity of the document as it represents a historical event and its integrity as a phys-

---

of a proof-reader can learn in two centuries." (These examples are quoted by James Thorpe in *Watching the P's & Q's,* 4–7.) Examples of nonsense readings abound in the apparatuses of most scholarly editions, though one should note that, while production crews can make silly mistakes, they can also make corrections. The main question here, however, is whether they have a legitimate role in suggesting or imposing revisions or "improvements."

ical unit connected to the author.[14] In the former the text of a document might be thought inviolable though reproducible, while in the latter the document itself is the important unit.

The third argument asserts that published texts have become culturally validated by the decades or centuries of readers who have come to know and love the work in this socialized form. If an editor changes the text so that the work means something new or different, these readers and their sense of the cultural heritage will be confused, if not absolutely violated. This dislocation occurs even when the changes are "restorations" of previously unpublished authoritative forms, which perhaps should have been a part of the original work, save for the interference of "unauthoritative" influences. It is remarkable, however, that those who argue on behalf of cultural continuity of the familiar seem never to consider the decades and centuries of readers yet to come who, perhaps, should not be forced to read mangled texts just because a few decades or centuries of readers already have.

Although, to my knowledge, literary editors do not use the second and third arguments (about the historicity and the cultural validation of texts) to support the idea that *no* emendation should be undertaken, that is, strictly, the logical conclusion of both arguments. That a first edition is a historical document, that it was the basis for the work's first readers' acquaintance, and that it can still so serve new readers are unquestionable propositions. That an emended edition would misrepresent the integrity of the historical document is also true—though not necessarily important. It would be ludicrous, however, to expect all students of a text to read only the first edition or some other authoritative edition that had comparable legitimacy—such as "the author's revised edition." One could, with the argument concerning cultural validation, opt for editions that were straight reprints (unedited) with the idea that the linguistic text, more or less as it was first published, is what has been validated. But as soon as emendations are introduced the center of this argument for "historical integrity" is weakened, and, in fact, some other notion of integrity has replaced it.

Editorial theorists inclined to accept a social validation for texts, such as Thorpe, Pizer, McGann, and McKenzie, may have tended to attack the "Greg/Bowers" authorial intention editorial theories in order to make room

---

14. Robert Taylor, quoting Max Beerbohm, refers to the latter when he describes the desire of book collectors to own first editions of works by authors they admire because "they give one a sense of nearness to him ... 'this is the binding *he* chose—perhaps. This—perhaps—is the fount of type that *he* insisted on. Here certainly is a typographical error that *his* eye overlooked—bless his noble spirit!'" That is to say, the document has integrity or authority as historical relic or icon, not because of the purity or inerrancy of its text.

for their own. In a sense editors are in competition for the attention of readers: each wants readers, scholars, and critics to think that her or his edition is the "standard" edition. Sometimes, therefore, arguments are used against other propositions instead of for the alternative proposition. The idea of historical integrity and cultural validation may be primarily arguments against the authority of authorial intention rather than for a social theory of texts. It is, in any case, contradictory to argue that the production process is good both because it helps (i.e., authors need help and textual critics can judge when that has happened) and because the production process validates whatever came out (i.e., authors get what they get as a social reality; sorry, judgment has nothing to do with it).

The fourth and fifth arguments for social texts are much more interesting and sophisticated and provide the proper ground for serious consideration of a social contract theory. The fourth argument focuses again on the production process. But rather than saying that editors and publishers help authors to implement their intentions in a physical book, or that there is an antiquarian integrity to the document containing the text, this approach sees the production process as a cultural phenomenon without which books do not exist. The influence of production on the book does not begin when the author hands a completed manuscript to the publisher; it begins when the author raises a pen for the first word of a work intended for publication, because of a consciousness of the way books get published. Publishers, too, are only part of an even larger phenomenon that includes language and usage and everything that forms the sociological context within which authors are enabled to write and can hope to be understood. Any legal contract that the author signs with a publisher is, in this view, merely a confirmation of a predetermined contract that exists, whether acknowledged or not, among authors, publishers, and readers. Publishers, therefore, are not primarily handmaidens to authorship exercising helpful servant roles, which they may fail to do well; they are, instead, part of the authoritative social complex that produces works of art. They are a fact of life that cannot be "edited out" of the text any more than the effects of an author's breakfast and subsequent indigestion can be edited out. There is no tangible support for this point of view. We are asked to acknowledge a higher order of historical determinism that operates regardless of individual intentions. We all know this in our bones, perhaps. We all see it working in "movements," be they political, moral, social, or aesthetic. The author becomes the pawn of time—as we all are. If one does not feel this argument in one's bones, I suppose it will not be very convincing. Frankly, it does not affect mine much.

There is a fundamental shift in the concept of authority involved in this argument. Rather than judging the effect of publication on the author's words, this argument simply vests authority for the text in a socioeconomic environment that "contains" the author's initiating creative activity *and* the publisher's ongoing process of moving composition into production. The textual changes introduced by the production process are accepted by the editor, not because they are better, not because they are historical, not because they are sacred, but because they are social—representing a necessary bio-socio-economic relationship between author, publisher, and audience (including the editor). The result of this argument is that the printed text is preferred as copy-text, emendation is discouraged but allowed to complete the socializing process, and the critical apparatus is seen as an important record of social/cultural dynamics. It seems to me, at least on the surface, that much of the appeal of these arguments derives from the quasi-philosophical high ground they assume. In fact they do not address matters that have been unknown to editors in the past, though it may be true that the importance of the social contexts and "contract" have been misjudged.

Intrinsic to this argument is a transference of authority from the author to the publisher. Different theorists would argue in different ways about how this transfer takes place; it is different, perhaps, for every author and work and, therefore, looks different to each editor. The evidence of transfer is not new, though the conclusion that the author transfers authority over the text to the publisher when "submitting" the manuscript is, perhaps, new in editorial theory.[15] It is, of course, a quite old idea in commercial practice. Editors who use this argument are, however, usually comfortable with it only as long as the production process changed insignificant details or "improved" the work. When actual damage resulted from the publication process, the theory ceases to be appealing, and recourse is taken to another.[16]

---

15. For Siegfried Scheibe, "authorization" emanates from the author and "endows the text" as that which is "willed by him or her." This odd way of putting it allows for primary and secondary authorization: the first being anything the author did to the text and the second being anything the author delegated to others to do ("Theoretical Problems," 172, 179).

16. Hans Zeller, for whom every ambiguous "textual fault" is authorized by the author's will to be published, supports a blanket rule for adopting uncritically the introduction of textual faults by so-called authorized (re)transmitters of the text. The rule is designed to prevent eccentric pursuits of authorial intention, but Zeller is unhappy with the result of his own recommendations: "A new problem presents itself here which I regard as fundamentally unsolvable. It is best known through M. Bernays's (1866) discovery of the fatal effect of Himburg's corrupt pirated editions (1779) on Goethe's revision of his *Schriften*, specifically on

An analysis of the author's "submission" to the publisher and the relationships represented by such acts can reveal useful distinctions that are usually overlooked in the arguments for a social contract. James West has developed this most persuasively by pointing out that the production crew's attempt to enhance an author's "active" intentions and its attempts to enhance the "programmatic" intentions might very well be at cross purposes.[17] Programmatic intentions refer to intentions to have certain effects on readers, to cause them to react; active intentions refer to intentions to mean certain things, to convey certain understandings, feelings, or actions. Thus, West argues, Dreiser's active intention to delineate certain sexual experiences may have been interfered with by an editor's programmatic intention not to offend. West's position was that only limited transfers of authority may occur and that it is part of the scholarly editor's duty to determine which were legitimate fulfillments of active intention and which were illegitimate attempts at programmatic changes. It is clear that the details of an individual case would influence any editor's assessment of the process. The argument in the hands of a "social contract" theorist would tend, however, to acknowledge the authority of the production process in all cases. McGann uses this argument to deal with Byron's works in *A Critique of Modern Textual Criticism,* but he is reluctant to apply it to Percy Shelley's works, in which the author was judged to have been more clearly in control of the effect of punctuation, and the publication process was judged to have marred that control rather than enhanced it (*Critique,* 102–9).

The fifth argument adds several new dimensions. Rather than focusing on the production process and its socializing influence, this argument focuses on the physical artifact that results. It does not argue that the "known" text is part of our cultural heritage to which we have become accustomed and which has influenced so much critical debate in the form it was produced. Rather, it says that the physical object is a version of the work that itself generates meaning. It argues that the linguistic text generates only a part of the meaning of a book; its production, its price, its cover, its margins, its type font, all carry meaning that can be documented. *Meaning* may be the wrong word to use here. *Implication* more accurately indicates the significance of design and price. The social, political, and economic implications of being published by a certain publisher or in a certain

---

the *Werther* of 1787. In the textual comparison with the initial edition of 1774 the corruptions are so blatant and scandalous that one would hesitate to allow the principles developed here to apply to this text" ("Structure," 116).

17. West, "Editorial Theory." West's major terms are borrowed from Michael Hancher, "Three Kinds of Intention."

series or in a recognizable format condition the reactions to the linguistic text for those persons able to recognize these implications. In short the physical book, of which the linguistic text is but a part, is important not because we have become accustomed to it, and not merely because it is a part of history, but because its form and historical entry into the culture determined the cultural acceptance it received. For example, the elegant first edition of Byron's *Don Juan* was received as a witty and spirited performance, but reviewers of the cheap pirated editions called it an immoral travesty. The same verbal text in differing physical formats meant different things (McGann, "Theory of Texts"). I do not know by what method McGann determined that the difference was actually occasioned by the physical appearance of the books rather than by the moral character of the reviewers. If a single reviewer reacted differently to each edition, the case would be strong. Similarly, if contemporary readers of Thackeray's *Henry Esmond* in old-fashioned Caslon type in three volumes (1852) read the book differently from those reading it in "modern" type in one volume (1858), there is no record of it, though there were reviewers of both formats who found it immoral and others who found in each a thoroughly good book. But if we grant the conclusion and add the observation that the pirated cheap "immoral" texts of *Don Juan* were the ones that most people read and that made Byron's "literary reputation and popularity," we have a very complex textual situation. The implications of this phenomenon to the social contract editorial school is that the physical books, as products of the social context and contract, are physically the works of art.

There is a basic validity to this argument that I think few persons would deny. One's reaction to a work is conditioned by the knowledge of a variety of factors having little if anything to do with the linguistic text itself. Book designers know this well; cheap literature in small type and double columns is printed on newsprint or other inexpensive paper. Lurid covers indicate something about how the publisher hopes readers will react to the text and may also indicate what kind of reader is being addressed. Likewise, hard covers, ample margins, generous leading, and heavy paper often imply a high social status for the publisher and for readers of such editions. They may also imply the literary value or durability of the work of art thus produced.

N. N. Feltes, discussing W. M. Thackeray's *Henry Esmond,* pursued this line of investigation, arguing that the novel represents "the establishment" by its physical format (a Victorian three-decker), its price (thirty-six shillings—out of the reach of most ordinary book buyers), its genre (historical fiction), and its publisher (George Smith, an executive member of the Booksellers' Association). It is, therefore, Feltes continues, unlike Thackeray's earlier parts-issued *Vanity Fair* and *Pendennis,* which represented the proletarian economic revolution by their price (one shilling per number), formats (paper-wrappered serials), and publisher (Bradbury and Evans, publishers of *Punch*) (Feltes 28–29). This is a very interesting approach to the meaning of *Esmond,* bringing into serious question the effect of reprinting the novel in modern dress (one volume, modern type font) and obscuring by that process these meaningful elements of the first edition. This is true even though Feltes's conclusion, that Thackeray's hand was limited by these establishment forces and that the meaning of *Esmond* is "determined" by the social contract over which Thackeray had no control, is unconvincing.[18]

It is one thing to recognize the implications of the physical embodiment of a linguistic text, quite another to identify the text in its physical format as the work of art, and still another to say that the social and economic context within which the work was published determined what the author would or could do or that it should determine what form of the work a reader should read. There may be some truth in all of these propositions, but it would be very hard to make a rule out of them that would apply well to many texts. In some ways this argument sounds rather familiar; in 1952, for example, Gordon Ray made much the same case but drew a different conclusion, since Ray saw the cultural history of books as external to authorial intention and as an added, rather than substitute, interest ("Importance"). Ray notes, for example, the reception of Zola's works reflected in the succession of physical formats in which they became available—from colorful, lurid paper covers to a "respectable" collected edition.

The concept that physical books have integrity and meaning in themselves bears more thinking about. The meanings referred to can be not only in addition to the linguistic text but also separate from or unified with that text. They can be meanings of which the author was unconscious or meanings the author consciously exploits or manipulates. There are many well-known instances of authors consciously seeking to enhance their text by controlling the physical form of the works: the green covers of *Leaves*

---

18. See chapter 6 of my *Pegasus in Harness,* 201–20, in which I argue that Thackeray, operating within the confines of socioeconomic forces, produced an *anti*establishment work—a wolf in sheep's clothing (213)—and that the determining forces of the social contract were not more restricting to authorial intention and individual meaning than the determining forces of genre are, for example, to the poet who "frets not in [the] narrow cell" of the sonnet.

of Grass, the shaped lines of George Herbert's "Easter Wings," the private limited printing in 1926 of Lawrence's book *The Seven Pillars of Wisdom,* Blake's lithographed combinations of text and illustration. Other cases are known of authors manipulating or taking advantage of reader reactions to physical formats: Thackeray's references to the jaundiced yellow covers of *Vanity Fair* and Trollope's remarks about the third volume of *Barchester Towers,* which became puzzling in reprints in other colors and single volume form. But for the most part authors do not control these matters, and the "meanings," or implications, of the physical text, if anything, reveal unconsciously things about the author or publisher.

Readers of classic texts in new editions are taught to ignore the extralinguistic contexts of the physical books in the same way that theatergoers are taught to ignore the stage relation to the audience through a willing suspension of disbelief. Thus, we read Tennyson's *In Memoriam* in the cut version in the *Norton Anthology* and "understand" the poem as if its placement had nothing to do with how we read the poem or what the poem means (willing suspension of disbelief, indeed). The social contract theory asks readers to pay attention to the physical setting of "authoritative" versions (not the *Norton Anthology*) of the physical work.

A summary of the five arguments surveyed might help in evaluating them:

1. Production crews improve works of art; the editor and critic recognize this improvement by judging the results.
2. Publication is a historical fact; emendation would violate the historical event represented by the published text. Critical judgment is not a factor.
3. Years of use have validated the familiar text; it has been appropriated by the cultural heritage. Emendation would confuse people.
4. Publication is an integral and necessary part of the social act of producing works of art; production influences pervade composition from its inception and should be accepted as social fact—as part of the definition of literary work of art.
5. The physically produced work *is* the work of art; its physical form reflects social contexts revealing the true character of the work.

The most important difference between the social contract approaches to textual problems and previous editorial principles lies in the radically altered definition of textual authority that they offer. Whereas earlier principles for critical editing accepted without question the authority of the author, differing primarily in determining what the authorial intention was, the social contract principle denies the author the pride of place and substitutes the social event that produced the book as the authority. In that complex the author is merely one of several authorizing forces; authorial intention may still have relevance to editorial practice, but it is no longer the central focus; other, "larger" issues enter the equation.

At first, looking primarily at the first three arguments for "social texts," it would appear that the principle of social contract would forbid critical editing because those arguments identify the work of art with the commodity offered for sale, the socialized product. In its most rigid form this principle requires that printed texts should be chosen as copy-texts and that emendations should not be allowed. But if those three arguments are disposed of, as perhaps they should be, and the last two arguments assessed critically, we can see that a concern for authorial meaning is merely different from the concerns emphasized here, not a concern denied by the arguments.

There is a sixth argument relevant to a social theory of texts, though in some ways it is merely an extrapolation of the fourth. Its summary for the previous list would be:

6. Texts are socially determined, not just in the contract between author and production crew but also from its conception and in its composition.

This concept seems to underlie a good deal of the thinking behind the other five arguments. This idea concerns the importance of the entire bio-socio-economic context in *determining* the work of art. If one fails thoroughly to understand this idea, one could believe that it has unqualified power or authority over texts, leaving us to conclude simply that whatever text was produced by the publishing or social contract is the right text. That conclusion appears contrary to any editorial principle in which authority is defined as author-centric. This idea is alluded to by McGann when, in reviewing McKenzie's *Panizzi Lectures,* he speaks of "the people who belong to the text" ("Theory of Texts," 21). The usual approach is to see things the other way round: the text that belongs to the author or to the publisher or to the reader. That has been the conventional way of seeing authority. That is the "old" way of shaping editorial policy—by reference to those persons who authorize or determine what the text should be. McGann and McKenzie seem to make the text and the social forces it represents larger than any person. They include the text itself as a part of the "contract," or the complex of social, political, and economic forces that determine life. Social determinism becomes literary determinism. The language speaks the author; the social complex makes the book. The book is not "a container or transmitter of meaning"; it is "a meaningful agent itself" ("Theory of Texts," 21). And what it has come to mean is not within the author's or any other person's control. N. N. Feltes concludes from his study of the "establishment" elements in *Esmond* that Thackeray was forced into uncharacteristic, reactionary meanings—that authorship is largely determined by economic forces and that these forces reduce or replace the play of individual judgment (29).

The idea of socially determined texts may best be understood by asking several related questions designed to clarify the way in which a definition of authority controls editorial decisions and to highlight the difference between author-centric and sociocentric approaches.

What happens when the contracted socializing process violates the confidence or trust that the author unwittingly placed in it? Is the social contract or the author's wishes of greater authority? Similarly, what is the status of the contract when the socializing process takes place without the author's consent, as in posthumous publications? Is there to be a presumption that the socializing process is proper, legitimate, and good unless something can be shown to be wrong with it? If the answer to this last question is yes, it follows that a publisher's punctuation would be preferred to an author's punctuation. One could ask why that must be so—what is the applicable rationale for copy-text, and what distinction is made in that rationale between accidentals and substantives? None of the theorists proposing arguments on behalf of the social contract seem to have a well-developed or convincing rationale for dealing with accidentals.

What happens when the succession of reprints that perpetuates and validates the cultural heritage perpetuates demonstrable flaws? Is a restoration of texts that creates an unfamiliar version disallowed because it violates the cultural artifact? Contrarily, what happens when the authorial intention is weak or flawed but is substantively improved by editorial advice, such as is claimed for works like *Look Homeward, Angel* by Thomas Wolfe (and Maxwell Perkins) and *The Waste Land* by T. S. Eliot (and Ezra Pound). Is the social contract, or in this case collaboration, acceptable only when the results are judged acceptable? Similarly, what happens when the authorial intention was strong and unorthodox but is substantively weakened by the publication process? Does that prove that no contract exists? If the results can be judged unacceptable, then the criterion is aesthetic, not social; there is no contract. And what if that impoverished text makes a cultural impact validated by large sales and broad influence?

What happens when a text considered as a cultural object with meaning and significance derived from its physical form becomes re-objectified in new editions? Is each re-objectification a new version of the work worth editorial attention? No one, I think, would deny that each is worth attention as a fact of cultural history, but does that make each publication a part of what the work of art is from a critical point of view? If the answer is yes, how does it affect editorial policy?

Listing these questions and contemplating their possible answers suggests that the social contract theory is just as complex and variable as the author-centric approaches have been. It would, therefore, I think, be shortsighted and narrow-minded to try to persuade editors that a social theory of texts with a definition of authority marginalizing the author is the only responsible way to edit.[19]

The common link of all these questions and of the theories available with which to answer them is the concept of authority. Authority is not something "out there" to be discovered and analyzed. It is a concept brought to the situation by the observer. It is whatever it is defined to be. The hesitation one has in answering these questions—and, therefore, of knowing whether authorial acts are determined or free—comes from the different definitions of authority implied by the way the questions state the supposed conditions.

The idea that authority is not intrinsic or discovered in the textual problems but is, instead, brought to the problem by the editor to help evaluate the problem is not generally accepted. Fredson Bowers, for example, in his address to the Society for Textual Scholarship in New York City in April 1987, discussed at some length the question of authority but did so from the point of view of a definition he wanted everyone to apply to that word. "We shall not get very far in examining any textual proposition," he said, "unless we can come to some understanding on what is meant by *authority.*" And the "moment that some agent like a typist, compositor, or copyreader interposes himself between the holograph and the disseminated document, the print, a diminution of authority occurs" ("Unfinished

19. Note how these questions have been addressed in recent years by Donald Reiman and Jack Stillinger (as demonstrated in chap. 9). The social or production contract reasoning permeates the work of contemporary German editorial theory (Gabler et al.) and crops up in Grigely and in McLaverty.

Business," 1). Given his definition of authority, that is true; the issue now, however, is whether that definition should be the standard one. It is worth, therefore, a separate discussion of authority before we can get on properly with the questions I have just posed.

The greatest obstacle to understanding differences in editorial principles, and in particular to understanding the claims of the social contract, is the word *authority*. I think this is so not only because it is used to denote several different things, which users suppose to be clear from the context, but because it is an emotionally loaded word that grants approval; it is not cleanly descriptive.

I would like to sort out various definitions of the word derived from its use to describe textual phenomena. I will, thus, show that it is used to indicate concepts at various levels of thinking, show that sometimes it is used as a specific description (as we use the word *yellow* in the phrase "that is a yellow school bus") and other times as a comparative word (as we use the words *clear* and *clearer* with an eye doctor to indicate which lens clarifies the eye chart better). This exercise will help to show how description of a text's derivation can be thought of separately from the approval or disapproval sometimes indicated by the words *authoritative* and *nonauthoritative*.

One meaning of *authority* is "deriving from the author." This usually means that a word, phrase, or point of punctuation can be shown to have been written or dictated by the author. Melville's *coiled fish* has authority; the compositor's *soiled fish* does not. Such words are said to have authority because we know they came from the author. One could call this specific kind of authority "primary authorial authority," which may sound redundant but is not when we consider other meanings for *authority*.[20] An author's manuscript, of course, has primary authorial authority. So do the autograph alterations in proofs or setting copies for revised editions and instructions in letters or notes to secretaries, compositors, or publishers.

Another meaning for *authority* is "having a demonstrable, though not precisely known, relation to the author." This usually means that it is generally known that the author did revise or proofread the text, which is said, therefore, to have authority. The specific words, phrases, or punctuation that have primary authorial authority are not known. One could call this "secondary authorial authority." Instances of secondary authorial authority can be seen in a scribal copy or typescript made from a lost manuscript or a magazine publication made from a lost revised carbon typescript for which

---

20. This is very like the term used by Scheibe in his discussion of levels of authority ("Theoretical Problems").

the fact of authorial revision is not in dispute but the details of specific revisions cannot be recovered.

Another meaning for *authority* is "deriving from a document with 'primary' or 'secondary authorial authority.'" This usually means that the text referred to is the closest known text to one the author wrote or otherwise supervised. It does not mean that the author necessarily had anything to do with the typesetting or proofreading. This could be called primary documentary authority to distinguish it from later editions. Instances of primary documentary authority would be the so-called good quartos of Shakespeare's plays or any first published appearance of a book for which prepublication forms have disappeared and for which it is reasonable to suppose that setting copy was the author's manuscript or fair copy made from documents with primary authorial authority.

Another meaning for *authority* is "having a precedent in a historical document." This usually means that the text, as preserved in physical documents that are probably "corrupt," has an unknown relation to the author and may or might not preserve the authorial forms as successfully as other documents with similar characteristics. An instance of this kind of authority would be the existence of, say, three syndicated magazine versions of a story no longer extant in manuscript. The differences between the versions probably originated in the composing rooms of the various publications. There is no other authoritative source for the story; hence, these three documents are the authorities. This could be called "radial documentary authority."

Supposing that one of these three radial documentary authorities corresponds in its pattern of punctuation more closely to the patterns familiar in the author's surviving manuscript, that document may be said to have "more authority" than the other two, at least with regard to punctuation. Notice that this brings into play the word *authority* in a comparative rather than a descriptive sense. Here the word is used evaluatively and reflects critical judgment in analyzing punctuation patterns. It would be more accurate to say that this one document is "more likely to be authoritative in its punctuation than the other two" than to say that "it is more authoritative," and it would be better yet to have a word other than *authority* or *authoritative* to describe what is being said. Perhaps it would be wise to revert to the terms *more or less sophisticated* to indicate the level of change resulting from ad hoc scribal or editorial interventions and *more or less corrupt* to indicate the level of error introduced by scribal or editorial carelessness or ignorance. These terms register an evaluative sense of the relative amount of intentional and unintentional alteration introduced by compositors or other production personnel. As such, they would have a bearing on our sense of the "authority" of a document without entailing that word in a confusion of meanings.

Another instance of "documentary authority" illustrates yet another way in which the word *authority* is used evaluatively. If one has a "difficult" reading in a text with secondary authorial authority or even with primary documentary authority that has been altered to an "easy" reading in a purely derivative nonauthoritative text, editors sometimes resist the temptation to adopt the easier reading by "sticking to authority." This use of the word *authority* places value on the tangible text over the critical conjecture of later compositors or modern editors. The possibility that the physical text might be wrong can never be proved, though there are some difficult readings that no one (so far) has tried to defend, but *Mne Seraphim* in Blake's "The Book of Thel," *spitting* rather than *splitting* in Shakespeare's *Henry VIII* (2.4.181), and the auctioneer who *repeated his discomposure* in Thackeray's *Vanity Fair* are just a few of a myriad of cases in which the editor is tempted to supply conjecture rather than stick to authority. Just as the documentary reading cannot be proved to be wrong, so the conjecture can never be established to be correct (if it could, it would cease to be conjecture). The point here is that the word *authority* is used evaluatively to defend an action taken, rather than descriptively to indicate the nature of a situation. It would be just as accurate to say that an editor who stuck to authority had knuckled under to the tyranny of copy-text or was a very conservative editor or was an unimaginative editor. All these terms are evaluative and not indicative of anything demonstrable. What can be said specifically and objectively of *Mne, spitting,* and *repeated his discomposure* is that they occur in texts with primary or secondary documentary authority—that and no more; anything else would be a matter of judgment.

All of the foregoing definitions reflect an author-centric view of textual criticism. Especially in the use of *authority* evaluatively and comparatively, one can see the controlling influence of an attitude of respect for authorial autonomy with regard to texts. There is, nevertheless, considerable room for disagreement within these views. Depending on the stress one puts on the authority of one document over another, depending on the sense of historical or documentary integrity one espouses, one can within these definitions be a documentary editor or a critical editor.[21]

---

21. See G. Thomas Tanselle's thorough discussion of documentary, historical, and criti-

Hershel Parker invokes yet another definition of *authority* when he limits it to the product of the act of creativity during the time that creativity as he defines it is in fact going on. According to this view, as the author works he or she imbues the work with intention and perhaps finds within the work its intention, which then takes over and becomes the controlling force of the work. That controlling force becomes the authority of the work and its intention—and it therefore becomes the editor's aim to edit the work in accordance with that authority. To do so, the editor might have to reject a good deal of "editorial" tinkering undertaken by the author after having lost the creative urge that produced the work.

A totally different level of meaning is invoked when one asks, "By what authority does the editor emend the text?" Here the word *authority* has no direct reference to the source of a specific reading; whether a word began with the author or a compositor or whether it is in a text with primary or secondary documentary authority are irrelevant questions. What this question asks is "What is the critical theory about works of art that leads you to believe that the text is in error here?" It is this question about the authority of the editor that leads to questions like "Why is it that the text you are trying to present need not have 'better' readings? why is it sufficient that they be authorial?"

Until editors were willing to consider the definition of *authority* at this level there was no point in wasting words about social theories of text or about the aesthetics of textual criticism. As long as the author-centric view was the only legitimate view, James Thorpe and Jerome McGann remained outsiders whose editorial principles did not need to be taken seriously. But in the late 1980s there was a great willingness to reconsider what was meant by *authority*.

It was initially painful, and for some editors it still is, to consider the question "By what authority does the editor emend the text?" because a serious analysis of potential answers required examination of fundamental assumptions about things that turn out to be problematic rather than solid and objective. As long as one remained settled inside the author-centric world of ideas, the concept of authority was very useful practically in the business of producing scholarly editions, documentary authority was a firm resting place, primary authorial authority was like being in clover. The problem with new editorial discussions was that they were successfully forcing thought to be expended on a higher level of authority. They

cal editing in "The Editing of Historical Documents," "Recent Editorial Discussion and the Central Questions of Editing," and "Historicism in Critical Editing."

succeeded because it became de rigueur to be self-conscious about one's critical theories.

In order for it to be acceptable to consider McGann's or McKenzie's editorial theories, author-centric editors had to put in abeyance their definitions of *authority* so as to consider the larger question of authority that a social theory of texts demanded, and they had to anticipate the possibility that author-centric definitions of the materials of textual criticism would have counterparts reflecting a different, higher-level concept of authority.

It would appear, therefore, that the major questions of authority are usually argued and settled before the evaluation of specific evidence concerning the composition and production of a given text takes place. Editors approach a text with preconceived ideas, about authority as it relates to the author or to a social contract or to publishers, that predispose them to interpret the evidence in certain ways. In general terms the evaluation of specific evidence is not determined by its intrinsic meaning—that which "the facts cry out"—but, rather, by some previous determination concerning authority and the nature of the work of art. For example, about *Sister Carrie* it could be argued that Dreiser's friend Arthur Henry gave him bad advice designed to help Dreiser avoid problems Henry himself had encountered but not designed to help Dreiser fulfill his own artistic intentions with regard to the novel. One editor will say, "Save Dreiser from his misguided friend"; another will say, "Henry is a fact of life; his advice was taken; the book that *Sister Carrie* would have become without his intervention is not recoverable." It could further be argued that Mrs. Page, the publisher's wife, influenced the book even more significantly than Henry, since by her insistence *Sister Carrie* was suppressed, though technically it was published. She did to the book something that can be measured in the circulation and reception of the book. Our first editor would say, "Rescue Dreiser's book from the publisher's influence"; the second might say, "The publisher is a fact of life without which *Sister Carrie* would never have become a suppressed book—along with all the meaning that condition adds to the book." My point is not to say which is right but to question the proposition that the facts of publication history "cry out" for a specific treatment. What an editor will see as appropriate treatment depends, instead, on a prior commitment to a definition of textual authority.

Seen from a sociological perspective, the specific evidence of the social context will cry out for attention and recognition as legitimate operants or influences in the production of texts. Given that perspective, those facts will cry equally loudly for a place in the reader's interpretation and appreciation of the work as a representation not only of the aesthetics of its time but of the economics and politics of its time. The word *legitimate* is not exactly right, for from this perspective the fact that production (the world of publishers, editors, and printers) is an acknowledged, normal part of the creation of book texts makes the participation of production staffs an integral part of the creation of the book, of the work of art. It is argued that authors write with the expectation of receiving production help in completing their art; therefore, the help they get is legitimate—that is, an integral, not external, operant or influence.

Further, given this essentially Marxist orientation and these principles, an edition that systematically eliminates the influences of all contracting parties but the author (such as was the goal in the University of Pennsylvania Press edition of Dreiser's *Sister Carrie*) will be seen as partial, distorted, and misrepresentative of the historical, socioeconomic, and political event that produced it.

Marxist critics take the social implications of texts more seriously than most critics. Insofar as they recognize the implications of editorial principles aimed at recovering the author's final intentions by eliminating the "external influences," they can be nothing less than disappointed and will more likely be enraged by what they will see as the desecration of texts. For the Marxist critic the editor's pursuit of the pure virgin text is a hypocritical, evil cover-up, unless it be an ignorant naive game.

The general rules, or orientations, that tend to predetermine how the evidence will be used, regardless of whether it is author-centric or socio-centric, are too often forced upon the evidence. One can have rules, said A. E. Housman about editors nearly a hundred years ago, but they will lead you wrong. That is, when an a priori set of principles leads to a mechanical or rigid manipulation of the facts of a given case, the potential provided by the overall view for generating exciting new insights is hobbled by an unexciting tyranny.

A look at specific cases will illustrate the uses and potential abuses of the fact that a general orientation predetermines the use of evidence. But first let me reiterate the basic questions that stimulated this discussion and encapsulate the competing and apparently irreconcilable general principles involved. The questions are: What is textual integrity (the unity and honesty and authenticity of the text of a work of literary art)? Is it possible for there to be more than one legitimate integrity for a single work? What is meant by textual authority? What should it be? Do editors influence interpretations (how do they do it, should they do it, can it be avoided)?

These questions arise because traditional consensus about the *real* nature of works of art has been challenged by a competing notion that is antithetical to it. Persons in our profession can no longer assume that everyone sees the work from a common point of view, but many of us act as though we still should be able to agree. This is not a question of standard interpretations; it is about a new failure to agree about the nature of literary works. It is also not about our failure to agree on the canon or on which works are literary; it is a new failure to agree about the foundation of words and linguistic meaning. One of these notions, the more traditional one, is that the work of art is a personal communication from an author to an audience. The assumption was that the author wished to communicate: when words were put on a page it was an attempt to create certain effects in readers; when an author developed the artistic and technical skill to create works of art, he or she was in control and did things deliberately. These assumptions represent a "commonsense" approach because, generally speaking, people think that way about their own speech acts. This view accords with the editorial principle of pursuing authorial intention and with the critical hermeneutic principles discussed by E. D. Hirsch Jr. in *Validity in Interpretation*. And this general notion of authorship views the production process of turning manuscripts into books as a service to the author helping to put the individual creative effort into a form for general dissemination.

The antithetical competing notion is that the work of art is social, not individual. Rather than the artist using language to create a new work of art, the language speaks the artist. Rather than the production crew being assistants in the author's effort to communicate though art, the publishing world is a cultural agency that employs authors to aid them in providing society with reading material. The domesticating act of actualizing art for society is, according to this view, the production function. Both the author and the production personnel are to some extent cultural puppets, products of their time producing inevitable art. The way we know that what came out of the process was inevitable is that something else did not materialize instead. The function of criticism in this view is to interpret the texts as cultural artifacts in their historical settings.

This survey of competing views of editing demonstrates that editing is a critical enterprise, not only involving criticism but also being a form of literary criticism. Criticism is interpretation; editions, like other interpretations, can be supported by evidence and argument, but they cannot be proved or validated. They are not definitive. Consequently, the editorial interpretive basis, like that of any interpretation, should be clearly acknowledged by the editor for the edition user. No editor should say that the method chosen is the only responsible one, though I think it is possible to discover that some methods are irresponsible.

D. F. McKenzie's remarks about the work of art as object suggest a parallel insight into the physical object that is the scholarly edition: it changes and enriches the work in its new form much more than it preserves or restores it. In critical editing not only is the edited text itself one that never existed before; it is surrounded by alter texts and related historical materials that have never before been attached to it physically. Scholarly editions invite a kind of reading no other textual form comes close to suggesting. As McGann has put it, scholarly editions invite the reader to read linearly, radially, and spatially all at the same time ("Theory of Texts," 21). Scholarly editors like to think of themselves as historians and preservers, when, in fact, they are the most progressive innovators of new texts and new contexts in the profession.

More questions become possible now: What is the textual editor's responsibility to the author *and* to the social contract? Is that one responsibility or two? If two, how can the editor balance them? Extended examination of specific actual cases is the only way to demonstrate how that can be done. To do so will lead to assessments of a related question: What is the importance of authorial intention *and* of the social contract to literary criticism? The most detailed examination of this question relative to a work that I know is my own treatment of the issues relative to editing Thackeray's *Henry Esmond*.[22] Much of the rest of the book provides examples and suggests refinements of the social contract.

One way to balance awareness of cultural context, including the ministrations of production crews, with a respect for authorial intentions was suggested by Fredson Bowers in his address to the Society for Textual Scholarship in 1987: "As a textual critic I am inclined to suggest that awareness of this phenomenon should encourage an editor to remove from the text as much as possible of this nonauthorial accretion *when it is actually of no material aid in assisting the latest original authorial intention*" ("Unfinished Business," 8; italics added). The suggestion is worth pondering, though it involves some contortion to believe original authorial intentions to be also final intentions and though the process limits critically the force of any supposed social contract.

There are serious, legitimate differences in point of view in these matters. We need, for certain important and rich works of literary art, several scholarly editions: the edition representing the author's final intentions,

---

22. See my book *Pegasus in Harness,* chapter 6.

the edition representing the historical event of first publication, the edition representing the thorough revision—each would possibly affect the student in a different way. None would of itself be *the* work of art. At the very least the facts of controversial cases point to the need for editors to be clear-eyed and honest about the particular principles they follow and to identify clearly those principles and the kind of edition they produce. It is not enough to call it a scholarly edition—even if it is approved by the MLA's Committee on Scholarly Editions. Ultimately, it is an impossible quest to produce "the edition that conveys the author's most comprehensive intentions"; what we can hope to do is produce "the edition that conveys the author's intentions most comprehensively."

Chapter 6

Individual and Collective Voices:
Agency in Texts

No, I am that I am, and they that level
At my abuses reckon up their own;
I may be straight, though they themselves be bevel;
By their rank thoughts my deeds must not be shown,—
Unless this general evil they maintain:
All men are bad, and in their badness reign.
—Shakespeare, Sonnet 121

The Voice that stands for Floods to me
Is sterile borne to some—
The Face that makes the Morning mean
Glows impotent on them—
—Emily Dickinson, Poem 1189

In the ten years since Jerome McGann's book *A Critique of Modern Textual Criticism* stirred an already simmering pot of discontent over the Pollard-McKerrow-Greg-Bowers-Tanselle school of editing, his socio-materialist views have nearly carried the field. For some people the shift from an old to a new view has "taken place" and is complete. Speed Hill documents the passing of intentionalist, author-centric approaches to editing (designed in their principles for choice of copy-text and for emendation to restore authorial practice and intention by eliminating the infelicities of the production process) in a review:

"Dead as a Dodo"—so Jerome McGann described the copy-text school of scholarly editing at the recent (October 1991) Ann Arbor conference, "Palimpsest." The Austin conference two years earlier, "New Directions in Textual Studies," was thus the first half of an extended wake for the once dominant school of textual and bibliographical studies inaugurated by Pollard, McKerrow, and Greg in England and situated so firmly in the practice of American scholarly editing by Bowers and Tanselle, whose final obsequies passed all but unnoticed at Ann Arbor.[1]

Hans Gabler's closing remarks at the "Palimpsest" conference suggested, too, that the principles associated with his old mentor, Bowers, were no longer applicable: that authorial final intention was not a Grail worth chasing.

McGann's *Critique* initiated the discussions that have catapulted modern editorial theory into its present varied and complex state. Complex theories tend in time, however, to be reduced to their most obvious features, and it seems important that we not allow reductionist views of authorial intention or social materialism to support oversimplified editorial policies. McGann has repeatedly insisted that he had not replaced authorial intention but put it on a par with other agencies of textuality. He acknowledged in a practical way that authorship is not a solitary occupation—and by the production approach and by emphasis on "bibliographic code" he acknowledged much of what is inherent in and sensible about the phrase "the language and culture write the author." Beyond that he acknowledged that a published text is a group project and that interpretation is multilayered, involving more than the linguistic text and more than authorial intention.

What McGann has done is to complicate the editorial problem by refusing to relegate anything to the realm of the insignificant. Editing, for McGann, must somehow reflect larger understandings about textuality, inscription, and the constructions of meaning. A theory of editing must be part and parcel of a larger theory or set of theories about textuality, communication, and hermeneutics. Where editors were, in recent memory, held to a rigorous standard of editorial policy, they now must be held accountable for theories of meaning, reading, perception, and reality. Editing must acknowledge how works relate to markets and to social relationships among authors, publishers, and their political friends and enemies. Editing must

---

1. Hill, 370. Bowers died in April 1991, but Tanselle and the Greg-Bowers school of editing survived the final obsequies alleged by Hill.

reveal, not suppress, the significance of the economics of publishing by assessing the meanings of paper, type fonts, margins, bindings, publisher's advertisements, and reviews. Somehow editing must find a way to incorporate these matters as "part of the work" or as the sociomaterial constituents of literature. The historical events of literary production at the point of social interaction (i.e., at publication) seem focal to these views.

From them arises a theory of copy-text privileging first publications or significant revised publications over manuscripts. Though I see McGann as one of the chief instigators of this larger view, the combative spirit with which he and those who agree with him emphasize the "new" at the expense of the "old" has polarized the thinking in ways I believe are reductive. That is, Bowers's position has been reduced and ossified as the pursuit of the author's final intentions, excluding the machinations of all other agents. That is not true. Likewise, the new wisdom has elevated the "production text" over the "intended text" in a way that reduces the usefulness of the new insights. While McGann has called for a larger more comprehensive editorial theory, what I fear has been celebrated, instead, is a victory over Greg-Bowers and a blanket approval of the production materialist text.

When the first part of this chapter was circulated, I was credited with providing the "social contract" theory of texts with a rationale it otherwise lacked (Eggert, "Document and Text," 16). I still think the theory lacks rigor and has not been integrated into a sufficiently comprehensive theory of texts or theory of communication. If we had a comprehensive view, it would show a continuum of theory and practice, both for text generation and for textual reception, from the author-centric views associated with Greg and Bowers to the sociological concerns of McGann and McKenzie.

If the social contract school of editing has in theory opened up the editorial field of vision by focusing on the significance of material texts and of production forces in the "acculturation" of texts, it has tended to shut back down in practice by overemphasizing the artifactual quality of texts and de-emphasizing the agencies of meaning. In fact, it is often difficult to see what role the scholarly editor has when the "means of production" is the legitimizing authority for text and the resultant artifact is physically and linguistically the signifier; any editing at all becomes tampering with the evidence. In other words, having noted that the dominant American editorial policy was denigrating a significant cultural activity by editing out the effects of production processes, the social contract theory legitimized production meanings of bibliographic codes in a general way. Perhaps the newness of the insight or the battle that it took to legitimize the view in any way at all led to lumping all production agencies into a single new dominant force for editorial policy.

Actually, however, McGann brought our attention to the *multiple* voices of texts. Thus, an editor editing the work to privilege one voice, whether the author's or the publisher's, runs counter to the new insight into how literary works work. If the new insight is that a work is the product of multiple voices, including nonauthorial ones, then the editorial policy must be one that enables readers to hear multiple voices. To supplant the authorial voice with the production voice or to imagine the work as the author's voice filtered and shaped by a social production process into a single composite voice is to deny the force of the new insight. Readers of every stripe continue to read books for a variety of reasons, looking for different sorts of evidence; therefore, an editor who privileges one reading over another without indicating clearly what has happened can only muddy the critical waters.

If the social contract school has a comprehensive theory of texts to help sort out the agencies of signification in texts, it has not surfaced in the editorial discussion, which has been dominated by the Marxist, or materialist, theory of production meanings.[2] I believe that communication theory provides interesting possibilities for such an integrating view. I argued, in chapter 3, first that texts have three forms: texts are *matter* (i.e., manuscripts, proofs, physical books of paper and ink or computer disks or Braille or phonograph records, etc.), and texts are *concepts* in authors', editors' and readers' minds, and texts are *events or actions,* like dance, that "exist" or come into effectual being only during performances such as authoring, manufacturing, and reading. Documents, I contended, are merely the evidence that such events have taken place, and they make new events of a similar kind possible. I also argued that the three basic kinds of events (authoring, manufacturing, and reading) dismantle the event that speech act theorists call "utterance." Utterance involves a speaker, a text in some medium, and a recipient, usually in one place and time, referencing a context of presuppositions that both speaker and recipient can take for granted.

---

2. Note the following from Paul Eggert's "Document and Text": "With some justice in 1983, McGann cast authorial intention as a Romantic abstraction we needed to be wary of. He recommended instead a respecting of the concrete, socio-economic relationships which an author, as a professional, typically engaged in. But when it comes to editorial practice, McGann's idea is as mystifying as the one it offers to replace: the term 'social production' shoulders aside 'individual creation' of text. So far so good. But in thus seeking an unidealizing clarity, McGann's approach runs together what I have argued are the distinguishable levels of text and document" (16).

Meaning (speaker meaning or utterance) takes place in a context of presupposition that forms an unstated but operative background that helps recipients distinguish between what was said and what was meant or helps them to narrow down the range of plausible significations for what was said. It is this basis of supposedly shared presuppositions that provides what "goes without saying" for each speech act. Texts reference but do not incorporate all the necessary presupposed background, though there are many rhetorical strategies for compensating. Few texts, however, manage to prevent all misunderstanding.

Authoring, manufacturing, and reading performances are seen more clearly if we keep in mind the distinction John Searle makes between *sentence* and *utterance*, terms first discussed in chapter 4. Sentence, we recall, is recordable as a series of words and is iterable; utterance is the intended meaning in a particular use of sentence, which means different things in different uses and is, therefore, not iterable. Utterance, not sentence, is the object of readerly interest, but utterance is reduced to sentence in written works.[3]

When the same sentence is used in two or more different utterances, the clues distinguishing the utterances are all extratextual. In speech these extratextual elements include tone of voice, gesture and body language, place and time, and actual (intended) audience; all of these help clue listeners to the "intended" meaning, regardless of what the sentence "actually" or literally says. The power to misunderstand sentence because of inadequate access to these extratextual clues is illustrated famously by Iago engineering a conversation between himself and Cassio to be overheard by Othello, who hears the sentences and fatally misconstrues the utterance (*Othello* 4.1.). In writing, the extratextual clues are less immediate than in speech but include the bibliographic code as a means writers, publishers, and readers use to help construct utterance from sentence.

Of the many extratextual clues the most important usually is the agent of utterance: who is speaking? It is that aspect of utterance that tends to blur in the blanket legitimization of the production voice of the social contract. The production voice is not *a* voice; its voices are legion. Furthermore, it is not an originating voice but a layered, or added, voice. Production always takes sentence, as originated by an author, and re-utters it in a new form. Time, place, texture, and speaker "become again" in publication, and, thus, utterance becomes multiple.

---

3. A rather different distinction between the work as artifact and the work as aesthetic object by Gunter Martens ("[De]Constructing," 128) reaches toward the same distinction between signifier and signified.

FOR NOW AND ALWAYS

I would like to hold you   bell that chimes in the underground
Bell wrapped in the vines of the afterlife
Made of smoke and hair
And dresses of pretty girls who would not undress for the commandant
But I can't   my hands have been cut off and are running away

I would like to hold you in my arms
Bell that waltzes in air the way bare feet touched these cold floors
I promise never to forget the sound that makes blood what it is
That icepick in the ear
I don't think that sound will ever melt

I would like to speak to you   sack of flour slung over a prisoner's
    shoulder
Powder-face of the dead in the baker's window
I would like to speak to you about large bodies of water
Breathing in and out ornate fans that keep them alive
About skyscrapers   tossing stars around in the heavens
Before falling asleep at the edge of town
I promise never to turn away   though my eyes are burning

And cloud   bright furnace of sunlight
Swinging back and forth in the sky as inside a great nightshirt
Like one large lung gasping for breath
I would like to see you again
Rather than go down to the sea and unlock icebergs
I have thought about it a long time
And that is what I want

Your silence is so peaceful   so restful
Any number of hats contain that silence   and go flying off in the
    wind
Any number of faces reflect its emptiness
That has escaped into the bones of sparrows already dead or still
    living on rooftops
It pushes a little flower cart across the prison grounds
Chases away bees that ring in the shadows

Starless night   I promise never to burn your photograph
My legs and feet are cold
Wire fences go travelling through my eyes as no travellers ever managed
    to before
Windmills tangle in my hair long into morning
Ashes   here is a kiss from the living
Impossible to see against the sky
                    (*Dachau, West Germany, 1979.*)

                                        —GARY MYERS

Gary Myers's poem "For Now and Always," *New Yorker,* 28 October 1985

One "sentence" stands as witness to multiple utterances. Even when author and publisher agree that they are saying the same thing, we might profit from distinguishing these voices. And often they are not saying the same thing, as I will show.

In a word the theory of texts that I think offers useful ways to integrate insights of the intentionalist and materialist "schools of editing" holds that material texts index a series of communicative events that signify intentionality by authors and by production personnel in a social complex that can and should be dissected in the ways utterances can be dissected: not only for what they say voluntarily (as Frank Kermode once put it) but also for what they say involuntarily. Acknowledging the exciting part of McGann's contribution (i.e., that texts have social histories, cultural implications, and that texts are material signifiers, not just linguistic ones) but rejecting the tendencies to follow these thoughts from one form of singularity (final authorial intentions) into another form of singularity (the production text), let us look at a few specific instances to see how broadened readerly perceptions of works might affect or even dictate the editorial principles we might prefer.

The poem "For Now and Always" by Gary Myers appeared in the *New Yorker* (28 October 1985) and was republished in a chapbook titled *World Effects* (1990). The time and place it recalls are clearly indicated by the last line, "Dachau, West Germany, 1979," referencing in this simple way a whole complex of well-known contexts that writer and reader access as the presupposed background for whatever the poem says. New readers might have to read the poem twice to access this background, unless their eyes caught the signature first. The poem's tone and general sympathies are clearly enough indicated by the linguistic text, but its appearance in the *New Yorker* reinforces its sad, ceremonial, elegiac, memorial intent. Its concluding image of "Ashes" reverberates with allusions to gas ovens, spent fires, lost opportunities, and funeral rites.

As one pulls meditatively away from the text of the poem, it is almost inevitable that the sketch of a brush and dustpan by Judith Shalin at the foot of the page will obtrude and pollute the image of ashes, reducing to absurdity, to triviality, the mood produced by the poem.

Immediately a question of agency arises. Who did this? Is this the social contract at work? Was it a mistake? An insensitive satiric comment? An adventitious concatenation of textual events forged into an intentionless exercise in bad taste? Is it ironic? Is it pernicious? The questions multiply as we glance at the "totally unrelated" prose text surrounding the poem,

WORLD EFFECTS

GARY MYERS

STANLEY HANKS CHAPBOOK   NUMBER FOUR 1990   ST. LOUIS POETRY CENTER

Titlepage and endpaper for Myers's poem in a new context (reduced from 11x14).

particularly to the narrow isthmus of letterpress separating the poem from dustpan, and we read that the author of that text was in Istanbul, where "the streets ... are crooked, filthy, dreadfully cobbled, and piled up with refuse, which is constantly rummaged through by ravenous local cats.... There was enough, in short, to pollute one's subconscious." Enough, indeed. Is this the social contract at work? Is this the bibliographic code that is an inextricable part of the work? Is this the contextualization that enriches the readerly interaction with the text in the performance that becomes the work in each reading?

A theory of editing that acknowledges socialization and production and materiality but that subordinates intention or agency by making the facts of production the important determiners of text runs a high risk of editing sentence without regard to utterance. Thomas L. Berger tells this story:

> I once met a woman who worked for *The New Yorker*. One of her tasks was to read each issue before it went to press. But she wasn't a proofreader. Rather, I guess you could call her a disaster reader. For example, she had to make sure that if on one page there was a touching poem about someone dying of cancer, there had better not be a particularly gruesome Charles Addams cartoon on the facing page. Similarly, Omaha Steaks advertisements were not to be placed in side columns next to stories about world hunger. Things like that. But suppose she failed, as indeed she tells me she did, often with hilarious and ghastly results. How are we to read that poem if the Addams cartoon is indeed present on the facing page? Do we read that poem differently when that poem appears in the author's *Collected Works*? I think we probably do. (195)

Well, yes, readers of "For Now and Always" in *World Effects* find it between "Ode to Sleep" and "Weeping Angel" in a chapbook with solid black endpapers. The effect contrasts starkly with juxtaposed brush and dustpan.

Of course, James Thorpe, Donald Pizer, Donald McKenzie, and others have given us numerous examples of benign, symbiotic cooperation between authors, editors, and printers, which they suggest represent normal practice. An isolated example like Myers's "For Now and Always," they might aver, cannot be the basis for elaborating a rule about the importance of agency in textual criticism. The rules should reflect normal practice, and is not normal practice cooperative? The rationale of copy-text (whether Greg's or Thorpe's) and the operative distinctions between form (accidentals) and content (substantives) are based on notions of normal conditions.

But, in fact, there is no generally agreed-upon notion of normal practice with regard to the so-called help or interference offered by publishers to authors. And as for rules of editing—designed to introduce standards or make it possible to proceed without thinking—A. E. Housman said, "you can have a hard-and-fast rule if you want one, but then you will have false rules, and they will lead you wrong; because their simplicity will render them inapplicable to problems which are not simple, but complicated by the play of personality" (132). Sherwood Anderson, in "The Book of the Grotesque" at the beginning of *Winesburg, Ohio,* tells of an old writer with the notion that there were hundreds of truths and "that the moment one of the people took one of the truths to himself, called it his truth, and tried to live his life by it, he became a grotesque and the truth he embraced became a falsehood" (5). Rules are made for use in moments of ignorance. Greg's rationale was to be invoked only when evidence was lacking upon which to make an informed decision. There is a difference between lack of evidence and ignoring evidence or "ruling" it out of court.

The linguistic text, the bibliographic code, the extratextual significance of contexts, must be tied to agency and therefore to intentionality in some way. We can do that in ignorance, like Othello overhearing parts of conversations, or we can try to sift and situate the voices indexed by our texts. Take the case of two poems by the Tasmanian poet Gwen Harwood, "Eloisa to Abelard" and "Abelard to Eloisa," published under the pseudonym Walter Lehmann in the *Bulletin* (a Sydney literary magazine) on 5 August 1961. Several years ago an Australian friend gave me a copy of these poems and told the following story: the author had already published under the same pseudonym in the *Bulletin* and had written a bitter complaint to the editor that her poem was distorted in publication by having all lines pushed over flush left, destroying, thereby, significant levels of indentation. The editor replied that the column format influenced the policy, which was applied indiscriminately to all *Bulletin* poetry. According to my informant, Harwood then wrote and submitted the two poems reproduced here. She submitted them, it was said, with varying degrees of indentation, and the editors predictably and indiscriminately "suppressed" the author's intentions by printing all lines flush left—creating, thereby, the "inadvertent" acrostic message, readable vertically down the left column: "So long Bulletin. Fuck all editors." From that story I concluded that texts are not agentless.

worship of power, and his early and emphatic rejection of Communism is one of the best things in his liberal-progressivist humanism.

In his more technical work, Russell's position in the history of philosophy is secure, although we can credit him only with high talent, not philosophic genius, which is a very rare thing. One point that emerged for me in reading over these extracts is the considerable carelessness of his thought and writing. Despite his concern with mathematics and his great contributions to symbolic logic, despite the clarity and ease of his style, there is some lack of rigor in his thinking. This can make him rather distressing reading for the professional philosopher. Indeed, to read Russell either when he is writing for a professional or a popular audience is, for me at any rate, to swing constantly between admiration and irritation.

DAVID ARMSTRONG

is Dead

and visits a prostitute who gives him rest when rest is all he needs. All the time his thoughts are of Tamar, the girl from his village whom he wants to marry before her illegitimate child, not his, is born. Morning comes, the eel is dead, and so, alas, are his hopes.

Despite a deadly seriousness which causes a dangerous teetering towards sentimentality and despite the conscious difficulties of style, West's novel is a fine achievement. He has tried to see Ireland as it is today, and through the eyes of someone to whom America is no longer the promised land, someone for whom there is no promised land. Above all, there is sympathy between West and his characters, a somewhat unfashionable thing these days when most novelists disgustedly hold their characters up with tongs for our bemused inspection.

Honor Tracy, who has taken several sharp and original glances at Dublin and Ireland, has turned her eyes from her own fair city towards the well-worked-over ground of the English home counties. The hero, if such he be, is Ninian La Touche, a noted art-dealer, past middle age, who thanks God he is an atheist and who has "great faith in Harrod's." The story is of his infatuation with his very young, remarkably silly, secretary, from whom he requires nothing more precious than a clearer recollection of what it felt like to be young.

Honor Tracy is quick, bright and expert. She can economically and brilliantly work up a scene which keeps a dozen or so characters moving at pace. She can snatch a character from the limited stock of English-county types, give him or her a quick coat of varnish so that the appearance is fresh.

However, most of Miss Tracy's admirers probably are happiest when she

is in her home territory. In "The Straight and Narrow Path" and "Mind You, I've Said Nothing" she stands alone; in "The Season of Mists" she is one of many.

PATRICIA ROLFE

Eloisa to Abelard

Solace and hope depart. God's finger traces
on fields of frozen darkness: You shall find
loss, absence, nothing. Walking on the wind
Our Lord speaks to a crowd of foolish faces,

no face that is not mine, while filtering through
gaps, honeycombs of memory you seem
but the faint ghost of a remembered dream.
Unveiled by pain, I bleed. My wound is you.

Lost in the well of space, my spirit hears
"Lucis creator optime . . ." The choir
entreats God, out of tune. I join my voice
to theirs. Nightfall's immense. I taste my tears.
I reap the harvest of my own desire.
No heart escapes the torment of its choice.

WALTER LEHMANN

Abelard to Eloisa

Far above memory's landscape let the fears
unlatched from thundering valleys of your mind
carry their lightning. Stare the sun up. Find
kinetic heat to scorch your mist of tears.

All that your vision limned by night appears
loose in dismembering air: think yourself blind.
Louder than death in headlines the unkind
elements hawk my passion: stop your ears.

Deny me now. Be Doubting Thomas. Thrust
into my side the finger of your grief.
Tell me I am an apparition frayed
out of the tattered winding-sheet of lust.
Recall no ghost of love. Let no belief
summon me, fleshed and bleeding, from the shade.

WALTER LEHMANN

33

Facsimile of the *Bulletin,* 5 August 1961

The agent of meaning, the reader's sense of who it was that "did" the text, has a great deal to do with one's enjoyment of or dismay with the text. When I was in Australia recently I found that no one, including the author, Gwen Harwood, remembers the sequence of events in the way I have described them. In fact, no one has the same story to tell.[4] At first, in dismay, I thought my point had been destroyed. But it has not. My point is that a sense of agency (whether the historically correct one or not) is a determining factor in every reader's interpretation of the text.

The questions prompted by the first, probably erroneous, tale remain the important ones: Whose intentions are fulfilled? Is this the social contract at work? Has cultural materialism expressed the mind of society? Has language spoken the author? Every interpretation of the poems implies or states answers to these questions. And for the editor the question is: Would the editorial principle that rescued "For Now and Always" from the inadvertent meanings of its *New Yorker* appearance be adequate or desirable for rescuing "Eloisa to Abelard" and "Abelard to Eloisa" out of the *Bulletin*? And is the latter an innocent pair of poems with a structural element of bad taste and bitter recrimination? or are there other interpretive matters at work here? When Eloisa says to Abelard "Solace and hope depart" is this the author's explanation for her decision to bid farewell to the *Bulletin*? When Eloisa calls Abelard "the faint ghost of a remembered dream" and concludes that she "reap[s] the harvest of my own desire," is the author really referring to this act of bibliographical revenge? Is the final line a warning to the editors of the *Bulletin* that "No heart escapes the torment of its choice"—in this case the choice to ram all lines flush left? These two examples demonstrate that we frequently take poems, and probably novels and short stories and plays, to be acts of communication subject to the dynamics of speech acts or script acts whose impact is determined by each reader within a sememic molecule—within the set of relevant contextual, extratextual, conventionalized presuppositions that help determine meaning.

An important conclusion to draw here is that the social contract, if there is such a thing, does not eliminate intentionality from editorial concerns. It may be true that the author is dead, that the culture uses authors to produce texts for social consumption, that the result of production processes is vital evidence of a collaborative process to create works of art, but none of that justifies the notion that intentionality or agency of communication is unimportant to the editorial or to the literary critical enterprise.

---

4. See, for example, Hoddinott, 87–89.

What has recently been called the social contract in our field should perhaps be divided into two separate areas of "textual authority": a *social contract,* using the term as Rousseau used it, to signal a willing alienation of individual authority to a social agency for the greater good of the whole, and a *production contract,* using the term as Marx might, to signal the economic and political exigencies of the marketplace in which forces greater than the individual determine outcomes.

In a classic case of the social contract at work Benjamin Franklin addressed his fellow Constitutional Conventioneers about the text of the proposed United States Constitution: he confessed that he did "not entirely approve of this Constitution," but he decided to agree to "this Constitution, with all its faults" because, he said, "I expect no better, and because I am not sure that it is not the best. The opinions I have had of its *errors* I sacrifice to the public good." And he concluded by "expressing a wish, that every member of the Convention who may still have objections to it, would with me on this occasion doubt a little of his own infallibility, and, to make *manifest* our *unanimity,* put his name to this Instrument."[5]

Here is an individual, an author, the drafter and reviser of a social document, agreeing to lay aside the individuality of the autonomous legislator or author, accepting for the good of the public compromises in wording and meaning to produce an instrument for public use. Suppose, however, that the document signed by the delegates, upon being turned over to the printer, were to undergo the socializing process of a copyeditor and printer who improved the prose or altered the meaning by judicious and injudicious changes, some on purpose, some inadvertent. Which is the Constitution of the United States, the signed manuscript or the printed version? The authors' acquiescence in language discussed and agreed to by compromise constitutes a social contract; their agreement to employ a printer in whose competence they have placed a perhaps injudicious trust to render the agreed-upon language into multiple printed copies constitutes a production contract. A social contract, so defined, should be binding on both the original printer and the modern editor. But a production contract has no more standing with a modern editor than the interference of any unauthorized third party, regardless of the benignity of their intentions.

My point is merely this: the social contract as a "school of editing" has not done away with agency for authority, it has not done away with

---

5. Benjamin Franklin, "Speech in the Convention, at the Conclusion of Its Deliberations," read to the convention by James Wilson of the Pennsylvania delegation.

personal responsibility for textual variation, it has not done away with intentionality, and it has not done away with the author.[6] What it has done
is complicate the editorial and readerly activity and demonstrate the inadequacy of the editorial and literary theories of thirty years ago. Those
theories and the practices they justified were inadequate because they defined the problem too narrowly, not because they mistook the object of our
interest altogether.

If modern editors believe that the production text has supplanted the
authorial text as the editorial goal, we will soon be hearing again about
the inadequacy of the current editorial theory and the narrow-mindedness
and shortsightedness of editorial practice. Editorial theory and editorial
practice must be elaborated in the context of theories of meaning, of communication, of history, of perception, and of reality. They must take into
account the different uses for texts, providing evidence so that questions
about authorial intention, production processes, and reader reception can
be asked and answered. They must not ignore questions of agency: who
did it, what was meant by it, and how was it taken. These remain the
questions readers need help answering.

Help. Readers should not have to take an editor's answer as if it were
unmediated.

---

6. Paul Eggert, remarking on the tendencies initiated by McGann in editorial theory, puts
it this way: "What his position requires before it can be taken seriously as a theory of editing
is a fuller and more conscious recognition of the responsibility of individuals for documentary
acts of inscription" ("Document and Text," 17).

Chapter 7

Textual Variants, Performance Variants, and the Concept of the Work

Till heaven and earth pass, one jot or one tittle shall in no wise pass from the law, till all be fulfilled.

—Matthew 5:18 (KJV)

Till heaven and earth pass away, not an iota, not a dot, will pass from the law until all is accomplished.

—Matthew 5:18 (RSV)

While Heaven and earth last, the Law will not lose a single dot or comma until its purpose is complete.

—Matthew 5:18 (Phillips)

So long as heaven and earth endure, not a letter, not a stroke, will disappear from the Law until all that must happen has happened.

—Matthew 5:18 (NEB)

An old question that reveals much about popular concepts of the nature of works of literary art is "When is a revised text a new work?" I believe the question suggests an identity between a stable physical object and the work. Such a view is consistent with other art forms such as paintings, sculpture, and pottery for which the popular conception finds nothing strange about asking, "Where is the *Mona Lisa*?" or "Where is Picasso's *Guernica*?" because there is only one of each, and its uniqueness can be authenticated. The distinction between the real painting or sculpture and copies of it can be demonstrated in many ways. And if the copy is a very good one and is

165

passed off as the real thing, there is a scandal about forgery. In short, the distinction between the authentic and the imitation has nothing to do with an aesthetic response to the physical object but has everything to do with a preconception about the nature or essence of works of art.

Laymen do, however, find it peculiar to ask "Where is *Moby-Dick*?" They are not bothered by the existence of multiple copies of *Moby-Dick* or even multiple editions of the work, but there is also in the popular mind a naive faith in the identity of the words of these copies and in the reliability of the physical objects.[1] When one points out to the popular consciousness that some copies vary textually from others, the usual desire is to know which copies represent the real thing and which are corrupt or inferior reproductions. This desire for authenticity is consistent with the attitude toward real and forged paintings.

When it is further pointed out that there may be a revised version of the work, the popular consciousness equates this phenomenon with the existence in the art world of multiple versions of some paintings or sculptures that the artist executed on more than one occasion—notorious cases include Edward Hicks's "A Peaceable Kingdom" and B. R. Haydon's "Napoleon Musing at St. Helena." Each "original copy" is authentic and interesting, though it is perhaps lamentable that the artist didn't "get it right the first time."

The idea of an artist's "getting it right" suggests two concepts that inform many persons' ideas of art. First, the idea suggests that art aims at some point of perfection that is "right," making all variants from it in some way "not right." And, second, the idea suggests that art is a frozen moment, a tableau, contained in and represented by the physical object that itself freezes and stabilizes the moment of perfection—or attempts to.

Thus the question "When is a revised text a new work?" reveals a concept of "work of art" that involves stability and perfection, allowing for the possibility of a second revised perfection that is different—a new work. But this question is not merely a notion in the popular mind. It has an impressive history of commentary in scholarly journals. Among the most influential discussions of it are those by G. Thomas Tanselle, Hans Zeller, D. F. McKenzie, Jerome McGann, Jack Stillinger, and Donald Reiman. Scholars, it appears, also hanker for a correct and, preferably, overwhelming answer. It seems more likely, however, that every answer is unsatisfactory, not just because each textual situation is so particular that no answer by rule will do

---

1. This question about the physical and conceptual identity of literary text is developed in chapter 3.

but because the concept of a stable work and a stable text is fundamentally flawed.

A brief review of some of the commentary on when revision produces a new work will prepare the way for some additional considerations that might indicate what kind of question this really is. Then, perhaps, specific examples, can demonstrate how even a work without written textual change can be different from itself. From these grounds we can search for the basic assumptions about works of art that make the question seem worth asking. And, finally, a guide can be elaborated for use in practical situations. That, of course, should be the last word on the subject, and we shall all live happily ever after.

First, however, we might ask, who wants to know when a work is a new work and why they want to know? Ever since Gordon Ray took F. R. Leavis to task for claiming that Henry James in his first work, *Roderick Hudson,* sounded like the mature Henry James—without realizing he was reading the heavily revised New York Edition—critics have known they should be careful about which *Roderick Hudson* they read. Which *White Jacket,* which *Red Badge of Courage,* which *Sister Carrie,* which *Prelude,* which *King Lear*—all these have become household questions for scholars and their students.

If it matters to scholars, it should matter to editors. Which version of the work shall be the reading text? This is a practical problem with serious consequences in the business of literary interpretation. Of course, there is no merit in deciding that the 1805 and 1850 *Prelude* are different works requiring separate treatment—or that Tennyson's "Oh, that 'twere possible" (1834) is different from *Maud* (1854) or that Marcus Clarke's *His Natural Life* is different in its Australian serial and English book versions. An editor with pudding for brains can see that the alternate versions of these works are radically different. The question becomes more difficult and more interesting in borderline cases.

In "The Rationale of Copy-Text" W. W. Greg says, the "reliance on one particular authority results from the desire for an objective theory of text-construction and a distrust, often no doubt justified, of the operation of individual judgment" (50). The tendencies to desire objectivity in text construction and to distrust individual judgment are alive and well a half-century later and have a bearing on the discussion at hand. But more to the point, in discussing rationales for emendation (once a copy-text is chosen), Greg distinguished between corrections and revisions, saying that all corrections from other sources should be incorporated. Revisions he divides into two rough categories, saying the editor should incorporate all "revisions, so long as this falls short of complete rewriting" (53). He does not discuss the borderline between "revision" and "complete rewriting"; I assume he left that to individual judgment. He does not clarify the issue in the brief example he raises to illustrate the problem. He notes only that in the folio version of Jonson's *Every Man in His Humour* "revision and reproduction are so blended that it would be impossible to disentangle intentional from what may be fortuitous variation, and injudicious to make the attempt" (57). These new distinctions between *revision* and *reproduction* and between *intentional* and *fortuitous variation* seem to focus on the difficulty of distinguishing authorial from nonauthorial alterations, rather than the difficulty of melding eclectically two authorial forms in which revision amounts to "complete rewriting." Ultimately, for Greg it appears that the decision to treat variant texts separately or eclectically is a practical one. If you can conflate the revisions into one version, then do it; if you can't, don't. I don't think that helps us much—perhaps because Greg was not faced with many instances of recognized revision in the texts he worked on.

James Thorpe is more specific. Discussing the question "When does a work become a work?" he remarks in "The Aesthetics of Textual Criticism" that the

> problem of identifying the "real" *Great Expectations* . . . was simplified when we insisted on respecting the public version to which Dickens gave authorial integrity. The application of this basic test will not select one or the other of Auden's "In Time of War," however, since each is a fulfillment of his intentions and each was communicated to his usual public. From our review of what takes place in revision *for* private and public versions, I think it is clear that the two versions of the Auden collection are equally "real." They stand, side by side, as two separate works, and each has every bit of the dignity and integrity with which an author can endow any work of art. (46)

This is both a romantic and a mechanical answer: whenever an author publishes a new revision, we get a new work, but, as long as the revisions remain unpublished by the author, we have only a private document, which is not yet a work. Authority, it appears, is something metaphysical that authors endow upon works (at publication?).[2]

---

2. Similar arguments proposed by Stillinger and Reiman are discussed in chapter 9, which revisits the question of editorial goals relative to the act of reading.

G. Thomas Tanselle finds Thorpe's formulation inadequate. He develops the idea that revisions designed to enhance an intention that remains basically unchanged can be called "horizontal" revisions and do not create a new work. Revisions that change the concept or purpose or intention, on the other hand, are called "vertical" revisions and create new works ("Editorial Problem," 334–45). He intends these categories of revision to help editors formulate general principles or guidelines subject to the exercise of individual judgment. Horizontal revisions, he implies, should be incorporated in the standard edition; vertical changes call for separate editions. One practical reason for these guidelines is that sometimes changes are so extensive as to make collation impossible; hence, preparation of separate editions, as Greg said, is the only practical or judicious way to deal with the problem.

Hans Zeller, pursuing theory where practical men fear to tread, notes quite logically that a work of art is a web of relationships among the signs that constitute it. The web becomes disturbed and realigned with every change. Thus, unrevised parts change their meaning or effect because their relationship to the revised passages is changed.[3] In editorial practice strict adherence to this theory would require parallel texts for every authoritative variant text. The idea is perhaps more palpable in poems than in prose and more intellectually feasible as an editorial principle in editing short poems than longer works and more economically viable in electronic than in print editions.

So far we have concentrated on "linguistically variant" texts in which some words are different. But emphasis in both textual and literary theory on the iconic character of literary art, the way in which the literary work means what it means bibliographically as well as linguistically, brings new factors to bear on the issue. For example, D. F. McKenzie and Jerome McGann have, in a sense, tied the work to the document that is its medium. In theory, at least, their arguments tend to make a new work out of every new physical manifestation of it, its physicality and historical context being inextricable parts of its literary existence. McKenzie says, "Each version has some claim to be edited in its own right, with a proper respect for its historicity as an artifact . . ." (*Bibliography*, x). Randall McLeod has demonstrated forcefully the way in which the Oxford editor of John Harington's English translation of *Orlando Furioso* ignored and violated the meanings of

---

3. "New Approach," 241. Similarly, Hershel Parker in *Flawed Texts* demonstrates the "adventitious meanings" resulting from the effects of revisions on interpretations of unrevised portions of a variety of American works.

the physical text chosen as copy-text and created nonsense by his ignorance of significant type forms ("from Tranceformations").

These iconic evaluations or interpretations of text are elaborated by Jerome McGann, who develops the additional idea that the circumstances of distribution determine the meaning of a work even when it is linguistically invariant. The physical book in its bibliographical integrity becomes the representative of the historical moment of distribution and of the production intentions that created that edition. He suggests that textually cognate editions of Matthew Arnold's "Empedocles on Etna" before and after Arnold's 1853 repudiation of it have different significances and that three textually invariant versions of Byron's "Fare Thee Well" have different significances deriving from the private and public nature of distribution and from the authorizing issuer of each text. The logical extension of this idea is that new scholarly editions are also new iconic representations of works representing the modern moment of republication in so-called corrected forms. The corrections, McGann points out, are only "corrections as they have been imagined and generated through a particular theory of the text" ("What Is," 27). The new scholarly edition means, then, what its producers intended it to mean, and it is therefore not "the work itself" but just another edition of the work.

It may be worth noting how radically different from one another are the bases for these theories. Tanselle's (and perhaps Greg's) test is intentional; Zeller's is semantic; McKenzie's is physical; McGann's is sociohistorical. Moreover, Thorpe's, Zeller's, and McKenzie's tests are mechanical: individual judgment is not needed to determine that the work is now a different work; judgment is employed only in determining what significance a semantic change has made or how a shift of physical perspective has altered the work. Editing, for them, becomes essentially a matter of tracing the history of change. Tanselle's test, however, requires judgment in determining if the alteration has really changed the work or just enhanced the old work. Editing, for him, is a matter of determining the best form the text should take to best represent the work as it should be (or should have been) according to some determination of authorial intention.

One might note that the range of editorial implications here can be seen as stretching between two poles: the one, usually associated with classical editing, of recovering a lost archetype that presumably did exist; and the other, usually associated with eclectic or critical editing, of recovering authorial or best intentions for a work when no existing text has yet achieved it.

Though it is sometimes clouded by other factors, the underlying assumption of some of these theories seems to be that a single text is more desirable than multiple texts, since it would be tidier (more convenient or less confusing) to have an edited standard text, which all readers and scholars could have in common, even though to do so would require that we trust the individual judgment of the critical editor. The equally clouded underlying assumption of the other theories is that multiple texts may be unavoidable, but, if we have multiple texts, let us not have the exercise of individual judgment in editing them.[4]

Jack Stillinger, opposing the first of these tendencies but falling into, I think, the latter, has coined the name "textual primitivism" for the tendency among editors to identify an author's early versions as the best representative texts of works. He advocates a multiplication of editions of Wordsworth's revised works on the grounds that

> Wordsworth did, after all, write the 1805 version [of *The Prelude*] *and* the 1850; and the 1798 *Peter Bell* and the rest of the versions including those of the printed texts of 1819, 1820, 1827, 1832, 1836, and 1845 ... each of these versions embodies some degree of the poet's intention and authority ... it is not, I think, possible to argue that authority resides in a single version, and that the rest of the texts in a series, whether early or late, should be banished to some limbo of poor relationship. ("Textual Primitivism," 27)

Whereas McGann seer ⌐o find a discrete work in each new edition because each represents a different production intention, Stillinger finds each revised edition interesting because it represents a different authorial intention. Neither man is impressed by the idea of a single eclectic text or by identifying a single edition as the best text—the one that *is* the work.

The tendency of Stillinger's and McGann's very different arguments is to promote multiple editions, each well labeled for its authorial or historical position of origination. These positions may at first appear to reflect the correlative idea in literary theory that literary works of art are primarily processes rather than objects—that writing and reading are action verbs describing processes that do not close. In fact, however, none of the textual

---

4. See the discussion forum with R. H. Miller, Peter Shillingsburg, and Joseph McElrath, in which Miller proposes the editor as archivist. He also proposes the editor as arbiter but then objects to the exercise of any judgment except in cases where the editorial goal is to recover a lost archetype.

critics surveyed have gone so far; Stillinger, McGann, McKenzie, and Zeller at most advocate a series of discrete historically extant objects that might have resulted from the fact that writing is a process. But they all stop short of saying that the work remains essentially a process rather than a stable object or series of stable objects.

One of the great strengths of Fredson Bowers's work on textual principles was that he focused on concrete examples rather than on abstract theories. In one of his last essays, "Authorial Intention and Editorial Problems," he lays out four instances in which the ideals of editing for authorial intention were challenged by textual revision by agents other than an author. As Bowers puts it, the editorial question concerns "whether in such circumstances an editor should observe the author's latest documentary intention, no matter how arrived at, or else restore what had originally been intended but altered for other than strictly personal literary considerations" ("Authorial Intention," 50). This is a specialized form of the question "When is a revised work a new work?" for in these cases the changes resulted from nonauthorial interventions. Nevertheless, the question hinges on the concept of versions of a work and leaves one, broadly speaking, with the choice of a work as intended by the author in some autonomous condition or as intended in a collaborative production process. The choice suggests either that the work in one version is *the* work and the other is a falsification or that the work exists in more than one form, each representing different (though obviously very similar) works.

In the fourth of his examples Bowers describes the conditions of composition, revision, and publication of William James's account of Thomas Davidson. Bowers indicates that the work was originally intended in 1903 for publication in a memorial volume. Such volumes have relatively homogeneous audiences, and James was occasionally technical in reference to philosophical positions and frank in reference to the subject's medical history. That intended volume was postponed for so long that, when the opportunity arose, James revised and published the piece in *McClure's* magazine for a broader audience. Several years later James's original version was printed in the memorial volume, apparently from a copy of the manuscript James originally had submitted and then had retrieved or copied to revise for *McClure's*. Thus, the last printed version is the author's original text; the first printed version, his last revised intentions. The different mediums of production imposed different influences on authorial intention.

From the way Bowers formulated this editorial problem we can deduce the underlying concept of works and the "proper goal of editing" that informed his decisions. First, he notes that, "whenever it is possible to substitute apparatus for parallel texts," one seeks the manuscript for authority in accidentals ("Authorial Intention," 58). That is, a single text is to be desired over parallel texts whenever it is practical to use an apparatus. This preference for a single text overrides any desire to see the work as two different works to be considered "separately in their own right." Second, Bowers formulated the question as one of determining James's "true intentions for the reminiscence" (59). It seems to go without saying that, if James had a *true* intention for the reminiscence, he couldn't very well wish posterity to read the essay in some untrue form. But Bowers raises as a complication the contradictory propositions that James's proofing and approving the memorial volume version "last" might indicate that it represented his "final" intentions, on one hand, and, contrarily, that James's true and final intentions are represented by the "revised" *McClure's* magazine version, prepared at a time when he believed that the memorial volume version had been aborted. Bowers's struggle over which was final and which was true demonstrates his resistance to the idea of two separate texts or two separate works. His solution indicated how thoroughly he was committed to the idea of a true version of the work, for he chose the *McClure's* as copy-text and restored from the memorial volume (later in publication but earlier in composition) those forms of the work that he believed to underlie or precede "the special self-censorship that James imposed on himself in view of his new audience." This he chose to do because "a reading text had to be prepared that to the best of my judgment represented what James finally wanted, free from a certain form of arbitrary restraint" (60).

The idea that there might be two separate texts representing what James "finally wanted" on two separate occasions, in two separate mediums, for two separate target audiences, did not outweigh the desire for one text whenever apparatus could substitute for parallel texts. The result is a third version of the work, which may very well approximate the text James would have wanted for Bowers's scholarly edition but which *in its reading text* fails to represent what James wanted on either of the two occasions when he designed a text for a particular form of publication. The ideal editorial goal for Bowers was, it seems clear, a single best text of the work. This should not be confused with earlier mentioned editorial attempts to simplify the work by ignoring or suppressing alternative forms, however, for Bowers did not withhold any textual information. At worst he privileged one version over others by foregrounding it; the others remain in the background, indicated by the pointing hand of the editor in the introduction.

We see then that the question "When is a revised work a new work?" has a variety of possible answers depending on one's theoretical position concerning the existence of literary works and that all the theories thus far examined share a basic focus on the work of art as a physical artifact. Even Tanselle, who distinguishes between the text of the work and the text of the document, sensibly finds both represented only in documents. The notion is that the text of the document, the physical copy, sometimes distorts the text of the work, which is the ideal text that might not be embodied perfectly in any document. When these physical copies vary, we think we have a problem. We resolve the variant texts by calling some of the variants "errors" and some "revisions," and we worry with the significance and importance of these variants—as well we should. But we seem not quite to understand the issue at hand if we think we have settled it all by correcting errors, conflating variant texts into a single standard text, or editing separate versions separately.

Let us ask one or two less frequently asked questions—asked less often probably because as editors we can do nothing about them and as bibliographers there may be nothing to record. Yet these questions are important to our concerns as editors and critics because we edit for the sake of the experience of reading. We want well edited texts *to read* not just *to have*.

McGann has already asked if a work that is textually unchanged can be two or more different works. His answer is that they can be and often are. He reasons from the "intentions of production" rather than from authorial intention and points to bibliographical differences as indexes (in C. S. Peirce's sense of the word) to the significance of the edition. T. H. Howard-Hill, probably misconstruing McGann's point, insists that the bibliographical elements of a work are not part of the meaning of the work because the author did not, in most instances, mean anything by them and because a bibliographical description of the book does not convey, as a text, the meanings about the text to which McGann alludes.[5] These two positions are different but not mutually exclusive. McGann is raising our consciousness about aspects of the work that "go without saying" and for which normally our reaction also goes without saying. McGann would have us examine the ways in which the bibliographical elements index social conditions and limitations and determinations. He attaches to the physical product the significance of the social conditions under which it was produced. Though he does not put it this way, I think when he refers to the

---

5. Howard-Hill, "Theory," 43. At least that is what I take Howard-Hill to mean when he refers the reader to a standard bibliographic description as if that were what McGann meant by the bibliographic text.

bibliographical meaning of the work he is referring to the intention of the producers of the edition. Authorial intention, he says, is one among several forces constituting a social contract adding significance to the production. If normally these things go without saying, McGann wants us to be aware of them in the same way that poststructural critics wish us to be aware of the consequences of similar conditions in discourses. Howard-Hill's insistence that they go without saying because they are without significance to the work itself is, in McGann's terms, simply declining to examine the significance of that which goes without saying.

Focusing for a moment on the work as a reception performance, let us shift our view from the context of origination—the author and the social complex of production—to the context of reception. It now becomes possible to ask, in a different sense, whether a single edition or even a single copy of a work can ever be a different work from the one it was at another time. This is difficult to say because we do not often think in this way. Can a single text of a document be the vehicle of performances such that a single invariant text can be said to represent two works? (I hasten to say the point of this argument is not going to be the obvious one, that different people read differently. Rather, we should observe the similarities between this form of the question and the ones we have previously considered in order better to see what concepts of a work of literary art underlie editorial concerns.) The text in a closed book can be corrupt or pure, singular or multiple, for all the difference it can possibly make. As long as the book is closed, the work is unknown. But a text read off the page becomes reality for readers in a variety of performances influenced by the text-on-the-page but not entirely determined by it.

When Ulysses, in Tennyson's poem, says in the fourth paragraph (line 33):

This is my son, mine own Telemachus,

does he say it with pride swelling his voice:

This is my *son,* mine own *Telemachus,*

or does he say it with simpering disdain:

This *is* my son [long pause while the sad fact and disappointed implications of this admission sink in before adding quietly], mine own Telemachus?

Does he say "Well-loved of me" (l. 35) with a heart full of pride and sorrow, or does he say "Well-loved of me" in ironic recognition of his neglected duties and hoped-for escape? When he says "He works his work, I mine" (l. 43), are we being told that each has a natural place or preordained goal in life, or is there a tone of disdain for the stay-at-home boy in his voice? The written text of the document does not give sufficient clues to the "correct" variant reading in these cases. Having a single standard text will simply not indicate which is the *real* "Ulysses" in a reading performance of the work.

So, let us go back briefly to Thorpe's distinction between private and public works in which we are asked to respect the integrity of a work only when the author has endowed it with such by publishing a text. Thorpe seems to say that readers are better off with a principle for dismissing a variety of versions of the work because they are private, not public. And let us look at Hershel Parker's preference for the text reflecting the peak of creativity over the mutilated revisions that cannot be read. He seems to say that readers are better off for having the revisions stricken from the work. Or look at McKenzie's or McGann's view that each edition represents its social existence as a work in ways the manuscript or other private or provisional versions cannot. They seem to say that readers are better off for having a principle for excluding textual information in the same way Thorpe suggests.[6] Are we better off with any other standard text, well edited and published on acid-free paper in library binding attesting the stability of the text within? We have in these cases a simplified text (i.e., rationalized from the extant variant forms), but do we have a *better* text? Is our reading and analysis of the text going to be better for being uncluttered by the facts?

One might object that scholarly editions are not uncluttered by facts. That is right. Scholarly editions are repositories of information concerning the multiple forms and developing forms in the past. They are also, in themselves, new "material texts." A scholarly edition is temporally and iconically different from the texts it purports to represent, but it also provides a great deal of information about authorial intentions, production interventions, bibliographical significance, revisions, corrections, and other important textual and metatextual events and circumstances. Why is it,

---

6. To do McKenzie and McGann justice here, they emphasize the integrity of each production performance. McGann's occasional denigration of manuscripts as copy-texts and of authorial intention as a guiding principle in editing probably results in part from the battle he is trying to wage on behalf of production intentions against the idea of autonomous authors, which tends to glorify manuscript forms. There is nothing in principle in McKenzie's and McGann's views that would prevent manuscript forms of works from being treated as products of a comprehensive context of origination similar to a social contract.

then, that scholarly editions are generally referred to as standard texts? Why do our references to them emphasize the edited text—the clear reading text? And why do critics and students who use scholarly editions focus on the edited text? Why do publishers of classroom editions reissue the edited texts without apparatus? Isn't it because we still generally think of a work of literary art in the way the popular mind conceives of it—as a single physical text that gets it right? or in a succession of single texts that each gets something right?

The question of when a revised work becomes a new work is both interesting and stupid. If the question emanates from a fussy concern over which variants are the correct ones and which can be ignored when reading a work, it is silly and schoolmarmish. If it emanates from a desire to know as much as possible about each text of the work, it is interesting and important. It is one, however, that can be answered only by the exercise of individual judgment. Critics worth their salt will want to know all texts and will be careful about which documentary text, out of the various available ones, their critical remarks refer to. Nor will they necessarily agree about which one should be the "standard" text.

It does not go without saying, however, that it is good to desire to know as much as is possible about all the variant texts and the contexts of their originations. It requires explanation to know why a text with an array of historical variants identified by originators is better than a single, correct, standard text purporting to be the work itself. Jo Ann Boydston has pointed out, with proper indignation, that many editors and critics still believe that a clean text with perhaps a few selected pieces of information about textual variants would be far more useful than an edition for which the editors "forgot to take down the scaffolding" when the editing was done.[7]

There is a very good reason, I believe, for wanting to know variant texts and for wanting to know who produced the changes and under what circumstances. Price Caldwell's theory of meaning, molecular sememics (discussed in chaps. 2 and 3), suggests that meaning is "determined" in particular communication acts by the relevant context (molecule) operant for speaker and recipient. Sememic molecules are conventionalized but not stable linguistic structuring elements shared by socialized speakers of a

---

7. "In Praise," 8. The unacknowledged exercise of phallic power involved in *not* disclosing all the information is clearly presented by Clayton J. Delery in "The Subject Presumed to Know: Implied Authority and Editorial Apparatus." Randall McLeod refers to similar editorial interference with the facts as "disambiguating" the text in "Information on Information" (252).

language. The specific molecule governing selection of language and determining its meaning is often indicated by the physical context as well as by syntax and by historical patterns of usage. For example, the phrase "He's out" has very different, specific, determined meanings when spoken by an umpire in a baseball game (not safe), a receptionist in a doctor's office (not in), an anesthesiologist at an operating table (not awake), or a radio sportscaster at a boxing match (not conscious). The relevant aspect of this theory to the problem of revised texts is that, in a given molecular structure of selection, there are a limited number of possible words to use at any point in a sentence, a limited number of possible phrases to use, even a limited number of sentences and paragraphs that can be chosen. An umpire cannot say "In" or "Still conscious" as an alternative to "Out" because the context rules out those possibilities. Further, and perhaps more important, the molecular structure of selection limits the number of meanings that can be conveyed by the chosen words, phrases, sentences, or paragraphs in a particular utterance. That is, context (semantic, physical, temporal, etc.) limits what can be appropriately said on any particular occasion, and it determines (in the sense of delimiting) what a particular locution means. A listener would understand, because of the physical context and identity of the speaker, whether "He's out" meant unconscious by reason of anesthesia or unconscious by reason of a violent blow to the head or not safe at home plate. Of course, nonsense can be produced (deliberately?) at any time and place, but even nonsense is recognized as nonsense because of the functioning molecular structure of selection (which nonsense violates). Furthermore, any locution hived off from its molecular origin can be made to mean an almost unlimited number of things. But a critic seriously considering the meaning of a particular work by a particular author published (or not) in a particular way has more to go on than the linguistic text as accurately reproduced in a scholarly edition. There are the bibliographical elements that McKenzie emphasizes, the production circumstances that McGann emphasizes, and the intentions (authorial and otherwise) that just about everyone refers to. Variant texts represent a number of possible kinds of activities. All of these aspects combine to form the context of origination for utterances. A knowledge of the context of origination is necessary in order to determine the structure of molecular selection that guided the generation of the utterance and determines its appropriate meanings.

Variants that result from an author's changing her or his mind about what is to be said and meant are different from variants that result from an editor's intervention about what should be written. Variant things to be said are different from variant ways to say the same thing, and these in turn are different from variants produced in the trial-and-error process of finding out what is to be said. If one assumes that an author is seriously contemplating variant texts, and if one can reconstruct the important parts of the molecular structure of selection, one might see more clearly from the variant texts what the author was trying to communicate. Hence, availability of variant texts is very helpful to analytical reading but only if the context of origination of each variant is taken into account.[8] Critics whose "play" with text is unimpeded by any knowledge of or concern for the contexts of origination are not explicating particular texts by particular authors. Like linguists contemplating the meaning of disembodied sentences or words, such critics are manipulating untethered sentence as "examples of utterance" rather than as utterances per se.

For example, if in "Ulysses" Tennyson had experimented with italics to indicate the old sailor's intonation, we would have some rough clues about what tone was being contemplated. An editor who eliminated such experimentation as trivial doodling or on the grounds that it was private documentation or that it was a pre-copy-text form would be eliminating data a good reader could use to generate a more author-determined reception performance of the work. Getting the text of the work "right" is not good enough. Identifying the best text of the work is not enough. Exercising editorial control over the individual judgment of readers is reprehensible. Just because some readers are asses does not mean we should treat all readers as if they were.

So, when asking, "When is a revised work a new work?" it is good to remember that this potentially interesting question is to be answered by each person individually. Each edition will reflect its editor's opinion in this matter, so editors should beware about foisting that essentially personal opinion onto readers by denying them the chance of judging the evidence for themselves (which happens every time variants or emendations are reported selectively). And when reading editions prepared by other editors, I would be careful not to accept without examination the choices made for the reader. I would also be careful not to ignore the data relevant to the reading of any text provided by the variants and their contexts of origination.

Editors who wish to enhance the work of good readers will forsake Thorpe's arbitrary distinction between private and public texts because it is a principle of exclusion; they will forsake Tanselle's distinction between

---

8. The notion of agency is developed in chapters 2 and 6.

horizontal and vertical revisions because it is a principle of separation; and they will be suspicious of every "standard" or "established" text in exactly the same way they are wary of a drugstore paperback. But these suspicions are not to be allayed by finally finding the correct or best text; they are to be satisfied by finding the record of revision laid out in the specific contexts that gave them being and that determined their significance. For practical purposes, of course, editors cannot be all things to all readers. Nor can they fail to make decisions simply because there is more than one feasible alternative. Scholarly editors who realize that their new editions are simply new editions may feel less pressure to insist on the correctness and universal acceptance of their editorial decisions.

Furthermore, editors are not in charge of the text's meanings, nor is it their responsibility to make its meanings clear. But by being clear about what they have done and being inclusive about information about variant texts, variant iconic formats, and variant contexts for authoritative source texts, editors seek to fulfill a responsibility for making sure that all the possible meaning indicators are represented, preserved, or transmitted. Editors are not asked by good readers to oversimplify the textual problems or to eliminate the anxiety of texts by pretending to have resolved for everyone what readers should resolve for themselves. I believe a good reader asks for clarity, not simplicity.

Chapter 8

Textual Ethics:
The Meaning of Editorial Work

For I testify unto every man that heareth the words of the prophecy of
this book, If any man shall add unto these things, God shall add unto
him the plagues that are written in this book: And if any man shall
take away from the words of the book of this prophecy, God shall take
away his part out of the book of life, and out of the holy city, and from
the things which are written in this book.
                                    —Revelation 22:18–19 (KJV)

I. THE LIMITS OF THE EDITOR'S RESPONSIBILITY

The righteous tone with which the last chapter ends reflects a common, if
dangerous, attitude among editors that stems, I believe, from a desire that
the fruits of such long labor as scholarly editing entails be valuable, useful,
right, and enduring. Consequently, editing has a long history of controversy over the right and the wrong ways to prepare and present editions.
Should one prepare a text that the author never intended? Should one prefer what the author did or what the publishing process produced? Should
one choose an early text or a late-lifetime text for copy-text? Should one
prefer authorial idiosyncrasy or consistency? Should one be able to reconstruct the copy-text from the apparatus? Should one report pre-copy-text
forms? What does the editor owe to the convenience of the modern reader?

Depending on one's particular answer to these questions in any given
circumstance, it is likely that persons choosing a different answer consider
one's own choices just plain wrong. Reviews of scholarly editions and
guides for editorial work are steeped in *should*s and *must*s. Much of such

language serves as shrouds and mists obscuring the ideological stances that make certain courses appear inevitable. But it may also hide shortcuts, elisions, and compromises embedded between the sturdy covers and between the lines printed on the acid-free paper of scholarly editions.

In *Scholarly Editing in the Computer Age* I tried to account for much editorial controversy and disagreement by identifying different notions of the source for textual authority and different ideas about what text readers might be interested in reading. Various orientations to editorial procedures and values have been defended persuasively and seem, therefore, legitimate. It may be that such questions are not actually ethical questions but, rather, choices among acceptable alternatives.

True ethical questions tend to involve discrepancies between declared purposes and achieved results: false advertising, untruth in labeling, false claims about fundamental research, inaccurate disclosure of methods and procedures. But what one tends to see in unfavorable reviews of new editions involves an editor who is accused of trying to impose principles and rules of editing onto materials that by their nature (so says the reviewer) demand different treatment. Such an accusation questions judgment, not ethics. Even when an editor is accused of claiming to do one thing while in fact doing something else, it is not necessarily the case that the editor realized the discrepancy. But to an edition user it can make little difference if the edition misrepresents itself by mistake or malice aforethought. Standards hold regardless of whether the accused intended to deceive. So, whether they are questions of ethics or mere competence, they are of concern to both editors and edition users.

The editing profession is not especially dogged by people who lack integrity, but it does attract a larger than average share of amateurs with more enthusiasm and sense of mission than training or talent. Furthermore, as our understanding of what we are doing changes and evolves, we see more clearly than we did before—which might lead us to denigrate work done before the dawning of the latest insight. Consequently interesting questions with ethical dimensions arise among perfectly good-willed people who have been blinded to the ethical significance of their work either by ideals that have unforeseen or subtle implications or by the common working expectations in the field. The questions are raised here for contemplation rather than for accusation.

The central idea of this chapter is that pursuit of the "pure virgin text" may, in the case of works for which differing authorial versions survive, lead an editor to make choices that should be left to each reader.[1] The desire for a standard text, moreover, might lead an editor to obscure genuine ambiguity by "clarifying" the text.[2] The point is that editors might be arrogating to themselves responsibilities they have no right to exercise. Secondary concerns include the way in which disagreements over the right way to edit a text depend on an editor's exceeding the limits of legitimate responsibility over texts.

Defining the editor's responsibility requires some sort of definition of the reader's responsibility or rights. The fact that many readers do not wish to exercise their right to know not only the alternative versions of a work but also the ambiguities of text when only one version exists probably derives in part from a textual and critical tradition in which works of literary art are considered stable and monolithic and in which the information about alternative versions and ambiguous texts is arranged in notes and tables designed primarily for other purposes, such as showing what the editor has done or tracing the "textual transmission"—both of which mix materials crucial to understanding the work of art as an authorial product with material relevant only to the history of the documents and their editorial treatment.

Although the bulk of this book is devoted to an analysis of basic assumptions about the nature of texts and basic issues in editorial theory and practice, it is not likely that the editorial community is now united in its understanding of these issues and assumptions. But one cannot explore the ethical implications of editing without some notion that is to be tested. The following, then, involves two propositions about works of literary art argued in earlier chapters: first, that they are essentially indeterminate textually (i.e., often plagued by what we call indifferent readings)[3] and, second, that they are multiple (i.e., often existing in more than one authoritative version). These two propositions are usually acknowledged in theory more than in practice. The emblems of both the CEAA (Center for Editions of American Authors) and the CSE (Committee on Scholarly Editions), for

---

1. This idea is the burden of chapter 6, which ends with a suggestion about what kind of help readers really need.

2. The idea that some ambiguity is intentional or provides desirable uncertainty or richness is not new, but ambiguity that dissolves upon further or closer reading will strike most editors and readers as a simple error.

3. Indifferent because the evidence is just as strong supporting one choice as it is supporting another but where doubt exists about authenticity or agency. Indifferent variants often involve substantives of great significance; the name derives from the "center of indifference" between magnetic poles and is not a value judgment.

example, label certain editions as "an approved text" (or "edition")—being careful to distinguish that from one that would be "the approved text" (or "edition"); yet to my knowledge neither organization has issued emblems to two competing editions of the same work. Furthermore, in practice it is common to describe the indifferent alternative that is not adopted as a "copying error" or a "scribal lapse," when, in fact, the evidence does not require or sustain such language.

The first of these propositions (that works are textually indeterminate) confronts uncomfortably the practical necessity of books in which texts are printed in a continuous line and hence can really present only one text. Attempts to do otherwise confront also the practical reality that readers tend to read continuously and tend to resist indeterminacy in texts. Readers can become irritated with editors who are unable to make up their minds what the text should be. Of course, these same readers can revel in the indeterminacy of the meaning of the text, but that is a different situation altogether, breeding the joy of freedom rather than the anxiety of uncertainty. Nevertheless, the stark fact of indifferent readings is that there is no firm ground for rejecting one possible reading and adopting another. Any editor who makes a decision about an indifferent reading is making a choice for the reader. No matter what choice is made, a distortion of the facts results. Confronted with an unsolvable dilemma, we solve it arbitrarily. This necessity has an ethical dimension.

The second of these propositions (that texts are multiple) presents us with a similar problem with potentially greater significance. Sometimes the editor must decide whether to produce a text the author never intended.[4] Sometimes authors intended more than one thing at different times. Sometimes their intentions were heavily influenced by considerations we think they should have been free of. Other times we think they did not give in sufficiently to influences that were in fact available to them. The resulting variant forms of a work all contribute, as we understand the context of each form, to our understanding of the work and of its origins, accomplishments, and failings. When an editor chooses one form or version over another to present as the text, a choice is made for the reader. It does not matter whether that choice is in favor of an orthodox author's final intention or for an unrevised initial authorial intention or for any other version.

---

4. The question was raised as an ethical issue by Stephen Parrish at the Society for Textual Scholarship convention in 1987. The idea that the editor can pit her or his judgment "against" that of the author is emphatically rejected by Donald Reiman (*Study of Modern Manuscripts,* esp. 103–4).

When a choice is made, the reader is likely to remain unaware of the resulting distortion of the facts.

This description of the basic textual situation also involves two common principles of editorial procedure: one is that, basing their work on an exhaustive examination of all available evidence, editors establish a text meant to be considered the standard in the profession, and the other is that editors provide a historical collation and record of emendations meant to report both the history of textual development and a record of the editor's interventions. The first of these principles reflects a high ideal: the pursuit of pure virgin text either in the form of the author's final or best intentions or in the form resulting from the social contract between author and publisher or as found in some specifically desirable document. No matter what the ideal, its pursuit as the established, or standard, text has been the ordinary editorial concern. That ideal has been appealed to when seeking funding. The Department of Health, Education, and Welfare (HEW) and then the National Endowment for the Humanities (NEH) gave money to produce editions that would "never have to be done again." It is easy to see that this principle of editorial behavior tends to aim at a single text and, therefore, tends to do all that it can to minimize or eliminate indeterminateness and multiplicity. In that tendency, combined with a blindness to the implications of indeterminacy and multiplicity, I see an ethical problem, an ethical lapse in our profession. If it is practically impossible simultaneously to establish a single standard text and to acknowledge multiplicity and indeterminacy, then I think we should seriously consider some major alterations in the way we present scholarly editions.

The principle for textual apparatuses also reflects high ideals: "laying the cards on the table face up"; making it possible to reconstruct the editorial work and to trace the history of textual transmission. In the early days of the CEAA, under Professor Bowers's highly influential editorial work of the late 1950s and 1960s, ethics was the strong point. Editorial work of the past was unethically shoddy. Bowers led the objections to editors who emended left and right, leaving little or no record of their improvements and regularizations. As editorial apparatuses grew, it became more and more apparent that the less editors told the reader about what had been done the more power the editor was, in reality, exercising over the reader's critical understanding of the work.

The theory and practice that brought the modern textual apparatus to its peak of development held that, while a definitive *text* might be impossible, a definitive *edition* (text and apparatus) was possible (Tanselle,

"Some Principles"). But that line of reasoning had at its core a flaw that there was no way to predict in advance. The flaw came in thinking that the integrity of the apparatus was the definitive answer to the weaknesses of earlier editorial practice. The purpose emphasized by the new apparatuses was to show what the editor had done and what the documentary evidence was. The idea was to lay out all the facts upon which the present text was based. The table of emendations, designed to show what the editor had done, however, mixed the record of the adoption of late authorial revisions (usually substantives) and the correction of "demonstrable errors" and sometimes the correction of "minor inconsistencies." The result was a list that came to be looked on as the record of rejected and superseded minutia.[5] The historical collation, mercifully omitting accidentals in most cases, was a documentary history mixing the editorial improvements and corruptions along with intermediate revisions by the author. The result was a list that, for all its high ideals and integrity, came to be seen as an exercise in bibliographical trivia.

That these two views of the apparatus are grossly unfair is beside the point. Critics and students often read readily available paperbacks and go to the scholarly editions, if at all, when their work is done, to check their quotations. The CEAA and CSE style apparatus did not do much to teach readers about indeterminate and multiple texts. The flaw was not in the integrity of the apparatus or in its failure to do what it set out to do. The flaw was that what it set out to do was not enough—a realization of which did not take place until the apparatuses did not have the desired result of getting literary critics to confront the implications of textual criticism. In addition to the records of editorial endeavor and documentary history, what was needed was a record of composition and revision that showed the indeterminateness and multiplicity of *authoritative* forms, swept clean of corruptions and corrections of demonstrable errors that interfere with assessments of significant variant forms. And in addition what was needed was a way to present the work as a series of bibliographical and social events that shaped the cultural history of each work. A systematic attempt to separate out the record of authorial composition and revision from the record of editorial and compositorial corruptions and copyediting and a systematic way to present the sociobibliographic history would go a long way to raise people's consciousness of the interpretive implications of textual

---

5. My own first significant realization of this flaw came when I tried to use the Wesleyan Edition of *Tom Jones* to trace Fielding's revisions. I do not think the splitting headache I developed was caused by allergies.

criticism. Furthermore, such an analytical presentation of variants would accommodate many of the diverse demands that varied readers make on literary texts.

The question is: what is the limit to which an editor can legitimately carry a desire for an established standard text in the face of the evidence that remains ambiguous? What right does the editor have to enshrine one particular version of the work over another? What responsibility does the editor have to those readers who would like to know about the authorial alternatives to the established reading text or to the production alternatives, as opposed to the whole plethora of documentary alternatives? Must each reader actually sort through the whole textual record to get an understanding or sense of the varieties of voices and agencies embedded in the text?

Do readers who are not editors of texts get what they want from the editorial work now available? Are they content with a standard single text? Do they ever wish that the record of composition and revision were available separate from the full record of textual variation? Do they object when they find that the editor has chosen for them from viable alternatives, which are then buried in a mass of other variations that are not really viable alternatives? And do they object when an editor cleans up ambiguities in the text even when there are no variants in the authoritative documents? The notion that works are textually indeterminate and multiple requires certain answers here that run counter to traditional editorial practice. Fredson Bowers's recommendation in the presidential address to the Society for Textual Scholarship in 1985 that we should pursue "the superior authority" does not address the problem sufficiently well. The nature of many works of art and the evidence concerning their creation is too complex for us to tell in every detail which is the superior authority. Besides, legitimate disagreement often exists over who or what is the authority.

These considerations of the ethical implications of editorial acts have already stimulated serious thoughts about altered methods of presenting scholarly editions. Some modern editions have abandoned the clear reading text with its strong implications that the text chosen by the editor was paramount and that the apparatus contains material of importance and interest only to trained scholars. The Australian Colonial Texts Series and its more ambitious companion project, the Academy Editions of Australian Literature, for example, put the records of authorial composition and revision at the foot of the page and the rest of the documentary record of textual transmission and editorial correction at the back of the book.

The idea that the presentation page of a scholarly edition should graphically portray and organize the multiple voices and the multiple performance events that constitute script acts is not a new one, but it will strike
commercial publishers and persons who read books once for pleasure as
pedantic, rather than ethically or even intellectually inevitable. Perhaps the
most complicated development of this idea in printed texts can be found
in the large scholarly editions of the Talmud (see fig. 5), in which the text
of central interest occupies a relatively small but central location. Attached
to it and surrounding the text like a series of receding moats and walls pro-
tecting the text from vulgar or naive readings or like a series of instructional
waystations preparing the reader for the central text are commentaries and
glossaries representing hierarchies of textual authorities. But to scholars
who reread and study a text such an arrangement of text and countertext
adds richness and convenience to the business of identifying the operant
performance events represented by the script acts known as the Talmud.

It is perhaps more significant that the advent of hypertext and multimedia electronic formats has greatly increased the options for text presentation. A brief description of an electronic reading experience can demonstrate how such editions can fulfill the ethical requirements surveyed here
and accommodate a variety of editorial orientations.[6] Imagine the reader
of *Moby-Dick* or *Vanity Fair* opening an electronic edition to a menu offer-
ing either the manuscript, proofs, first edition (first state or second state),
the author's revised edition, or a newly edited critical edition. Suppose the
reader chooses the edited text and begins reading. Suddenly, wondering
what the passage on the screen looked like in the manuscript, the reader
touches a key or "clicks on" an icon to open either a virtual representation
of the corresponding page of manuscript or a transcription (diplomatic or
fair), which appears in a second window. Arranging the size and shape of
the windows to suit taste, the reader notices that certain parts of the text
are highlighted in both versions, indicating points of variance. Scrolling
through the text of one window causes the text in the other window to

---

6. See my book *Scholarly Editing*, particularly chapter 14. Finneran's *Literary Text* offers
a variety of views on electronic editions, including my own set of standards for the ideal elec-
tronic edition. See also Robinson, ed., *Wife*, a brilliant presentation of an electronic edition
on compact disk. Internet discussion lists relevant to electronic scholarly editions include:
  SEDIT-L@IUBVM.UCS.Indiana.Edu (Scholarly Editing);
  ETEXTCTR@lists.princeton.edu (electronic text centers);
  ESE@ra.msstate.edu (Electronic Scholarly Editions);
  TEI Listserv@UICVM.UIC.Edu (Text Encoding Intiative); and
  CETH Listserv@PUCC.Princeton.Edu (Center for Electronic Texts in the Humanities).

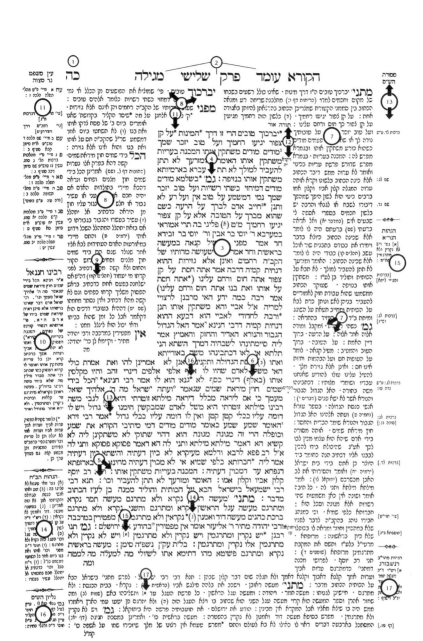

Detailed explanations of these numbers are to be found in the following pages. Large circles indicate the various texts appearing on the Talmud page. Small circles with arrows indicate references to the texts.
1) Page number. 2) Page heading. 3) Talmud text. 4) Indication of the Mishnah and the Gemara. 5) Punctuation. 6) Parentheses and correction of the Talmud text. 7) Rashi's commentary. 8) Tosafot. 9) References in Rashi and in Tosafot. 10) Rabbenu Hananel. 11) *Ein Mishpat Ner Mitzvah*. 12) *Torah Or*. 13) *Masoret HaShas*. 14) *Haggahot HaBah*. 15) *Haggahot HaGra*. 16) *Gilyon HaShas*. 17) *Haggahot Rav B. Ronsburg*.

Fig. 5
The Talmud: The Steinsaltz Edition (New York: Random House, 1989), p. 48.

keep pace. Seeking further information about the textual history, the reader points to a highlighted area and opens, in another window, a historical collation or a textual note or an explanatory annotation. Satisfied, and wishing to continue reading, the reader closes all windows but the edited text (or some other "unedited" representation of the text).

What began as a clear reading text experience of the work for the reader became a richly embedded and contextualized reading experience with information about the performative events for which the surviving texts were the residual spoors. An editor's decision to provide a critical edition in a clear reading text following the dictates of one or another editorial orientation need not restrict the reader, who can choose to ignore that text in favor of another historical text (edited, of course, by some other editor, who may or may not be identified) or who can cause the clear reading text to be surrounded with pointers to the contexts that help determine the text and its meaning according to the script act or utterance performance one chooses to explore.

II.   MULTIPLE TEXTS, MULTIVOICED TEXTS,
      AND CLEAR READING TEXTS

> *The stronger the writing, the sharper the definition in the place. The direction of the piece combs the word into the single one of its meanings intended like a hair. Some would have it that the words are cowlicks that won't be combed straight in a direction.*
>
> —Robert Frost, *Prose Jottings*

It is not always clear to students and scholars why such complicated experiences of texts are valuable. The traditions of reading have all tended to focus on "a text" as "the text": the author's name on the titlepage announces the work as her or his work. The notion that a published text is a cooperative product of a series of (not necessarily well-coordinated or harmonious) performative script acts still requires explanation, for it is not difficult to treat texts as if they were univocal and to interpret their subtleties and complexities as those of one agent.

Let us agree, then, for the sake of argument that the three major categories of performances outlined in chapter 3 do, in fact, constitute the experiences of literary works of art: their creation, production, and reception. Suppose further that texts merely represent more or less accurately the work, rather than "being" the work, because there are not only inaccurate copies but also legitimately variant copies. It seems plausible to say, then, that the literary work of art is—or becomes through revision, production, and reception—a multivoiced medium. One can, in the terms of good old-fashioned historical criticism and textual scholarship, say that the primary voice is that of the author (and those voices the author consciously controls, the narrator and characters). Such a view holds that the primary goal of textual and literary criticism is to establish the author's intentions, first, intermediate, and/or final. Or one could—in the terms of poststructural, particularly deconstructive, criticism—say that the reader is free to find whatever voice and meaning pleases him or her and to construct or reconstruct the contexts that make such meanings currently plausible and significant. Such a view holds that textual criticism is relevant only in that it provides more material for the joy of text. Though any text will do as well as any other, variant texts will do different things. Or one could say with Umberto Eco, in the *Times Literary Supplement* for 22 June 1990, in which he backs away from the ideas he propounded in *The Open Work* (1962), that, though the text is free of its author's intentions, it is bound to a limited range of voices and meanings by its syntax and vocabulary and by the demands of (reasonably[?] coherent and plausibly historical[?]) contexts—that it, therefore, cannot mean just anything, though it need not mean "what the author intended." Such a view, sounding a great deal like warmed up New Criticism, holds that, if textual criticism is relevant at all, it is only to establish an error-free and hence reliable text of the work. Or one could say with the New Historicists or the textual sociologists that the voices of a variety of individual but social beings blend together or sing in more or less harmony in the published book, making it possible for the critic/historian to read the linguistic text as a social artifact containing not only what the author wrote but also the utterances of the editor and typesetter, the printer and binder, and perhaps even the bookseller, all of whom influenced the copy in hand. Such a view holds that the work *becomes* a work of art when it becomes a commodity. Textual criticism is of no particular relevance to the study of such commodities, though scholarly editing may itself be an interesting social activity that generates new commodities. All four of these approaches imply a definition of literary art in which texts are to be viewed, as G. Thomas Tanselle suggests, as sequential verbal art, which he distinguishes quite usefully from static visual art—the first existing in a linguistic medium, while the second exists in a material medium ("Textual Criticism and Deconstruction").

A fifth approach (this list of possibilities might be endless) treats the literary work as visual art. In this view the work is coeval with the book or document. Each particular manifestation of the work is potentially a unique work in which can be read the significance of the type font, the leading, the width of the margins, the thickness of the paper, the quality of the binding, and even the typos and bowdlerizations. Advertising blurbs and booksellers' stickers become in this view significant parts of the book, which is the work. The reader becomes a kind of literary archaeologist experiencing and understanding the work as physical object while at the same time decoding the linguistic text in an overall response to the work of art.

Unless one ignores all interests in texts other than one's own noble aspiration to read the text as ——— (fill in the blank from the previous list), if, in short, one accepts both that texts speak many voices and that readers have a variety of interests in hearing those voices one at a time or in symphony, then a single text edition is doomed to confuse the voices or reflect only one of many voices and serve only one of many audiences. What is the responsibility of the scholarly editor? Remember that this poor mortal is also just a reader performing reception texts and exercising human and, therefore, partial judgments on every detail of the work being edited.

Several options face the sophisticated reader/editor, some more practical than others: one could insist on reading only original editions, trying to create the illusion of reading as an original reader; one could promote the publication of multiple editions (presumably inexpensive ones) of "standard" texts of various versions of the work—Jack Stillinger seems to see merit in that proposition ("Textual Primitivism"). Or one could try to put between one set of covers every version of the work and describe or reproduce all significant formats—as, for example, the Cornell Wordsworth edition seems to be attempting. In short, a scholarly editor who is trying to serve the profession as comprehensively as possible is required by the propositions I began with to produce editions that make as many as possible of the creative and production performance voices palpable, not as a cacophony of sound or chaos of texts (which, ironically, is what happens in single clear reading texts) but as an orderly arrangement of data that makes it possible to read and reread the work in its multiple versions and for its multiple voices.

That has not been the usual aim of scholarly editing. The original "Statement of Principles" of the MLA's Committee on Scholarly Editions says:

> If the audience for the edition is to be the general reading public as well as students, teachers, and scholars, if the text is a literary work of

the kind normally published in final form, or if the editor and his publisher intend to produce a text that can be reproduced by photo-offset printing or can be reset with maximum accuracy for wide distribution and sale, the editor will choose clear text. (*Center for Editions,* 8)

A revised statement acknowledges that "varying editorial projects require varying editorial policies and procedures," but it also expresses the belief that "some issues are common to almost all scholarly editing (the choice and/or treatment of the reading text, for example...)." What that probably means becomes more evident in the part of the statement concerning the CSE's aim to "foster the dissemination of reliable texts in editions appropriate for classroom use and available to the general reading public." Such texts, the statement claims, "do not ordinarily contain textual essays or apparatuses," and therefore the CSE urges scholarly editors "to bear in mind the advantages, for reprint purposes, clear reading texts" (Committee 446).

That statement seems to me to imply, if it does not say it explicitly and clearly, that readers need texts without errors. But it also suggests that readers need only one text. Multiple texts and multiple voices are not high priorities for "classroom use" or for "the general reading public." But responsible editors cannot any longer pretend to edit a single clear reading text that is to be the standard scholarly edition text of the work to be reprinted sans apparatus for study by students, unless by the word *student* we mean a creature who is fully satisfied with a partial engagement with a single text—in other words, if by *student* we mean New Critic.

Patricia Ingham—after an extended discussion of Thomas Hardy's novel, *The Well-Beloved,* which she distinguished from the serialized version, called *The Pursuit of the Well-Beloved*—commented that the strategy she had employed to examine textual revisions is "not at present critically acceptable. Though tempting to many, it is usually made in equivocal parentheses. For though the author, we know, is, critically speaking, dead when the narrator takes over, he does not die until he has made all the changes which create finally that synchronic slice, the last revised version as the author intended it" (Ingham 52). It is a pity that one cannot pursue the implications of multiple texts "because it is not critically acceptable to do so." It is a pity that those bold enough to attempt the task anyway should stumble over themselves so clumsily with oversimplified allegiances to so-called final intentions simply because they have no taxonomy with which to distinguish between the work of art as the author "uttered" it at one time or another for one audience or another and as the reader recreates or performs the work and as the production crew packages it in a variety of ways so easily identifiable by time, country, and social class or aspiration toward the "intended" market. But the greatest pity of all is that even the critic with a scholarly edition in hand is often using a work in which certain voices and texts have been systematically obscured and denigrated at the behest of a misguided and misguiding principle: the clear reading text sans apparatus. It is a principle that implies by its very structure that there can be a single, authentic, and adequate text—one in which all the voices speak with one voice, one for which all else is ancillary and dispensable.

Time and again what textual critics have found in their research is richness, not purity, and too often they have directed their editorial efforts toward reducing that richness to a single clear reading text representing a limited potential for the text. The arguments about purity of text and finality of intention are weak efforts to defend a narrow-minded editorial theory. Furthermore, they represent a tendency among teachers to "dumb down" to their students, particularly but not only their undergraduate students, who are often treated as fragile minds to be entertained and coddled into an appreciation of great art—oversimplified, sanitized, purified, and enshrined on an altar to culturally derived, local, and temporary values represented in the single uncluttered sacred text.

Textual critics have no place on the pedestals of cultural heritage. They should expose their discoveries (if possible) on the same page with the text, acknowledge that a new scholarly edition adds to the pile of existing texts rather than sweeping all before it, and provide editions (physical objects) that attest to the complexity and richness of the work of art (mental projects and historical events). Scholarly editions should provide orderly access to multiple texts and multiple voices within texts. That is the editor's responsibility. The editor should forget about being an arbiter of final texts—unless, that is, the editor enjoys forever failing.

With these notions of texts and editions designed for rich scholarly engagement, one could turn directly to an exploration of the potentials and problems of electronic editions to fulfill desires arising from these considerations. But it might be of some interest to explore the implications of the reading potentials surveyed here as they affect a reading of the monuments that dominated scholarly editing in the third quarter of the twentieth century.

III. THE MEANING OF A SCHOLARLY EDITION

There are many kinds of texts that serve many different uses and the
editor alone has the right to choose the kind that he will produce, just so
he announces his procedure in a preface and then sticks with thorough
scholarly integrity to his own rules.
—Robert E. Spiller, "The Impossible Dream:
Adventures in Editing American Literary Texts"

That scholarly editions have meanings by their "being" occurred to me
as a whimsy, but examination revealed it to be important both to edition
makers and edition users. This is a meditation about ideologies. It would
not hurt, however, to treat the subject as a whimsy, which allows us to
ask questions that might not appear to be serious. The questions can be
divided into groups. The first has to do with the meanings of the physical substance and appearance of the books—questions like: What is the
meaning of the binding, of the dustwrapper, of the height, thickness, and
weight of the book, of the cover design, of the titlepage, of the paper stock,
of the width of margins, of the spacing between lines of text, of the type
fonts? The second group has to do with the institutional relations of the
book—questions like: What is the meaning of the publisher's imprint, of
the presence or absence of the Modern Language Association's seal of approval, and the institutional affiliations of the editor and editorial board
members? Closely related is a third group of questions about the market status and market strategies of the book—questions like: What is the
meaning of the price of the book and of the advertisement fliers? Finally,
there is a group of questions about internal arrangements that indicate certain things about the relation between the author's text and the editor's
texts—questions like: What is the meaning of the table of contents, of the
position given to the listing of editorial board members and other acknowl-
edgments, of the size and position of the textual apparatus, of the presence
or absence of explanatory notes and critical introductions? Are there footnotes or only endnotes? Do the historical and textual essays precede or
follow the text of the work?

There are, of course, other kinds of questions to ask, but we have been
asking them for decades: What are the editorial principles? Did the editors
work from originals or photocopies? Did the collations include all lifetime
editions, did they include multiple collations within editions? How many
proofreadings by how many teams of proofreaders assured the accuracy of
the product?

I will not speculate on whether the meanings surveyed here were consciously intended or merely unconsciously present and revealing. Once one starts asking about the meanings of the books, as opposed to the meanings of the texts they contain, one becomes aware of the potential implications of the book as a text, and, then, an editor might try consciously to shape the book in the hopes of producing desired effects. It is not clear whether the editors and designers of monumental scholarly editions anticipated a deconstruction of the scholarly edition as text.

We are all already familiar with some of the meanings of books: with the associations that have attached themselves to books in such a way that we know what is meant, at least generally, by terms such as *yellowbacks, sleazy paperbacks, hardbound editions, gift books, coffee-table books,* and *textbooks.* From these terms we can guess, with some degree of accuracy, both the contents and the prices of the books indicated. Many of the meanings of scholarly editions will pop out at us, so to speak, just by asking the questions posed. It appears obvious, for example, if the book is tall and thick and substantial, with an elegantly plain dust wrapper, issued from a reputable press, edited by a professor at a reputable university, attested by famous editorial board members, why, then the user can feel confident that this edition of the work is the established, the standard, the safe, in short, the best edition to use.

The conclusion does not necessarily follow from the evidence, but, generally speaking, we allow the conclusion until such a time as it is disproved. For example, the Ohio University Press edition of the works of Robert Browning, under the direction of Roma King and with editorial board members including Morse Peckham, began publication in 1969 with all the appearances of scholarship. The books were big, well printed, well bound, and well marketed. It took a series of hostile reviews, indicating that the research had been sloppy and sketchy and, finally, the public repudiation of the first two volumes by editorial board member Morse Peckham before the meaning of the books as physical objects was belied. Then it began to dawn on folks that the Ohio University Press was not the same as the Ohio State University Press, which was already world famous for the majestic Nathaniel Hawthorne edition boasting Fredson Bowers as textual editor. When King left the project that phase was over, and the Browning edition could begin again. This new conclusion, by the way, does not follow from the evidence any better than the first, for the first two volumes of the Browning edition in their pristine bindings still stand on the shelves of the libraries that first bought them beckoning users with the meaning of their spines and of the entries in the card catalogs, which do not call attention to reviews or repudiations. Perhaps we are lucky that the works involved are *Pauline, Paracelsus, Strafford,* and *Sordello,* not *Bells and Pomegranates, Men and Women,* or *The Ring and the Book.*[7]

The Browning example indicates one of the reasons we might be interested in the meaning of the scholarly edition. We want to know if that meaning is accurate, justified, or deserved. Generally speaking, we have granted the meaning of the tall, thick, reputable object, and we want to feel justified in trusting it. When betrayed we get very indignant. We see John Kidd, for example, doing his best to discredit the work of Hans Gabler on the Garland edition of Joyce's *Ulysses,* and we find, in addition to the quibbles about editorial decisions and about the error rate, that the ultimate objection Kidd has to the Gabler edition is that, as a book—in three tall, thick volumes and in one "corrected" volume—it has usurped the physical spaces that might have been occupied by other editions (perhaps one to be edited by Kidd). The physical space is limited, in the case of Joyce, because copyrights still restrict his works from the free market, which otherwise probably would easily accommodate rival editions of *Ulysses.* To displace the Gabler edition Kidd must persuade people to believe that the Gabler edition does not deserve the "establishment" meanings of the physical book.[8]

But finding whether or not the shape and weight and reputation of a scholarly edition is deserved is only one reason to be interested in the meaning of the scholarly edition. So, for the duration of this whimsy it is assumed that the editions have been scrupulously edited and produced and are the epitome of the ideals of scholarship as understood by the editors. In what other ways does the shape of a scholarly edition make some responses easier than others?

The Northwestern/Newberry (NN) edition of *Moby-Dick* looks like an *established* text. Its thickness (573 pages of Melville's text, 570 pages of apparatus); its type font and spacing between lines; its margins; its dust wrapper; its black, red, and gold binding; and its colophon all attest to its establishment character. Its opening credentials certify the volume's authority, beginning with the announcement that this is volume 6 of a com-

---

7. See reviews of the Browning edition by Thomas J. Collins, John Pettigrew, and Michael Hancher. See also Roma King's defense and John Pettigrew's response.

8. See the recurring debate in *Irish Literary Supplement* (Autumn 1985 and Spring 1986); *TLS,* 1, 8, 22 July, 12 August, 2, 8 September, 7 October, 4 November, 2, 9, 16 December 1988; and *New York Review of Books* 30 June, 18 August, 29 September, and 8 December 1988. See also essays by Hans Walter Gabler, John Kidd, and Charles Rossman.

plete works and followed by two separate, slightly variant, full-page listings of nineteen editors, associates, board members, and contributors.

Nothing else stands between the reader and the text to indicate which *Moby-Dick* is contained here. Readers who work their way through from the beginning find no notes, no commentary, no instructions, no external facts, to interfere with an untrammeled access to the text. The CEAA emblem says, correctly, that it is "an approved text," but the volume's physical appearance and arrangement proclaims that it is "the novel itself." Is it likely that many readers will doubt that this text is *Moby-Dick* as Melville wanted it to be?

But the NN edition produces a third *Moby-Dick*, not an established *Moby-Dick*. It represents the notion one group of editors has of what the text would have been had the first New York edition incorporated authorial revisions or had the first English edition not been copyedited and bowdlerized by the publisher. This is a 1960s edition fully deserving the CEAA emblem. There is nothing to prevent the first 573 pages from being detached for separate sailing in a sea of readers ready and willing to accept it as *the text itself* of *Moby-Dick*. That is both the tragedy and triumph of CEAA editions.

Of course, no reader of this 1,043-page book can long remain ignorant of the last half of the book, in which the edition redeems itself from the arrogance of it pristine text. Though the editorial principles of this edition commit it to establishing a reading text of *Moby-Dick* that presents itself with monolithic confidence, and though huge portions of the editorial appendix are devoted to justifying that text as the best reading text over all others, this edition also offers to the most demanding skeptic nearly all the materials needed to rectify its own ideological stance.

The pursuit of pure virgin text or author's final intentions is fraught with decisions that depend entirely on critical interpretation. The editor of a critical edition cannot avoid making decisions others would make another way. The resulting edition is an interpretation and must be supported by arguments based on evidence. As its reading text, the NN edition prints a critically determined compromise between the two original versions of the work, thus creating a third version; the decisions are extensively, if not always convincingly, argued. The beauty of this edition is that the salient features of both original texts are easily available as well. If the editors seem strenuously to invite readers to accept their text as the best possible text, they also invite (or at least allow) them to disagree, and they provide the wherewithal to do so. In that regard the NN editors have exercised professional ethics, but at the same time they have allowed the book itself to say that which they had no right to say: to wit, this *is Moby-Dick* as it should be.[9]

In an extended discussion of the consequences of editing Wordsworth as the Cornell edition has chosen to do it, Jack Stillinger comes round, finally, to the question of the appearance of the volumes as it affects their use. Stillinger was unhappy about the Cornell edition's tendency to foreground early, unrevised texts.

> Let us imagine a student in the library seeking a respectable text of, say, *I wandered lonely as a cloud*. Let us further imagine the student standing in front of the twenty or so grayish-green volumes of the Cornell Wordsworth, and somehow (by luck or by means of a general index in the final volume) managing to locate the poem in Curtis' volume [*"Poems, in Two Volumes," and Other Poems* (1983)], on pages 207–8. In this version the poem is eighteen lines long (not twenty-four, as formerly in the standard texts); has "dancing" instead of "golden" daffodils in 4; has "Ten thousand dancing" instead of "Fluttering and dancing" in 6; has a "laughing" instead of a "jocund" company in the fourth line of the second stanza (what standardly used to be the third); and has lost the following stanza that formerly constituted 7–12:
>
>> Continuous as the stars that shine
>> And Twinkle on the milky way,
>> They stretched in never-ending line
>> Along the margin of a bay:
>> Ten thousand saw I at a glance,
>> Tossing their heads in sprightly dance.
>
> Reading the shorter, plainer text in the Cornell volume, the student may well wonder how the poem came to be so famous. It is an attractive piece, certainly, but somehow not so vivid and imaginative as one had thought it would be. ("Textual Primitivism," 19–20)

The second conclusion of this whimsical survey is, then, that the meaning of the scholarly edition might, in Jack Stillinger's terms, inadvertently standardize one of several equally viable or defensible texts, making other versions of the work too hard to access, even though no deliberate malice

---

9. I comment more fully on the NN edition in "The Three *Moby-Dicks*."

in that regard might have been intended and high standards of accuracy were maintained.

A third reason to be interested in and concerned about the meaning of the scholarly edition has to do with the relation between the author's text and the editor's text. In this regard the NN Melville and the Cornell Wordsworth editions are poles apart. I have noted that the NN edition offers the author's text first. This is typical of CEAA editions of the 1960s and early 1970s and has become a standard of American critical editions. The practice has several possible meanings, some of them apparently contradictory. First, it seems to mean that the author's text gets pride of place and is "foregrounded." The editor's role is "backgrounded" to demonstrate a lower status, that of a servant of the author and of the text. It also means that the editors trust the readers to deal directly with author and text without officious intervention by the editor. Finally, it means that the text can be reprinted easily without any editorial apparatus, which the format announces is of negligible importance after all. All of these meanings point to the humility of the editor. A contradictory meaning, however, is equally operative though not so obvious. The total separation of the reading text from the editorial apparatus hints broadly that the reading text *is* the author's and not the editor's. If it is a critical edition, however, that is not true. From this point of view the backgrounding of the editorial work—hiding it from sight—is the most arrogant thing an editor can do. Structurally, the book says for the editor, "I have done it right; trust me."

Let us look by contrast at the Cornell Wordsworth. Although it has some appendices and though the mechanical transcriptions of documents are slightly separated from the reading texts, the edition never lets the reader forget that this is an edition of the poems and that other forms exist. The recto running heads proclaim the pages to contain "reading texts"— the clear implication being that there must be other texts to do other things with. At the bottom of every page are the alternative readings; these also are parts of the reading text. To be fair to the Cornell edition the student Jack Stillinger imagines pulling down Jared Curtis's edition and reading "I wandered lonely as a cloud" in its eighteen-line form need only look to the foot of the page to find the omitted stanza. The student may resist doing that or be timid about putting back that which the editor has dropped down but cannot escape the fact that the editor has been at work. One could say, then, that the meaning of apparatuses on the page itself is either that the editor is proud of the work and wants the reader to be constantly aware of it or that the editor is honest about the interventions in the text and anxious to give the reader all the information possible relevant to the reading text or texts.

I say all these things in spite of the format and meaning of the first four volumes of the William M. Thackeray edition, of which I am general editor. I only became aware of the important meanings of the relation between author's and editor's texts after the format for the Thackeray edition was set. My initial solution was twofold. First, there is a prominent notice to the reader at the beginning describing the purpose of the edition and drawing attention to the existence and uses of the textual apparatus. Second, I divided the apparatus into the part relating to what the author did to his text and the part that editors have done to it. Beginning with the fifth volume, the Thackeray edition has a new publisher (University of Michigan Press) and the first part of the apparatus, describing composition and revision, is now presented at the foot of the reading text, constantly reminding the user that the reading text is a construct that need not be taken as gospel. Concern about this possibility does not represent fear that some editorial decisions were wrong choices (no doubt some were) but that, inevitably, editors make choices where other "correct" options existed. That these choices can make significant differences in reader responses is amply demonstrated by the editors of the NN *Moby-Dick* when they trace the general tenor of reviews of the English and American first editions in part to the differences between the specific texts under review.

Between the poles represented by the Melville and Wordsworth editions is an infinite gradation. Like the Melville edition, the Cambridge Lawrence edition presents what it hopes will be taken as *the* text of Lawrence's works. The "General Editor's Preface" precedes the text in each volume, emphasizing the corruption and censorship Lawrence's texts have suffered and claiming that all that could humanly be done to rescue the texts has been done so that they "are as close as can now be determined to those he would have wished to see printed." But the presence of the editor is, after all, thus foregrounded; there is an editorial introduction preceding the author's text; and the text itself has line numbers in the margins, which any discerning reader must soon figure out are to aid in the cross-referencing of "author text" in the main body of the book and "editor text" in the apparatus.

By contrast, the meanings of the scholarly edition of Ada Cambridge's novel *A Woman's Friendship*, edited by Elizabeth Morrison as the first volume in "The [Australian] Colonial Texts Series," are anything but pretentious. Any Australian will know better than I the implications of the publisher's imprint, University of New South Wales Press, and of the series' institution of origin, the English Department of University College at the Australian Defence Force Academy. But it will be immediately apparent to any user in the world that this work is not long on pretension. It is a paperback, shorter and thinner than any of the other editions I have mentioned. It is an elegant paperback, with flaps like a dust wrapper, but the flap text does not claim anything extravagant for the edition—only that it is "a careful rendering of the newspaper text, with an extended introduction and notes." In short, the book does not claim much for itself by its outward appearance. One clutches at straws to see ways in which it could be thought to be bold: it is part of a series calling itself "The Colonial Text Series" (CTS)—is that bold because it is "the" series, not merely "a" series? Is it brash because it left out the word *Australian* to distinguish itself from other English-language colonies? These are hardly worth dwelling on. But *A Woman's Friendship* is, nevertheless, a scholarly edition and a careful rendering, indeed—though, for honesty's sake, I will admit that I found one typo in the text and disagreed with one niggling editorial intervention I thought unnecessary. Could it be significant that I waited to make specific complaints until I got to an edition that lacked a magisterial presence and that was edited by a woman? But these matters, too, are my subject: the meanings of the scholarly edition includes our reactions to the pretensions of the book and to the editor.

The text of *A Woman's Friendship* is lodged in this edition between the introductions, including the general editor's remarks and the explanatory notes and appendices. The general editor focuses on the series as a means to make reliable texts available where there were none available. As for the texts, he says they should "be considered as a combination of the copytext and apparatus." Although there is only one source text for *A Woman's Friendship*, the sincerity of the general editor's claim is attested by the fact that note numbers are used in the text to call the reader's attention to relevant editorial texts in the apparatus.

My sense of what this book means by its physical presence and its arrangement is this: here is a useful, inexpensive, unpretentious, clear, and scholarly presentation. It does not ask to be admired; it asks to be used. In this I see a bold statement. Here is a scholarly edition that is a "working copy," not a showpiece for the shelf. For years the textual critical establishment in the United States has been groaning and complaining because critics have not properly used the scholarly editions provided by the CEAA and CSE. They complain that critics prefer to cite paperback editions, either because the critics find them handier or because the critics want to cite what everyone is using. And as they complain they go on validating their own critical efforts by publishing monuments: tall, thick, heavy, respectable editions. It is pleasingly Australian that the Colonial Texts Series has taken a democratic course. Whether the Australian academic community realizes what a treasure, both real and potential, is represented in this series remains to be seen.

These editions have been examined in relation to the third reason for paying attention to the meaning of the books, particularly the implications of arrangements of author and editor texts, but a fourth and fifth reason have been obtruding themselves all along. The fourth relates to the questions: What books have been chosen? and do the choices deserve to be "edited as scholarly editions"? If we think that the editorial effort, the care for research and proofreading involved, the elegance of design and quality of printing and binding, is deserved only by our sacred texts or by texts of our sacred authors, then several propositions would follow: one is that, if there is a tall, heavy, reputable edition of a text, that text and its author have been canonized. By this standard *Wieland* by Charles Brockden Brown was for twenty years a more sacred or at least more honored work than Marcus Clarke's *His Natural Life*, for which there was no scholarly edition until the late 1990s, or even than Ada Cambridge's *A Woman's Friendship*, for which the scholarly edition is a paperback. Miles Franklin's *My Brilliant Career* is even further down the canonical ladder, by this standard, for, though it has been republished and is in print, it is a "mere reprint" without introduction or notes or any other editorial validation.

Second, it might seem logical to conclude that the honor of a full-scale edition on good paper, etc., is a tribute to the author and the text, whereas, in fact, it serves more effectively as a monument to the editors and the presses, demonstrating their mastery. Thus, many of the big American editions have been virtually ignored by the public to whom they were addressed but who go on preferring cheaper paperbacks and who seem content with available editions of authors not yet dignified by a scholarly edition.

These possible subtexts raise a fifth reason to be interested in the meaning of the scholarly edition, relating to the implied audience. Traditionally, the scholarly edition is undertaken and designed to "make the author's text more accurately and/or fully available to the reader." I think it is usually assumed this means that the edition user is one who reads the author's text or at least wishes to. But if we think of the author or "implied author" as addressing an implied reader through the text of the original edition, perhaps we should consider the editor or "implied editor" as addressing not the author's implied reader but the edition's implied user. What, in short, does a scholarly edition imply about its users, or what does the editor assume about the edition user?[10] The answer to this question will be different for each edition, but among the common ones are, surely, that the edition user will be grateful for the editorial effort, will study the text in relation to the apparatus, does not mind obfuscation from suppression of ambiguities or the physical contortions required in holding one's place in three or four sections of the book at once. Further, the assumption seems to be that the user is wealthy or does not mind checking a book out from a library for extended use in study.

These assumptions about edition users seem, of course, farfetched in some ways, and it is not uncommon to hear arguments in favor of reprint series emerging from these views of the reading public. We are told that readers use cheap books that they can own themselves and mark in, and we are told that the important thing is the author's text, not the elaborate apparatus obviously designed for scholars only. Two approaches to reprinting are defended in this way: one is to produce cheap reprints with perfunctory introductions designed to make the texts available as quickly and cheaply as possible (which is exemplified by the Virago series and Picador imprints); the other is to strip the scholarly edition of its scholarly apparatus and make the "established text" available by itself or with a simplified introduction in paperback. The latter approach is slower but only slightly less reprehensible than the former.

It is difficult to calculate the damage done by Virago, Picador, and other reprint houses. Their naïveté, often combined with an exploitive commercial motive, provides poorly proofread texts based on poorly selected source texts inadequately described. The user spends her or his money and gets who knows what—something that can be treated as the work of art but which all modern textual criticism indicates is not the work of art and which cannot be read by the vast majority of buyers with any sense of the provenance or operative contexts relevant to the works. Buying a cheap reprint of a book is rather like buying a cheap VCR with no instructions. Perhaps one of its functions can be fulfilled, but the full range of satisfying use is inaccessible. Not only has the cheap reprint closed doors

10. This idea was suggested to me by Stephanie Trigg, who heard a shorter presentation at the Bibliographical Society of Australia and New Zealand (BSANZ) conference, October 1989.

for the person who buys it; it closes the doors for replacement texts more intelligently and carefully produced because the temporary marketplace for those better texts has been usurped by material that any responsible consumer protection group would have recalled from sale.

Without going into tedious detail, one could point out that cheap reprints perpetuate texts with variant readings of which the user is unaware. For the user such reprints make a more or less shoddy linguistic text equivalent with the work itself. And it appears in new covers and a new date, having, in a sense, shrugged off the contexts of its origination. The importance of these deficiencies was brought home to me during a year teaching in Australia, when for the first time in my life I began reading Australian fiction. First on my list was Ada Cambridge's *A Woman's Friendship* in the Colonial Texts Series. The newspaper origins, the historical social setting of the work, the critical reception and reputation of the work, were described in the introduction, and a wealth of local references were explained in the notes. Further studies were indicated in the notes to the introduction. My experience of reading that book was made rich and satisfying without diminishing the pleasure of trying to work out the highly problematical ironic, or at least potentially ironic, "intent" of the text. From that experience I went to Miles Franklin's *My Brilliant Career* and Henry Handel Richardson's *The Getting of Wisdom*, both of which are available only in cheap reprints without introductions, notes, or description of the text. Both were curious and wonderful texts, but neither gave anything like the satisfaction of *A Woman's Friendship*, for, without the aid of additional materials, I was required to hunt contexts and explanations on my own. And yet it could be argued that, as literary works, both are as good as or better than the Cambridge novel and are equally deserving of the status given by a scholarly edition—even a paperback one like the CTS provides. Cambridge's *The Three Miss Kings* is equally poorly served by its cheap reprint incarnation, though my opinion is that there are other books better deserving scholarly editorial attention—one of them being Cambridge's magnificent *A Marked Man* (or *A Black Sheep*, to use its proper title) available in the late 1980s from Pandora with a perfunctory introduction more critical than informative and a short note on the text more remarkable for its textual naïveté than for any helpful description of the provenance of the text. My reading of these two additional Cambridge works was influenced more by the edition of *A Woman's Friendship* than by any editorial expertise evident in the reprints.

Australia's literary heritage, before the advent of the Academy Library Edition, was not well served, reprints standing in where scholarly editions are needed; the literary heritage of the United States has suffered a different fate, being appropriated by monument builders.

Chapter 9

A Whirlwind of Possibilities

Therefore am I still
A lover of the meadows and the woods,
And mountains; and of all that we behold
From this green earth; of all the mighty world
of eye and ear—both what they half create,
And what perceive;

—William Wordsworth, "Tintern Abbey"

Disputants over the nature and goals of scholarly editing have arranged themselves on either side of a fault line separating the concrete from the ideal. One side maintains that texts are documents, concrete, real— immutable or in need of preservation from mutability. The other side holds that texts as documents are merely vehicles for the really real work, which remains an abstraction in relation to which documentary texts are always fallible instruments in need of restoration or else of improvements to fulfill an as yet unrealized potential. A consequence of this opposition is that questions about editorial tasks tend to suggest binary options: Is it the editor's job to find or to construct texts? to preserve or to restore? to archive or to emend? to chronicle the history of texts or to correct the ravages of fate and time? to preserve achievement or to pursue intention? Editors cannot do both simultaneously.

The outlines of such disputes become clearer when seen from the broader perspective offered by a meditation on the relations among imagination, perception, and "the concrete." Concepts useful to such a meditation include fancy, judgment, criticism, and understanding. Failure to meditate on and clarify these concepts leaves them lurking obstacles to clear thinking.

The Romantics considered imagination to be a faculty of mind enabling the apprehension of truth. Coleridge famously defines imagination as the power of mind to find coherence in the chaos of sensations. Imagination, however, was for the Romantics not a creative faculty as such; it allowed one to discover the coherence that is there (not to construct a coherence that will do). The "coloring of the imagination," which Wordsworth praises so, is less an admission that imagination provides us with a way to hold the concrete—thus, a biasing faculty—than it is a heightening instrument accenting the truth in order to enable our perception to penetrate to "true" significance. Even Shelley's less hopeful vision of imagination in the guise of intellectual beauty maintains the notion that perception enabled by the imagination is truth gathering about a mutable, transient, variable world that *is there*.

Coleridge and his contemporaries were well aware of the fundamental problems of perception—the inability of the subject to prove (test or demonstrate) the object, the impossibility of verifying the accuracy of one's perceptions and communicating them to another person. But faith in imagination and rationality was strong, and there were few if any who were willing to say that pragmatism would suffice in the absence of absolutes. The desire to know for sure, or to operate as if one did know or could know, dies very slowly and revives with each generation.

Nevertheless, a general faith in the magical ability of the imagination to reveal inherent truth has all but disappeared. Perception's limitations are more difficult to ignore. Relation (relativity) has become more important than object (objectivity). Imagination is understood to be the faculty of constructing our universe or, perhaps more pointedly, the faculty of holding and understanding our world in ways we also recognize to be culturally, experientially, and psychologically tailored. Truth has become relative as confidence fades in our ability to apprehend the concrete unmediatedly. But the desire for absolutes, for stability, for the integrity guaranteed by "solid facts" continues and may in fact grow as theories of uncertainty continue to undermine confidence in truth seeking and truth saying.

Imagination remains an organizing faculty with the capacity to produce insights that make the worlds of our experience cohere, but our sense of what it is that has cohered is less grandiose, less certain. We seem more willing to hold the world tentatively, to subject our insights to truth tests; particularly, we hold them to pragmatic standards. We seem always to search for the new imaginative insights that will replace or at least improve the old—even as we realize the new one may not be the true one.

Just as religious orthodoxies in Victorian England rigidified in both dogma and behavior when under attack from theories of evolution and the higher criticism, so modern editorial theory and practice, at a time when new visions arise to question the nature of physical texts, has tended to rigidify in some circles, in which texts are treated either as literary icons, raised to a level of sanctity, or as material objects whose historicity and stability serve as anchors to the unbridled imagination of interfering editors. The questions, however, seem inevitable, and it seems the better part of wisdom as well as of valor to face them and accept the consequences of thought. Recently, the questions have focused on the relations between physical texts (documents) and abstract concepts of them. Which is the "work"—what the author intended or what the reader appropriated? And do documents constitute the work, or do they just represent it?[1]

Imagination has a two-tiered role to play in the case of written texts. The first, almost universally acknowledged role of imagination in interpretation holds that the meanings or significances of texts are explored, expanded, extrapolated, and all but determined from one or more of a vast array of critical positions in currency, from old to new historicism, from New Criticism to Marxism and feminism, from deconstruction and reader response to psychological and mythographical approaches. Each methodological approach puts a perceptible, analyzable "spin" on a text. It is easy to see that the imagination is a constructing, sorting, organizing faculty when one assumes that an interpretation is "predetermined" by the ideology that generates it. Literary criticism is self-consciously imaginative—that is, constitutive of meanings and significances in a world that is made, not found.

But the second-tier role of imagination relative to written texts is far from universally recognized, though it may, on examination, seem more fundamental. Literary critics frequently take texts (documents) as givens, unproblematical and trustworthy. Textual critics, on the other hand, practice the art of constituting texts from the coincidental combination of lacuna and plethora of textual material that did not or did survive. Where the evidence is lacking, textual critics supply learned conjectures; where it is

---

1. See, for example, Tanselle, *Rationale;* and "Textual Criticism and Deconstruction"; and David Greetham's response, "[Textual] Criticism." See also West, "Fair Copy, Authorial Intention, and Versioning"; Donald Reiman, "'Versioning': The Presentation of Multiple Texts"; Paul Eggert, "Document and Text: The 'Life' of the Literary Work and the Capacities of Editing"; Tim William Machan, "Work and Text"; and Gunter Martens, "What Is a Text?"

overabundant, they sort and select. How such textual construction is done depends significantly on how the relations between documents and works have been imaginatively conceived. For the trusting reader who believes textual criticism to be an arcane specialization best left to others, the effects can be quite significant, though many remain unaware of them.

A brief, oversimplified survey of alternative ways to imagine the coherence and integrity of texts at the level of textual criticism will demonstrate the effects of textual criticism's imaginative frameworks on what "the text" is considered to be. There was a time when the text was almost universally conceived as the product of an author who, over time, worked toward the fulfillment of a work's potential perfection. Composition went through drafts, each better than the last, till publication made the work complete. Revised editions usually were thought to continue the process, so that a scholarly editor of fifty years ago would routinely pick as base text the last publication in the author's lifetime to insure that the author's final intentions would be incorporated. It was a matter of faith that the process of creation was continuous and progressive. Such editors imagined the product of composition to be the fulfillment of an ideal. Some of them imagined the editor's role to be that of a ministrant who continued the process by taking as a starting point the most advanced form of the work produced with authorial input and continuing, by editorial action, to polish and hone the finer points of grammar, spelling, and punctuation.[2]

Reacting against this imaginative vision of things, the "new bibliography" of McKerrow, Greg, and Bowers rejected the impressionism and cavalier ignorance of the facts of textual transmission that characterized the work of their predecessors.[3] They demonstrated that authorial input in the creative process was restricted in most cases to prepublication activity, that compositorial and editorial input was often contrary to the continued development of authorial intention, and that the processes of reprinting, even in the case of revised editions, was frequently one of increased corruption, particularly of a text's "accidentals" or "formal elements." They argued that editors had been choosing the most corrupted form of the work as their starting point—perhaps because they couldn't be bothered to determine exactly what had happened, for that would require full collations of manuscripts, proofs, and all the extant "authorized" editions of the

2. See, for example, Saintsbury's Oxford edition of the works of W. M. Thackeray; Brett-Smith and Jones's Halliford edition of the works of Thomas Love Peacock; or, very recently, Haight's Clarendon edition of George Eliot's *Mill on the Floss*.

3. See, particularly, R. B. McKerrow; W. W. Greg, *Calculus;* and "The Rationale of Copy-Text"; and Fredson Bowers, *Bibliography and Textual Criticism;* and his widely distributed essay "Textual Criticism."

work. Thus, both science and righteousness were on the side of a positivist new bibliography. Significantly, however, the overall imaginative vision of the relation between document and work remained unchanged: the editorial goal was to capture or recapture the work as it had developed under conscious authorial control toward the fulfillment of artistic potentials. The editor's task remained to produce the "best" or "most reliable" text of the work and to provide in apparatuses a record of the editorial process. Briefly in the late 1960s and early 1970s there seemed to be consensus among American editors, particularly those associated with the Center for Editions of American Authors (CEAA), that *best* and *most reliable* were synonymous with the author's final intentions.

A major shift in imaginative vision and editorial goals occurred with the growing consciousness that for many works the goal or intention of the author was to fulfill the needs or demands of a particular audience. The process of revision was not, in such cases, dictated solely by an abstract artistic potential for the work of art, conceived as some muse-directed or mystical activity that would end in a well-wrought urn or sacred literary icon. Instead, the writing was directed toward a specific market and would change not only because of political, moral, aesthetic, or intellectual changes in the author but also because of the publisher's sense of new target audiences. This altered vision of textual production affected textual critics in various ways: editors might with justice produce multiple texts for the same work, each edited to reflect a particular moment in the "life" of the work. This was not a simple shift from one paradigm to another, for it remained obvious that authors and compositors occasionally worked at cross-purposes, that any publication is susceptible to flaws rendering the intentions of authors—and of publishers, too, for that matter—unrealizable. Thus, authorial intentions for each version became a thread to extract (or construct) from surviving documents.[4]

Two other problems faced editors pursuing practical ways to implement their new imaginative vision of works into printed scholarly editions. The first is that multiple texts in printed form cannot avoid hierarchic presentation. Alternate texts might be of equal validity and interest, but they cannot be presented equally: even parallel texts have a first and a second, and sometimes other readings; and parallel presentation of most long

---

4. See, for example, Jerome McGann, *The Textual Condition;* and *Black Riders;* George Bornstein, "'It is myself that I remake'"; and C. Deirdre Phelps, "The Edition as Art Form"; and "The Edition as Art Form in Textual and Interpretive Criticism." Fredson Bowers provides an excellent example, which he tries to arbitrate into a single text in "Authorial Intention and Editorial Problems." I comment on Bowers's example in chapter 7.

works is too expensive. Footnotes and apparatuses at the back of the books are obviously in subordinate positions. The second problem was that the scholarly edition had itself become a discrete entity. A scholarly edition of *Moby-Dick* or *Ulysses* or any other work was, willy-nilly, an edition of the work and not the work itself. Self-consciousness alone precludes the presentation of the work itself.[5] And yet the idea of works in multiple forms coexisted with the insights that the new bibliography revealed about conflicts between composition (authorial) and publication (production) processes, so the task of editors just became more complex.

The more complex the imaginative vision of the relations between documents and works became, the greater became the pressure to cut through to a simpler vision. Editors needed a way to avoid the complexity of juggling too many textual versions of a work at once. I remember the mingled exhilaration and dismay with which it first dawned on me, in editing the works of W. M. Thackeray, that, if I were to maintain not only that the final manuscript form but also that the first edition form and the revised edition form of his works all had textual and artistic integrity, I would have to edit each version in turn and provide an apparatus that would make each text equally available to users of my edition. Without that simple insight editors could treat the apparatus as a dumping ground for superseded textual forms; in the light of that insight the apparatus comes to bear the functional weight of an ordered, imaginatively coherent set of alternatives to the reading text. The apparatus can no longer be a record of what the editor had done or what the editor had considered and rejected in the process of "determining" the final text; it became a guide to the progression of composition and production processes creating a succession of versions. Reading text and apparatus text combine to represent the whole work.

Textual histories of Thackeray's works were simple compared to those of James Joyce or William Wordsworth. It dawned on many editors that the concept of multiple alternative texts also multiplied the editorial task as long as it was conceived in the imaginative framework provided by the new bibliography: each work became a series of versions, each represented by flawed texts in need of editing. Furthermore, the new vision of multiple texts in process, rather than finished works as products, surpassed the limits of mechanical printing to accommodate a scholarly edition. There was no "fair" way to present multiple versions in printed form without implying

---

5. Hans Zeller arrives at the same conclusion on different grounds when he distinguishes between "Record and Interpretation," noting that an editor cannot (re)present "record" but can only "describe" it or "interpret" it (42–44).

a hierarchy. Practical and material considerations dictated that it was time for another major paradigm shift.

And here is where the fault line between the concrete and the ideal in textual studies is most palpable. It is here that the imaginative vision that had provided the organizing and energizing force for two generations of editors was put most fiercely to the test of pragmatics. If the imaginative framework in which the basic editorial problem was conceived in terms of a belief that concrete documents normally fail to represent fully the ideal work could be replaced by an imaginative framework in which that failure could be erased, editing would become possible again.

The first step in effecting such a shift was to discredit the standard view of editorial goals and procedures—those championed by Greg, Bowers, and Tanselle. Hubris being what it is, it was not difficult to find vulnerable points in the language supporting editorial work of the type that has unfortunately been dismissively called the Greg-Bowers school of editing. "The calculus of variants" and "definitive editions" were just two of many phrases taken to suggest that Fredson Bowers, G. Thomas Tanselle, and the Center for Editions of American Authors all thought (wrongly, of course) that their brand of scholarly editing was scientific, reliable, and definitive. With one exception the attackers seemed carefully or perversely to avoid mention of the central phrase of the new bibliography: "critical editing." But when the task is to make room for a new paradigm, it is, of course, counterproductive to be fair; one focuses on the weaknesses of prevailing thought that will make a new position not only viable but also inevitable.[6]

The most important document in the attack on the new bibliography or the "Greg-Bowers" school was Jerome J. McGann's *Critique of Modern Textual Criticism* (1983). There McGann tried to show that, historically, the concept of ideal texts fulfilling a potential indicated by documentary texts was a modern anomaly, a blip in the history of textual editing. He claimed that the term *critical editing* had been appropriated and redefined by Bowers to accommodate this Johnny-come-lately form of editing. Bowers had defined a critical edition as one in which critical judgment was employed in the process of emending a copy-text to produce

---

6. The apparent rejection of "copy-text editing" was more apparent in the discussions at the Palimpsest conference at the University of Michigan in November 1991 than in the published proceedings, edited by Bornstein and Williams, but the demise of such editing and of the influence of Fredson Bowers was prematurely announced in the proceedings of the 1990 Texas editing conference, edited by Oliphant and Bradford. See Hill's and Greetham's reviews of Oliphant.

an edited, eclectic text. McGann claimed that the term *critical editing* historically meant no more than reconstructing the texts of lost documents. Critical judgment in his view was restricted to inferences about what lost documents had said. Any attempt to guess at what the text should have said or was meant to have said, but never did, was an arrogant, misguided editorial activity.

The second step in preparing the way for a new vision of editorial goals was to establish some alternative to authorial intention as the central focus of editorial endeavor. Marxist criticism provided a useful concept: economic social materialism. Building on the idea that multiple texts are justified in part because authors and publishers enter agreements to reach certain audiences, it was an easy leap to the conclusion that the author never had been, in fact, and so should no longer be considered, the central player in the production of texts. Social and economic forces combine not only to shape the products we call literary art but to make these products possible in the first place. In this view authorship as a profession has grown because markets made it a viable profession to follow. Authors, to be successful, must write what the public wants to read. Publishers help authors understand what must be written. In short, publishers hire authors to fulfill the needs of the public. Authors are, therefore, not romantic geniuses, pursuing the dictates of the Muses and exercising their roles as the unacknowledged legislators of the world; they are employees in a corporate world helping to package a salable commodity.[7]

It follows from this extraordinary, imaginative transformation of the author from controlling genius to hired hand that the physical documents produced by socializing book production processes *are* the works of art. According to this view, until the social and economic forces have combined to produce the work, it remains unfinished, unfulfilled raw material. But when author, publisher, and production crews have coalesced, they finish the work together. It is, therefore, not the task of the editor to ask if the author's intentions have been fulfilled. By the light of this perception it is patently the case that the material text *is* the work. It follows that multiple texts result from new marketing opportunities, rather than from new promptings by the Muse.

---

7. One might note that the history of copyright legislation has involved a steadily increased rejection of the "work for hire" concept implied by this argument (by which the publisher as employer should own the rights). The law establishes authorial rights in "intellectual property"—an abstraction with multiple potential but, in every case, incidental physical manifestations.

What needs teasing out at greater length is the implications of the controversy over whether written works of art are primarily documentary (i.e., material) or primarily ideal (i.e., critical or conceptual). The three relatively recent paradigm shifts in editorial theory relevant here have been described in detail in previous chapters. A brief summary will introduce a closer analysis of the imaginative dimensions of editorial theory. The first, initiated by Greg's "Rationale of Copy-Text" (1950) established the ground on which the pursuit of authorial intention (an ideal not yet achieved) was distinguished from the reconstruction of a lost archetype (a historical text to be restored) as an editorial goal. The second paradigm shift, celebrated without conscious orchestration at the 1985 conference of the Society for Textual Scholarship, established the ground on which multiple texts, versions, and process were distinguished from single, definitive editions as editorial responsibilities. This second paradigm, however, remained authorial in orientation. The third shift has yet to be properly named. Its source, quite different from the second, resides in the recognition of the social implications of production processes and in the material significance of literary artifacts. Its emphasis is not on creative processes fulfilling an ideal but on the meanings of production—its processes and its outcomes—as a social element.

Having provided the initial shockwaves that created the movement away from ideal texts toward concrete texts, Jerome McGann has continued to write influentially about a vision for editing that consists primarily of archiving and annotating existing documentary texts. He is implementing that vision in the Dante Gabriel Rossetti archive, which has attracted attention and imitators.[8] And there are other theorists who have bolstered the division between the concrete and the ideal in textual criticism.[9] It is a dichotomy worth exploring, for the motives that drive the new theories seem at times inadequate for the effects being wrought.

Jack Stillinger, for example, provides what he calls a "practical theory of versions," in which he distinguishes between "Ideal texts: versions of the mind" and "Real texts: versions on paper." In doing so, he attempts to elaborate a rationale for practical editorial procedures. In place of the critical examination of textual evidence to ferret out the processes or sequences of authorial intentions, we now are encouraged to posit a "critical" sequence of documents in such a way that each new document is seen as a new version of the work with dimensions both linguistic and bibliographic. That

---

8. http://jefferson.village.virginia.edu/rossetti/rossetti.html

9. See especially essays by Hans Zeller, Gunter Martens, and Siegfried Scheibe in Gabler, Bornstein, and Pierce, eds., *Contemporary German Editorial Theory.*

is, the work is seen as consisting not only of its verbal elements but also of the implications of its physical embodiment, for which type font, leading, width of margins, quality of paper, type of binding, and publishers' imprints become significant indicators of how the work is to be taken.

As I have pointed out briefly elsewhere ("Editing Thackeray," 366–67) but wish to elaborate here, this shift from "multiple intended versions" to "multiple sequenced documents" is not always accomplished cleanly or convincingly. Stillinger distinguishes theoretically between multiple versions and sequenced documents, but in practice he invariably equates the two. He writes, theoretically, "I have arbitrarily taken substantive difference—that is, difference in wording—as the principal rule for distinguishing one version from another" (*Coleridge,* vii). But his listing of versions of "Frost at Midnight" notes that version 5 is "substantively identical" to version 3 (p. 55), version 9 is "substantively identical" to version 7, and version 10 is "substantively the same" as version 9 (p. 56). It would seem, by his theoretical statement, that documents 7, 9, and 10 represented the same version, but, instead, he has each, though substantively identical, represent its own version. Regardless of his theoretical distinctions, version and document are, in his practice, coeval; each new document is a new version. Perhaps, each production constitutes a new version because the meaning of the edition is defined to include the ways in which it indexes the economics of marketing and the reception of a literary work of art.

A question one might want to ask at this point is: Why does the recognition of the social implications of production seem to lead editors like Jerome McGann and Jack Stillinger and, more recently, Donald Reiman, in *The Study of Modern Manuscripts,* to equate the work with the documents? McGann insists that the textual condition is physical, Stillinger finds a new version in every reincarnation of the text, and Donald Reiman deplores editors who emend. Why is it important in this paradigm for editors *not* to edit documents? Why and how does the recognition of the materiality of the symbols on the page entail the conclusion that the work is coeval with the document?

A partial answer might be found in some of the basic reasons this recent editorial fashion is attractive: first, since each document has its own "versional" integrity, emendation is no longer an important editorial task; no mixing or melding of variants is required or justified; therefore, agonizing over indifferent variants (those for which the evidence for intention is equally divided between two or more forms) is unnecessary. Second, refusal to emend avoids the charge that emendations made in the text represent nothing more than editorial preference—avoids it by agreeing with the charge. And third, the ideals of this new vision of texts can be adequately and elegantly presented in hypertext, multimedia computer formats.

There is a significant difference between Greg's editorial paradigm in which the *work* was "intended" and the *document* was an attempt to "represent" the intention, on the one hand, and this most recent materialist editorial paradigm in which the work is coeval with the document. In one the editor takes all the responsibility to produce the text the author wanted the public to have; in the other the editor abjures all responsibilities except that of collecting the evidence and giving a guided tour.

Put in this way, it looks like a choice between assuming a godlike authority, on the one hand, and adopting the coward's stance, on the other. The first choice entails pretending that the editor can know things no one can know, in order to make decisions on the reader's behalf, keeping readers ignorant, barefoot, and dependent. The second choice entails pretending that we know less than can be known, so that we will not have to make decisions that other editors or readers might find faulty.

The controversy is miscast when put in that way, for it reduces the alternatives to two, the adherents of each considering the other wrong. It is more productive to articulate clearly a variety of ways to define the work and then trace the consequences of each method of definition—the consequences of thinking, for example, of a work as existing in various versions, each identical with the document that contains it, represents it, or *is* it, and then, by contrast, to trace the consequences of thinking of a work as a voice that is embodied and re-embodied more or less well and with more and more attendant voices as the work is transmitted through various physical media.

Let us look at three fundamentally different ways of "locating the work." Using three methods, each with the potential to represent the work in a special way, seems less simplistic than using two methods, one of which must be wrong.

First, consider the idea that the work is either really or potentially equivalent only with its perfect embodiment, the well-wrought urn. This idea is currently out of favor, but for the sake of contrast we can contemplate it briefly. Consider what the editorial and interpretive implications would be if we believed that there might *be* a perfect work, a Platonic ideal, a potential perfection toward which author and collaborators worked, toward which the scholarly editor might lend a hand, and toward which the reader might aspire. This is a purely idealist conception. If one adopts it, then physical texts are merely (flawed) representations of "really real" texts that lie behind or beyond physical texts. The ideal reality of works would be the editorial goal—unreachable in objective terms though that might be.

Such an idea of texts seems quaint, if not downright eccentric these days. Flight from it to a second way to locate the text seems all but inevitable. The simplest positive statement of the social materialist position is that the work exists in multiple versions, each stably represented by a physical document: version and document are coeval. The arguments for this position I have summarized in *Scholarly Editing in the Computer Age* (chap. 8). They offer cogent objections to the idealist position, but reviewing them revealed why a simple leap from idealist "versions in the mind" to "real versions on paper" is also inadequate. Without repeating the analysis in *Scholarly Editing*, the arguments for the position are that physical documents are stable, works of art (normally) do not exist without them, arguments about the text can be referred to documents, authors are limited to that which can be represented in documents, and they cannot (or usually do not) write what the social engines of production will not print in documents, and the documentary products were originated and authorized by authors and hence represent the social consequences of authorial acts. It follows, therefore, that versions of the work are coeval with documents of the work and that disputes over *version* can be anchored, in the same way as disputes over *text,* in the physical document.

It strikes me, however, that the most compelling argument in favor of this conclusion is the unattractiveness of its popularly conceived alternative. To speak of the "intended text" as the version, the materialists point out, is to speak of a nonextant form about which no two people are likely to agree. Agreeing on a starting point, a reliable text, is an obviously desirable thing for anyone who accepts the notion that discussion should arise from common ground and that disagreements that stem from dislocated sources are a waste of time. If critic A argues for a position relative to text A, and critic B refutes the argument relative to text B, the critical debate becomes a laughingstock. To argue against intended texts and in favor of material texts serves doubly to simplify the editorial task and solidify the base of critical activities.

To the idea that a newly edited, scholarly, eclectic edition provides such a solid basis for critical disputes, the anti-idealists can reserve the right to assess the authority by which each production process was undertaken, choosing to value the social contracts between the authors and their original publishers more highly than the (spurious?) authority claimed for the new edition.

It appears to me that social materialists, pursuing the concrete, can be as arbitrary as proponents of any other imaginative vision of the relation between documents and works. In fleeing the idealists' imaginative construction, one is not limited to believing that the work is coeval with its physical documents. That is one alternative, but it is not, in my opinion, the best one and certainly is not the only one.

I come, then, to a third position—one that I believe both repudiates the idealism of which Greg and Bowers have been accused and recognizes the importance of the facts pointed out by the social materialists. Moreover, it repudiates the social materialists' implicit claim that equating version with document achieves objectivity.[10] This position occupies middle ground, both theoretically and practically, between the positions represented by the so-called Greg-Bowers-Tanselle school on the Right and the so-called social materialists (McGann, Stillinger, and Reiman, to mention only the Romanticists) on the Left.

This view holds that there is a significant distinction to be made between works and physical representations of them. It does not hold, however, that there is any essential or "extant" conceptual or performance work that is the real work. It cannot, therefore, hold that such an abstract ideal can serve as the standard by which physical representations of the work should be or could be measured. It is fundamental to this view that the "textual condition" be fully recognized as participating in a variety of larger "human existential conditions": physical, social, performative, conceptual, and communicative conditions. The physical copies of the work "index" (point to and result from) these other conditions in which works exist.

It is, for example, an undeniable fact that readers "read through" the physical text to a text of their own imagining, including the correction of typos and supposed typos. This text of their own imagining is not a pre-existing text "out there" that the reader's imaginings match; it is a product both of their skill in performing the text from the physical object given to them and of their personal experiences and their presuppositions about texts. Amateur readers or experienced textual editors or much-published literary critics—all, in their access to works, are limited to the text produced by their performance of the work relative to the physical document

10. No editor I know explicitly claims that any form of editing is "objective." But nearly every editor who has argued against idealist pursuits of authorial intentions has done so on the grounds that such pursuits are subjective and variable. The claim is that limiting editorial activity to archiving and annotating avoids the evils of subjectivity inherent in emending. The implication is, therefore, that equating work with document is not subjective, that is, objective.

before their eyes, performances influenced by their experiences and notions. These are ideal texts in the sense that they lack concrete existence, but they are *not* ideal in the sense of a perfection that transcends the limitations of the merely concrete.

It would be absurd, as Stillinger has already amusingly pointed out, to equate any reader's performance, complete with distractions and interruptions, with "the work itself," but it remains true that any reader's experience of the work is limited to his or her performance, sifted as much as possible from distractions and interruptions. To say the work is coeval with the physical copy of it is, in practical terms, to say that it must remain forever on the page—usually about eighteen inches away from the reader—objective, inert, and inaccessible. It may be important to note that works are external to readers who can "look at a book" in the way one looks at a vase, painting, or sculpture and that they can "listen to a book" in the way one listens to music, but it is also important to note that readers create an internalized form of text by "performing texts," interpreting as they go, with far greater responsibility for the experience than is involved in listening and looking.[11] And editors are readers before they are editors.

If we look for analogies, it might be better to say that the text for a poem or for a novel is like a recipe for a cake. The author probably "made a cake" and wrote out the recipe for it. Now the reader comes and uses the recipe to make the same cake or reasonable replica of it. A reader who wants to have the cake again must go to the recipe and follow it again to produce a new replica of the original. No two cakes are the same cake. The real cake is not any one of the recipes for it, nor is it any of the cakes produced from the recipes. One who eats a cake and then eats another cake made from the same recipe might pronounce judgments about which cake was better. Different eaters can make pronouncements about the cakes they have made and eaten. But these judgments are not the cake, nor are they verifiable. All another person can do is perform the acts involved in turning the recipe into an experience of it and judge other critics' accounts of their experiences by comparison.

Manuscripts, proofs, first editions, reprints, revised editions, and scholarly editions are physical documents that are indicators or recipes for further literary experiences. Any reader is dependent on the particular physical copy that is the basis of her or his performance. Variant documents can

11. This is not to say that personal skills and physical limitations are unimportant in visual and audial arts. But the visual arts are more immediate than textual ones, and audial arts are "aided" by performers (frequently very skilled performers). Reading a poem is a closer equivalent to reading a musical score than to listening to a recording.

have significant variant effects on a reader's performance of the work. But so too does any reader's skill in reading, any particular understanding of the social implications of the material work in hand, and any perception of the communicative conditions of the work.

It is this last element of the 'textual condition that has gotten short shrift from the social materialists. The communicative conditions are complex, and I have touched on a number of them in chapter 3, but I would like to focus here more meditatively on two issues: First, that of agency, or speaker, and, second, as suggested at the outset of this chapter, on the concept of understanding.

We all recognize the ways in which our understandings of given texts are agent dependent when we say, "That argument sounds like so-and-so" or "Smile when you say that, stranger" or "Coming from you, that is a compliment." Readers of novels and poems always posit a speaker for the text of the work and judge what they read by the character of the speaker. Watchers of plays must pay attention to which character speaks, or they are lost. Playgoers often also create an "agency filter" for understanding what the characters are saying by remembering that the author made them say it. My experience, for example, of David Mamet's *Oleana,* while not very sophisticated, was very much filtered by the fact that the argument between the teacher and the student had been constructed. My point is *not* that Mamet alone constructed the argument; he may, for all I know, have had help writing those texts. My point is that readers and even playgoers find their experiences of texts to be agent dependent.

Agency—who said it, to whom, in what tone of voice, to what purpose —is a slippery concept when applied to written texts. It opens that ugly can of worms intention again. Many critics are willing to leave "meaning" in a sort of limbo in which critics grapple for the most interesting or persuasive or exotic or practical interpretation without claiming authorial authority for their endeavors. But they want the words on the page—the basis from which critics begin—to be stable and reliable. They wish to be able to take the text for granted while being free to find (or create) meaning by whatever interpretive strategies.

Now it may not matter to the social materialist or the deconstructionist who the author was, but, if it were a communication that mattered to them, they would want to know "who said that" and they would want to know whether the words could be relied upon. But the social materialists' insistence on accepting the document as produced by the prevailing means of production is equivalent to accepting potluck texts. The idea that the document is the only thing with textual integrity reflects a very limited understanding of the textual conditions (plural). The integrity of documents is easy to see, to hold, to contemplate. In fact it takes only the most rudimentary intelligence to understand documentary integrity.

The integrity of agency is not much more difficult to understand in ordinary life. All we have to do is be accused of having said something we did not say or of having done something we did not do in order to understand and feel the significance of the integrity of agency. But not even a court of law can insure the integrity of agency. Producing a text that says what the author said or what the author wanted to say or what the author wanted help in saying—none of these can be done with surety. But that does not mean that the integrity of agency is not important or that it should not be pursued by editors. There may be other valuable ways to edit, but they need not be supported at the expense of editions that emend texts so that they more accurately represent the voice of one or another of its authorizing agents.

Given the slipperiness of the concept of textual agency and given the virtual impossibility of objectivity in producing a text that is "true" to one of its authorizing agents (such as the author), it is understandable that editors and readers should want some solid, reliable, concrete ground. But I think the desire for such a footing does not make the social materialists' offer of the document a logically acceptable solution. A brief meditation on "understanding" suggests an imaginative view of the textual condition that precludes solidity and concreteness.

Most, if not all, reactions to any text can be subsumed under one of three headings: understanding, misunderstanding, and failure either to understand or to misunderstand. Responses to texts fit into these categories or a combination of them (partial misunderstanding, etc.).[12] Misunderstanding, unless it is willful and deliberate, feels like understanding, being recognized as misunderstanding only when a new understanding replaces the old or when someone we take to be an authority refutes our understanding. A refuted understanding (i.e., a misunderstanding now recognized as such) may be replaced by confusion (failure to understand) or by a new understanding—which may itself be a new misunderstanding. A failure to understand may result from irreconcilable signals or from indifference. The author of the text might deliberately send irreconcilable signals, or a reader might just find them to be irreconcilable, either through lack of patience or lack of knowledge, skill, or experience.

---

12. The idea, basically John Searle's, is initially mentioned in chapters 3 and 4.

The concept of "mis"-understanding presupposes that a "correct" understanding is desirable. Such a presupposition is not universally subscribed to, but strong inclinations to seek a correct understanding attend certain kinds of communicative acts. Promises, treaties, and contracts, for example, are worthless without a concept of correct or at least reliable mutual understanding. The arcane language of legal contracts, often taken by ordinary folk to be obfuscation designed to render lawyers necessary, is usually defended as an attempt to render only one understanding of the text possible. Disputes over contracts or treaties demonstrate both the importance of reliability and the difficulty of attaining it. Letters, whether informal or formal, carry a signature that usually indicates a guarantor of the message incorporated. Public letters, such as those to the editor of a newspaper, carry the form of signed letters, but one wonders occasionally whether the guarantor can be serious, as in letters to advice columns signed "Lonely in Peoria." Ransom notes are usually unsigned and are often made out of other messages, as when the words or letters are cut from newspapers and rearranged to make the new message (thus rendering them both anonymous and unoriginal), but these attempts to disguise the guarantor do not diminish the intense interest of involved parties in the correct understanding of what was meant by the "writers" of the ransom messages. Sermons, political speeches, and sweepstakes announcements (that you may already have won five million dollars) are always problematic. Some texts, not outright lies, were meant to be misunderstood or to be misleading. Does the text mean what it says literally, or must it be interpreted? (To the laity some texts do not need to be interpreted, that activity being needed only for texts that cannot be trusted or easily understood. Bus tickets, for example, are usually thought not to need interpretation because their message—date, destination, price, bus company—are unproblematic, unambiguous, not deceitful.) Graffiti is frequently unsigned and insincere, its authors apparently not caring if any particular reader "gets it" so long as some reader gets a kick out of it. Some forms of art objects fall in the same provocative rather than communicative mode. Sacred texts are often thought to be literally true and, hence, are said not to need interpretation, but for the most part one person's literal interpretation appears to others, especially unbelievers, to be a rigid or narrow interpretation.

In all the examples given so far, except some kinds of graffiti, the desire or need for a correct or mutual interpretation generally leads participants in the script acts to find satisfaction only in what they can consider correct understanding. Such readers generally abhor misunderstandings, disagreements about understanding, or puzzlement. The characteristic indications of satisfaction by participants is a nod of the head, a smile, or a grunted "Aha!" But one should note that satisfaction is available to those who misunderstand as long as they think they understand. Hence, one could say that satisfaction, not actual communication, is the mark of a successful reading performance. "Actual communication" might take place, but one could not know for sure that it had.

So-called literary texts are always problematic. Were they meant to mean something in particular? Were they meant to provoke meanings of various kinds? Does it matter whether they were meant to mean anything if, in fact, they can be made to mean either something in particular or various things?

When one considers both the indeterminacy of the *meaning* of texts and the mixed and indeterminate *agency* of the texts, it is small comfort that documents offer relatively stable, material, objective, immutable texts. "So what?" one asks. What have we gained by observing that a document is physically stable? A document amounts to no more than a snapshot in the production processes of texts, a snapshot that frequently obscures or fails to identify the authorizing agent for any particular physical sign on the page. If we don't know who authorized it, how can we know what it signifies? The textual condition is one of abstraction, suspense, and tension. Texts, communications, interpretations, and satisfactions about them take place in a whirlwind of possibilities.

The editor who stops with saying that the social contract validates the product that is the first edition is absolved of responsibility for the integrity of the agency of the texts. So, too, is the editor whose work stops with archiving and annotating the concrete documentary texts, rejecting "ideal" concepts of the work. Such editors perform valuable work, but they offer no more than starting places, and they leave much of the really significant editorial task undone.[13]

It takes courage, criticism, intelligence, and humility to edit a text so that it represents integrity of voice or agency. And it is not damaging to

---

13. In fairness one should note that archiving texts is a difficult, expensive operation that can be done sloppily or well and that annotation can be far more useful and revealing than the critical melding of all source texts into one eclectic text. It should further be acknowledged that the editorial task I see unfulfilled in "archival editions" is considered by its advocates to be a task readers should be free to undertake for themselves. Yet, having produced a number of critical editions myself and having reviewed a number of them, I know the task of editing for the integrity of agency or voice is frequently a monumental task that few if any readers could undertake. Readers can, however, understand what an editor has done to a text and why; they can find the results of critical editing that produces texts that never achieved fulfillment before to be very useful.

admit that a courageous editor who creates such a text has created only another recipe for the work. Even editors who avoid emendation, perhaps in the hope of avoiding subjectivity, can do no more than provide a recipe—a text—that readers can use to perform the work and to compare their performance of that edition with their performances of other editions or with the accounts other readers have given of their own reading performances.

Editors who acknowledge the complexity of the textual conditions (emphasis on the plural) will include preservation and replication of significant documentary texts among the important goals of editing. And they will include production of newly edited texts emended to represent, as best they can, the integrity of one voice or a collection of certain melded voices, even when that means mixing the texts of several documents.

Perhaps this would be a good place to admit that the fault line between the concrete and the ideal does not actually exist. It is a metaphor that leads us as much astray as aright. McGann's campaign against Bowers's conception of the textual condition mirrors the view he opposes. The binary opposition of the idealist and materialist views seems constructed as much by the need to have an opposing or reflective view as by any need to understand the functions of writing, publishing, reading, and editing texts. The insights that energized Greg and Bowers by initiating their reactions to previous editorial endeavors are no less enabling because subsequent editors have encrusted "copy-text editing" with rigid methods and unrealizable goals. The insights that enabled McGann's, Reiman's, and Stillinger's (indeed, Gabler's, Robert Miller's, Speed Hill's, and myriad others') materialist views have already seen their own rigidities form and their own unrealizable goals formulated.

Editions, regardless of how they are perceived, are half-created by methods and goals. Each derives its coherence and its energy from an imaginative construction of textual materials and of the spaces they occupy. The text of each edition is determined by the coherences imagination casts in the form of editorial principles by which editors undertake the practical task of relating the work to the documents. Each procedure has its goals and its limitations. Right or wrong can be determined only within the limits of an "imaginatively" defined way of viewing texts and their functions.

Works Cited

Anderson, Sherwood. *Winesburg, Ohio.* 1919; reprint, New York: Boni and Liveright, 1922.

Austin, J. L. *How to Do Things with Words.* Oxford: Clarendon, 1962.

Baender, Paul. "Megarus ad lunam: Flawed Texts and Verbal Icons." *Philological Quarterly* 64 (Fall 1985): 439–57.

Barthes, Roland. "The 'Death' of the Author" (1968). *The Rustle of Language,* trans. Richard Howard, 49–55. New York: Hill and Wang, 1986.

———. "From Work to Text" (1971). *The Rustle of Language,* trans. Richard Howard, 56–68. New York: Hill and Wang, 1986.

Battersby, James. *Paradigms Regained.* University Park: Pennsylvania State University Press, 1991.

Beardsley, Monroe. *The Possibility of Criticism.* Detroit: Wayne State University Press, 1970.

Berger, Thomas L. "The New Historicism and the Editing of English Renaissance Texts." In *New Ways of Looking at Old Texts: Papers of the Renaissance English Text Society, 1985–1991,* ed. W. Speed Hill, 195–97. Binghamton, N. Y.: Medieval and Renaissance Texts and Studies, 1993.

Bloom, Allen. *The Closing of the American Mind.* New York: Simon and Schuster, 1987.

Booth, Wayne. *The Company We Keep: An Ethics of Fiction.* Berkeley: University of California Press, 1988.

Bornstein, George. "'It is myself that I remake': W. B. Yeats's Revisions to His Early Canon." In *Victorian Authors and Their Works: Revision Moti-*

228 / *Works Cited*

vations and Modes, ed. Judith Kennedy, 41–56. Athens: Ohio University Press, 1991.

Bornstein, George, and Ralph Williams, eds. *Palimpsest: Editorial Theory in the Humanities.* Ann Arbor: University of Michigan Press, 1993.

Bowers, Fredson. "Authorial Intention and Editorial Problems." *Text* 5 (1991): 49–61.

———. *Bibliography and Textual Criticism.* Oxford: Clarendon, 1964.

———. *Essays in Bibliography, Text and Editing.* Charlottesville: University Press of Virginia, 1975.

———. "Multiple Authority: New Problems and Concepts of Copy-Text." *Library,* 5th ser., 27 (1972): 81–115.

———. "Regularization and Normalization in Modern Critical Texts." *Studies in Bibliography* 42 (1989): 79–102.

———. "Remarks on Eclectic Texts." *Proof* 4 (1974): 13–58.

———. "McKerrow Rivisited." Review of Phillip Gaskell *New Introduction to Bibliography. Papers of the Bibliographical Society of America* 67 (1973): 109–24.

———. "Textual Criticism." In *The Aims and Methods of Scholarship in Modern Languages and Literatures,* ed. James Thorpe, 23–42. 2d ed. New York: Modern Language Association, 1970.

———. "Unfinished Business." *Text* 4 (1988): 1–11.

Boydston, Jo Ann. "In Praise of Apparatus." *Text* 5 (1991): 1–13.

Brantlinger, Patrick. "The French Lieutenant's Woman: A Discussion." *Victorian Studies* 15 (1972): 339–56.

Brett-Smith, H. F. B., and C. E. Jones, eds. *The Halliford Edition of the Works of Thomas Love Peacock.* 10 vols. London: Constable, 1924–34.

Brooks, Cleanth. *The Well-Wrought Urn.* New York: Harcourt, Brace, 1947.

Brown, Charles Brockden. *Wieland.* Ed. Sydney Krause and S. W. Reid. Kent: Kent State University Press, 1977.

Caldwell, Price. "Molecular Sememics: A Progress Report." *Meisei Review* 4 (1989): 65–86.

Center for Editions of American Authors (CEAA). *The Statement of Editorial Principles and Procedures.* New York: Modern Language Association, 1972.

Center for Scholarly Editions: An Introductory Statement. New York: Modern Language Association, 1977.

Clarke, Marcus. *His Natural Life.* Ed. Lurline Stuart. St Lucia: University of Queensland Press, forthcoming.

Cohen, Philip, ed. *Devils and Angels: Textual Editing and Literary Theory.* Charlottesville: University Press of Virginia, 1991.

Collins, Thomas J. Review of Browning edition. *Victorian Studies* 13 (June 1970): 441–44.

"Committee on Scholarly Editions: Aims and Policies." *PMLA* 100 (1985): 444–47.

Conradi, Peter J. "The French Lieutenant's Woman: Novel, Screenplay, Film." *Critical Quarterly* 24 (1982): 41–57.

Crane, Stephen. *The Red Badge of Courage.* Ed. Henry Binder, for *The Norton Anthology of American Literature,* 2: 802–906. New York: Norton, 1979.

Davis, Herbert. Review of *Studies in Bibliography,* vol. 15. *Review of English Studies* 12 (1961): 324–25.

Davis, Tom. "The CEAA and Modern Textual Editing." *Library* 32 (1977): 61–74.

Delery, Clayton J. "The Subject Presumed to Know: Implied Authority and Editorial Apparatus." *Text* 5 (1991): 63–80.

Doyle, Jeff. "McLeoding the Issue: The Printshop and Heywood's 'Iron Ages.'" In *Editing in Australia,* Ed. Paul Eggert, 163–65. Kensington: University of New South Wales Press, 1990.

D'Souza, Dinesh. *Illiberal Education: The Politics of Race and Sex on Campus.* New York: Free Press, 1991. Excerpted in the *Atlantic,* March 1991, 51–79.

Eaves, T. C. Duncan, and Ben Kimpel. "Richardson's Revisions of 'Pamela.'" *Studies in Bibliography* 20 (1967): 61–88.

Eco, Umberto. "After Secret Knowledge." *TLS* 22 June 1990, 666.

Eggert, Paul. "Document and Text: The 'Life' of the Literary Work and the Capacities of Editing." *Text* 7 (1994): 1–24.

———. "Social Discourse or Authorial Agency." Paper delivered at the ASPACLS conference, University of Sydney, 24 September 1993.

———. "Textual Product or Textual Process: Procedures and Assumptions of Critical Editing." *Editing in Australia,* 19–40. Kensington: University of New South Wales Press, 1990.

Eliot, George. *The Mill on the Floss.* Ed. Gordon Haight. Oxford: Clarendon Press, 1980.

———. *Romola.* Ed. Andrew Brown. Oxford: Clarendon Press, 1993.

Embree, Daniel, and Elizabeth Urquhart. "The Simonie: The Case for a Parallel-Text Edition." In *Manuscripts and Texts: Editorial Problems in Later Middle English Literature,* ed. Derek Pearsall, 49–59. Cambridge: Brewer, 1987.

Erdman, David V., ed. *The Complete Poetry and Prose of William Blake.* Berkeley: University of California Press, 1982.

Feltes, N. N. *Modes of Production of Victorian Novels.* Chicago: University of Chicago Press, 1986.

Fielding, Henry. *The History of Tom Jones.* In *The Wesleyan Edition of the Works of Henry Fielding.* Ed. William B. Coley et al. Middletown: Wesleyan University Press, 1975.

Finneran, Richard, ed. *The Literary Text in the Digital Age.* Ann Arbor: University of Michigan Press, 1996.

Foucault, Michel. "What Is an Author" (1969). Trans. Josué Harari. *The Critical Tradition,* ed. David H. Richter, 978–88. New York: St. Martin's Press, 1989.

Franklin, Benjamin. "Speech in the Convention at the Conclusion of Its Deliberations [read to the Convention by James Wilson of the Pennsylvania delegation]." *Writings,* 1139–41. New York: Library of America, 1987.

Gabler, Hans Walter. "Joyce's Text in Progress." *Texte: Revue de Critique et de Théorie Littéraire* 7 (1988): 227–47.

———. "On Textual Criticism and Editing: The Case of Joyce's Ulysses." In *Palimpsest: Editorial Theory in the Humanities,* ed. George Bornstein and Ralph Williams, 195–224. Ann Arbor: University of Michigan Press, 1993.

———. "The Text as Process and the Problem of Intentionality." *Text* 3 (1987): 107–16.

———. "Textual Studies and Criticism." In *Editing in Australia,* ed. Paul Eggert, 1–17. Kensington: University of New South Wales Press, 1990.

———. "Unsought Encounters." In *Devils and Angels: Textual Editing and Literary Theory,* ed. Philip Cohen, 153–66. Charlottesville: University Press of Virginia, 1991,

Gabler, Hans Walter, George Bornstein, and Gillian Borland Pierce, eds. *Contemporary German Editorial Theory.* Ann Arbor: University of Michigan Press, 1995.

Gaskell, Philip. *From Writer to Reader: Studies in Editorial Method.* London: Clarendon Press, 1978.

———. *A New Introduction to Bibliography.* Oxford: Clarendon Press, 1972.

———. "Night and Day: The Development of a Play Text." In ed. *Textual Criticism and Literary Interpretation,* Jerome J. McGann, 162–79. Chicago: University of Chicago Press, 1985.

Gatrell, Simon. "Hardy, House-Style, and the Aesthetics of Punctuation." In *The Novels of Thomas Hardy,* ed. Anne Smith, 169–92. London: Vision, 1979.

Gilbert, Sandra M., and Susan Gubar. "Masterpiece Theatre: An Academic Melodrama." *Critical Inquiry* 17 (1991): 693–717.

Goldfarb, Sheldon. "Repeated Discomposure: A Vanity Fair Textual Problem." *English Language Notes* 24 (1987): 34–36.

Greetham, David C. "Enlarging the Text." Review of Oliphant, ed., *New Directions. Review* 14 (1992): 1–33.

———. "Politics and Ideology in Current Anglo-American Textual Scholarship." *Editio* 4 (1990): 1–20.

———. "A Suspicion of Texts." *Thesis: The Magazine of the Graduate School and University Center* (City University of New York) 2, no. 1 (Fall 1987): 18–25.

———, ed. *Scholarly Editing: A Guide to Research.* New York: Modern Language Association, 1995.

———. "[Textual] Criticism and Deconstruction." *Studies in Bibliography* 44 (1991): 1–30.

Greg, W. W. "Bibliography—an Apologia." In *Collected Papers,* ed. J. C. Maxwell, 239–66. Oxford: Clarendon Press, 1966.

———. *A Calculus of Variants: An Essay on Textual Criticism.* Oxford: Clarendon, 1927.

———. "The Rationale of Copy-Text." *Studies in Bibliography* 3 (1950–51): 19–36; reprinted in *Bibliography and Textual Criticism,* ed. O M Brack Jr and Warner Barnes, 41–58. Chicago: University of Chicago Press, 1969.

Grigely, Joseph. *Textualterity: Art, Theory, and Textual Criticism.* Ann Arbor: University of Michigan Press, 1995.

———. "The Textual Event." In *Textualterity: Art, Theory, and Textual Criticism,* 89–119. Ann Arbor: University of Michigan Press, 1995.

Groden, Michael. "Contemporary Textual and Literary Theory." In *Representing Modernist Texts: Editing as Interpretation,* ed. George Bornstein, 259–286. Ann Arbor: University Michigan Press, 1992.

Hancher, Michael. Review of Browning edition. *Yearbook of English Studies* 2 (1972): 312–14.

———. "Three Kinds of Intention." *Modern Language Notes* 87 (1972): 827–51.

Harkness, Bruce. "Bibliography and the Novelistic Fallacy." *Studies in Bibliography* 12 (1958): 59–73.

————. Review of *Jane Eyre,* ed. Jack and Smith, *Nineteenth Century Fiction* 25 (1970): 355–59.

Harris, Wendell. *Interpretive Acts: In Search of Meaning.* Oxford: Clarendon, 1988.

Hernadi, Paul. "Literary Theory." In *Introduction to Scholarship in Modern Languages and Literatures,* ed. Joseph Gibaldi, 98–115. New York: Modern Language Association, 1981.

Higdon, David Leon. "Endgames in John Fowles's *The French Lieutenant's Woman.*" *English Studies* 65 (1984): 350–61.

Hill, W. Speed. Review of Oliphant, ed., *New Directions. Text* 6 (1994): 370–81.

Hirsch, E. D., Jr. *Cultural Literacy: What Every American Needs to Know.* Boston: Houghton Mifflin, 1987.

Hoddinott, Alison. *Gwen Harwood: The Real and the Imagined World.* North Ryde: Angus and Robertson, 1991.

Housman, A. E. "The Application of Thought to Textual Criticism" (1921). In *Selected Prose,* ed. John Carter, 131–50. Cambridge: Cambridge University Press, 1961.

Howard-Hill, T. H. "The Author as Scribe or Reviser? Middleton's Intentions in *A Game at Chess.*" *Text* 3 (1987): 305–18.

————. "Modern Textual Theories and the Editing of Plays." *Library,* 6th ser., 11 (June 1989): 89–115.

————. "Theory and Praxis in the Social Approach to Editing." *Text* 5 (1991): 31–48.

Ingham, Patricia. "Provisional Narratives: Hardy's Final Trilogy." In *Alternative Hardy,* ed. Lance St. John Butler, 49–73. New York: St. Martin's Press, 1989.

Jack, Ian, and Margaret Smith. "The Clarendon *Jane Eyre:* A Rejoinder [to Harkness's review]." *Nineteenth Century Fiction* 26 (1971): 370–76.

Jack, Jane, and Margaret Smith, eds. *Charlotte Brontë's Jane Eyre.* Oxford: Clarendon, 1969.

Kidd, John. "An Inquiry into *Ulysses: The Corrected Text.*" *PBSA* 82 (1988): 411–584.

King, Roma. Defense of the Browning edition. *Essays in Criticism* 24 (1974): 317–19.

Kramer, Dale. "The Compositor as Copy-Text." *Text* 9 (1996) 369–388.

Leithauser, Brad. "Notions of Freedom." *New York Review of Books* (15 February 1996): 34–36.

Lorsch, Susan. "Pinter Fails Fowles: Narration in *The French Lieutenant's Woman.*" *Literature Film Quarterly* 16 (1988): 144–54.

Machan, Tim William. "Work and Text." *Textual Criticism and Middle English Texts,* 136–176. Charlottesville: University Press of Virginia, 1994.

Mansfield, Elizabeth. "A Sequence of Endings: The Manuscripts of *The French Lieutenant's Woman.*" *Journal of Modern Literature* 8 (1980–81): 275–86.

Martens, Gunter. "(De)Constructing the Text by Editing: Reflections on the Receptional Significance of Textual Apparatuses." In *Contemporary German Editorial Theory,* ed. Hans Walter Gabler, George Bornstein, and Gillian Borland Pierce, 125–52. Ann Arbor: University of Michigan Press, 1995.

———. "What Is a Text? Attempts at Defining a Central Concept in Editorial Theory." In *Contemporary German Editorial Theory,* ed. Hans Walter Gabler, George Bornstein, and Gillian Borland Pierce, 209–231. Ann Arbor: University of Michigan Press, 1995.

Mazis, Glen. "The 'Riteful' Play of Time in *The French Lieutenant's Woman.*" *Soundings* 66 (1983): 296–318.

McGann, Jerome. *Black Riders: The Visible Language of Modernism.* Princeton: Princeton University Press, 1993.

———. *A Critique of Modern Textual Criticism.* Chicago: University of Chicago Press, 1983.

———. "Theory of Texts." Review of McKenzie's *Bibliography and the Sociology of Texts. London Review of Books,* 18 February 1988, 20–21.

———. *The Textual Condition.* Princeton: Princeton University Press, 1991.

———. "*Ulysses* as a Postmodernist Text: The Gabler Edition." *Criticism* 27 (Summer 1985): 283–305.

———. "What Is Critical Editing?" *Text* 5 (1991): 15–29.

McKenzie, D. F. *Bibliography and the Sociology of Texts.* The Panizzi Lectures. London: British Library, 1986.

———. *Oral Culture, Literacy, and Print in Early New Zealand: The Treaty of Waitangi.* Wellington: University of Victoria Press, 1985.

McKerrow, R. B. *Prolegomena for the Oxford Shakespeare.* Oxford: Clarendon Press, 1939.

McLaverty, James. "The Concept of Authorial Intention in Textual Criticism." *Library* 6, (1984): 121–38.

———. "Issues of Identity and Utterance: An Intentionalist Response to Textual Instability." In *Devils and Angels: Textual Editing and Literary Theory,* ed. Philip Cohen, 134–51. Charlottesville: University Press of Virginia, 1991.

————. "The Mode of Existence of Literary Works of Art." *Studies in Bibliography* 37, (1984): 82–105.

McLeod, Randall [Random Clovd]. "from Tranceformations in the Text of Orlando Fvrioso." In *New Directions in Textual Studies,* ed. Dave Oliphant and Robin Bradford, 60–85. Papers from The Harry Ransom Conference, University of Texas, 30 March–1 April 1989. A special issue of *Library Chronicle of the University of Texas at Austin* 20, no. 1/2 (1990).

————. "Information on Information." *Text* 5 (1991): 241–81.

———— [RandyM cLeod]. "Or Words to that dEffect." Photocopy, 1985.

Miller, J. Hillis. *The Ethics of Reading.* New York: Columbia University Press, 1986.

————. "Presidential Address 1986. The Triumph of Theory, the Resistance to Reading, and the Question of the Material Base." *PMLA* 102 (1987): 281–91.

Miller, R. H., Peter Shillingsburg, and Joseph McElrath. [Forum] "The Place of the Received Text in Editorial Theory." *Analytical and Enumerative Bibliography* 3 (1989): 89–107.

Modern Language Association (MLA). *Professional Standards and American Editions: A Response to Edmund Wilson.* New York: MLA, 1969.

Mumford, Lewis. "Emerson Behind Barbed Wire." *New York Review of Books* 18 January 1968, 3–5.

Ohmann, Richard. "Speech Acts and the Definition of Literature." *Philosophy and Rhetoric* 4 (1971): 1–19.

————. "Speech, Literature, and the Space Between." *New Literary History* 4 (1972–73): 47–63.

Oliphant, Dave, and Robin Bradford, eds. *New Directions in Textual Studies.* Papers from the Harry Ransom Conference, University of Texas, 30 March–1 April 1989. A special issue of the *Library Chronicle of the University of Texas at Austin* 20, no. 1/2 (1990).

Olshen, Barry N., and Toni A. Olshen. *John Fowles: A Reference Guide.* Boston: G. K. Hall, 1980.

Parker, Hershel. *Flawed Texts and Verbal Icons.* Evanston: Northwestern University Press, 1983.

————. "The 'New Scholarship': Textual Evidence and Its Implications for Criticism, Literary Theory, and Aesthetics." *Studies in American Fiction* 9 (Autumn 1981): 181–97.

Parrish, Stephen. "Foreword." In *The Salisbury Plain Poems of William Wordsworth,* ed. Stephen Gill, ix–xiii. Ithaca: Cornell University Press, 1975.

Peckham, Morse. "Reflections on the Foundations of Modern Textual Editing." *Proof* 1 (1971): 122–55.

Pettigrew, John. Review of Browning edition. *Essays in Criticism* 22 (1972): 436–41.

———. Response to Roma King's defense. *Essays in Criticism* 25 (1975): 482–83.

Phelps, C. Deirdre. "The Edition as Art Form: Social and Authorial Readings of William Cullen Bryant's Poems." *Text* 6 (1994): 249–85.

———. "The Edition as Art Form in Textual and Interpretive Criticism." *Text* 7 (1995): 61–75.

Pizer, Donald. Review of the Pennsylvania *Sister Carrie*. *American Literature* 53 (January 1982): 731–37.

———. "Self-Censorship and Textual Editing." In *Textual Criticism and Literary Interpretation*, ed. Jerome J. McGann, 144–61. Chicago: University of Chicago Press, 1985.

Rajan, Tilottama. "Is There a Romantic Ideology: Some Thoughts on Schleiermacher's Hermeneutic and Textual Criticism." *Text* 4 (1988): 59–77.

Ray, Gordon N. "The Importance of Original Editions." *Nineteenth-Century English Books*, 3–24. Urbana: University of Illinois Press, 1952.

Ray, Gordon N., ed. *The Letters and Private Papers of William Makepeace Thackeray.* 4 vols. Cambridge: Harvard University Press, 1946.

Reiman, Donald. *The Study of Modern Manuscripts: Public, Confidential, and Private.* Baltimore: Johns Hopkins University Press, 1993.

———. "'Versioning': The Presentation of Multiple Texts." *Romantic Texts and Contexts*, 167–80. Columbia: University of Missouri Press, 1987.

Robinson, Peter, ed. *The Wife of Bath's Prologue.* CD-ROM. Cambridge: Cambridge University Press, 1996.

Rossman, Charles. "The Critical Reception of the 'Gabler Ulysses': or, Gabler's Ulysses Kidd-napped." *Studies in the Novel* 21 (1989): 154–81.

Saintsbury, George, ed. *The Oxford Thackeray.* Oxford: Oxford University Press, [1908].

Scarry, Elaine. "*Henry Esmond*: The Rookery at Castlewood." In *Literary Monographs Volume 7: Thackeray, Hawthorne and Melville, and Dreiser,* ed. Eric Rothsheim and Joseph A. Wittreich, Jr., 3–43. Madison: University Wisconsin Press, 1975.

Schiebe, Siegfried. "Theoretical Problems of the Authorization and Constitution of Texts." In *Contemporary German Editorial Theory,* ed. Hans

Walter Gabler, George Bornstein, and Gillian Borland Pierce, 171–92. Ann Arbor: University of Michigan Press, 1995.

Searle, John R. *Expression and Meaning.* Cambridge: Cambridge University Press, 1979.

Shaw, Peter. "The American Heritage and Its Guardians." *American Scholar* 45 (1974–75): 733–75.

Shillingsburg, Peter L. "Authorial Autonomy vs. Social Contract: The Case of *Henry Esmond.*" *Editing in Australia,* 33–47. Kensington: University of New South Wales Press, 1990. Also In *Devils and Angels: Textual Editing and Literary Theory,* ed. Philip Cohen, 22–43. Charlottesville: University Press of Virginia, 1991.

———. "Editing Thackeray: A History." *Studies in the Novel* 27, no. 3 (1995): 363–74.

———. "Ideal Texts." *Scholarly Editing in the Computer Age,* 75–91. Ann Arbor: University of Michigan Press, 1996.

———. "An Inquiry into the Social Status of Texts and Modes of Textual Criticism." *Studies in Bibliography* 42 (1989): 55–79.

———. "Key Issues in Editorial Theory." *Analytical and Enumerative Bibliography* 6 (1982): 1–16.

———. *Pegasus in Harness: Victorian Publishing and W. M. Thackeray.* Charlottesville: University Press of Virginia, 1992.

———. *Scholarly Editing in the Computer Age.* 3d ed. Ann Arbor: University of Michigan Press, 1996.

———. "The Three *Moby-Dicks.*" *American Literary History* 2 (1990): 119–30.

Skinner, Quentin. "Conventions and the Understanding of Speech Acts." *Philosophical Quarterly* 20 (1970): 118–38.

Stillinger, Jack. *Coleridge and Textual Instability: The Multiple Versions of the Major Poems.* New York: Oxford University Press, 1994.

———. *Multiple Authorship and the Myth of Solitary Genius.* New York: Oxford University Press, 1991.

———. "Textual Primitivism and the Editing of Wordsworth." *Studies in Romanticism* 28 (1989): 3–28. Revised as chap. 4 of *Multiple Authorship and the Myth of Solitary Genius.* New York: Oxford University Press, 1991.

Sutherland, John. "Thackeray's Errors." In *Victorian Fiction: Writers, Publishers, Readers,* 1–27. New York: St. Martin's, 1995.

Tanselle, G. Thomas. "The Editing of Historical Documents." *Studies in Bibliography* 31 (1978): 1–56.

———. "The Editorial Problem of Final Authorial Intention." *Studies in Bibliography* 29 (1976): 167–211. Reprinted in *Selected Studies in Bibliography,* by G. Thomas Tanselle, 309–353. Charlottesville: University Press of Virginia, 1979.

———. "Historicism and Critical Editing." *Studies in Bibliography* 39 (1986): 1–46.

———. *A Rationale of Textual Criticism.* Philadelphia: University of Pennsylvania Press, 1989.

———. "Recent Editorial Discussion and the Central Questions of Editing." *Studies in Bibliography* 34 (1981): 23–65.

———. "Some Principles for Textual Apparatus." *Studies in Bibliography* 25 (1972): 41–88.

———. "Textual Criticism and Deconstruction." *Studies in Bibliography* 43 (1990): 1–33.

———. "Textual Criticism and Literary Sociology." *Studies in Bibliography* 44 (1991): 83–143.

———. *Textual Criticism since Greg, A Chronicle, 1950-1985.* Charlottesville: University Press of Virginia, 1987.

Taylor, Robert. *The Common Habitation.* Princeton: n.p., n.d.

Thackeray, W. M. *The History of Henry Esmond.* Ed. Edgar F. Harden. New York: Garland, 1989.

———. *The History of Henry Esmond.* Ed. John Sutherland. Harmondsworth: Penguin, 1970.

——— *The Newcomes.* Ed. Peter L. Shillingsburg. Ann Arbor: University of Michigan Press, 1996.

———. *Vanity Fair.* Ed. Peter L. Shillingsburg. New York: Garland, 1989.

Thorpe, James. "The Aesthetics of Textual Criticism." *PMLA* 80 (1965): 465–82. Reprinted in *Principles of Textual Criticism,* 1–49. San Marino, Calif.: Huntington Library, 1972.

———. *Principles of Textual Criticism.* San Marino: Huntington Library, 1972.

———. "The Treatment of Accidentals." In *Principles of Textual Criticism,* 131–70. San Marino, Calif.: Huntington Library, 1972.

———. *Watching the P's & Q's: Editorial Treatment of Accidentals,* Library Series no. 38. Lawrence: University of Kansas, 1971.

Trigg, Stephanie. "The Signature of the Editor: Towards a Theory of Editorial Intention." *Meridian* 5 (1986): 169–74.

Urkowitz, Steven. *Shakespeare's Revisions of "King Lear."* Princeton: Princeton University Press, 1980.

Warren, Michael. "Textual Problems, Editorial Assertions in Editions of Shakespeare." In *Textual Criticism and Literary Interpretation,* ed. Jerome J. McGann, 23–37. Chicago: University of Chicago Press, 1985.

West, James L. W., III. "Editorial Theory and the Act of Submission." *Papers of the Bibliographical Society of America* 83 (1989): 169–85.

———. "Fair Copy, Authorial Intention, and Versioning." *Text* 6 (1994): 81–89.

———, ed. *Theodore Dreiser's* Sister Carrie. Philadelphia: University of Pennsylvania Press, 1981.

Whall, Tony. "Karel Reisz's *The French Lieutenant's Woman:* Only the Name Remains the Same." *Literature Film Quarterly* 10 (1982): 75–81.

Wilson, Edmund. "The Fruits of the MLA." *New York Review of Books,* 26 September 1968, 7–10; and 10 October 1968, 6–14.

Wimsatt, W. K., and Monroe C. Beardsley. "The Intentional Fallacy." *Sewanee Review* (1946): 468–88. Reprinted in *The Verbal Icon.* Lexington: University of Kentucky Press, 1954.

Zeller, Hans. "A New Approach to the Critical Constitution of Literary Texts." *Studies in Bibliography* 28 (1975): 231–64.

———. "Record and Interpretation: Analysis and Documentation as Goal and Method of Editing." In *Contemporary German Editorial Theory,* ed. Hans Walter Gabler, George Bornstein, and Gillian Borland Pierce, 17–58. Ann Arbor: University of Michigan Press, 1995.

———. "Structure and Genesis in Editing: On German and Anglo-American Textual Criticism." In *Contemporary German Editorial Theory,* ed. Hans Walter Gabler, George Bornstein, and Gillian Borland Pierce, 95–123. Ann Arbor: University of Michigan Press, 1995.

Index

Jakobson, Roman, 57–58
James, Henry, 167
James, William, 91, 172–73
Jonson, Ben, 168
Joyce, James, 18, 93, 126, 197, 212

Keats, John, 13, 18
Kermode, Frank, 157
Kidd, John, 197
Kimpel, Ben, 89
King, Roma, 196–97
Kramer, Dale, 17, 126

Lawrence, D. H., 201
Lawrence, T. E., 137
Leavis, F. R., 116, 167
Leigh, Percival, 20–21
Lévi-Strauss, Claude, 52, 54, 64
linguistic text, 71, 83
Lorsch, Susan, 117
Lowry, Malcolm, 25
Lytton, Bulwer, 129

Machan, Tim William, 209
Mallarmé, 14
Mamet, David, 221
Mark Twain, 12, 90, 96, 129
Martens, Gunter, 125, 155, 215
Marx, Karl, 163
Marxist criticism, 28, 53, 55, 83, 146,
    209
material texts, 71, 73, 76
material base, 83
Mazis, Glen, 117
McElrath, Joseph, 171
McGann, Jerome, 10–12, 31, 33, 39–40,
    55, 59, 61, 65, 71, 73, 75, 85, 91,
    93, 96, 126–35, 138, 144, 152–54,
    157, 164, 166, 169–71, 174–78,
    211, 213–16, 219, 225
McKenzie, D. F., 31, 33, 65, 73, 91,
    110, 128, 131, 138, 145, 148,
    153, 159, 166, 169–70, 172, 176,
    178
McKerrow, R. B., 49, 151–52, 210
McLaverty, James, 61, 65–66, 85, 87,
    91, 93, 106, 125–26, 140
McLeod, Randy, 32, 34, 169, 177
mediums, 107
Melville, Herman, 141, 167, 197, 201,
    213; Moby-Dick 166, 197, 199, 201

Meredith, George, 129
Middleton, Thomas, 31
Miller, R. H., 171, 225
Miller, J. Hillis, 8, 42, 83
minoritist, 29
Modern Language Association (MLA), 9
molecular sememics, 34–36, 54, 80, 177
Mona Lisa, 165
Moore, Marianne, 86
Morley, Christopher, 67
Morrison, Elizabeth, 201
Mudrick, Marvin, 37
multiple texts, 33
Mumford, Lewis, 122
Murray, John, 129
Myers, Gary, 156–59

National Endowment for the Humanities
    (NEH), 26, 127, 185
New Critics, 27, 125
New Criticism, 27, 209
New historicism, 53, 191, 209
New Bibliography, 26, 28, 210
Newby, Thomas, 129

Ohmann, Richard, 99
Oliphant and Bradford, 213

Page, Mrs., 145
Parker, Hershel, 55, 59, 90, 96, 125–26,
    144, 169, 176
Parrish, Stephen, 33, 184
pathetic fallacy, 9
Paul Hernadi, 63
Peacock, Thomas Love, 210
Peckham, Morse, 125, 196
Peirce, C. S., 174
performance text, 84
performances, 107
Perkins, Maxwell, 129, 139
Pettigrew, John, 197
Phelps, C. Deirdre, 211
Picasso, Pablo, 165
Pinter, Harold, 110–11, 117
Pizer, Donald, 123, 129–31, 159
Pollard. A. W., 151–52
poststructuralism, 52
potential version, 68
Pound, Ezra, 139
process editing, 33
production contract, 163
production performance, 76–77

Peter L. Shillingsburg is Associate Director of Graduate
Studies and Research at Lamar University.